A WRITER'S WORKBOOK

An Interactive Writing Text

Third Edition

A
WRITER'S
WORKBOOK

An Interactive Writing Text

Third Edition

TRUDY SMOKE
Hunter College, CUNY

St. Martin's Press
New York

Sponsoring editor: Darcy Meeker
Managing editor: Patricia Mansfield Phelan
Senior project editor: Erica Appel
Associate project editor: Jennifer Valentine
Production supervisor: Joe Ford
Art director: Lucy Krikorian
Cover design: Patricia McFadden
Cover photo: Tony Stone Images
Illustrations: Anthony A. D'Amico and Alan Robbins

Library of Congress Catalog Card Number: 94-80174

Manufactured in the United States of America.

0 9 8 7 6
f e d c b a

For information, write:
St. Martin's Press, Inc.
175 Fifth Avenue
New York, NY 10010

ISBN: 0-312-11508-3

Acknowledgments

Joe Klein, "The Education of Berenice Belizaire," from *Newsweek,* August 9, 1993. © 1993 Newsweek, Inc. All rights reserved. Reprinted by permission.

Anita L. Wenden, "How to Be A Successful Language Learner," pages 103–107 from *Learning Strategies and Language Learning.* © 1987. Reprinted by permission of Prentice Hall, Upper Saddle River, New Jersey and Simon & Schuster International.

Nancy Duke S. Lay, "Learning from Natural Language Labs," pages 74–81 from *Journal of Basic Writing* 11.2 (Fall 1992). Reprinted by permission of the author and the Journal of Basic Writing.

Ernest Hemingway, "A Day's Wait," from *Winner Take Nothing* by Ernest Hemingway. Copyright renewed © 1961 by Mary Hemingway. Reprinted by permission of Scribner, a Division of Simon & Schuster and the Ernest Hemingway Foreign Rights Trust, Bozeman, Montana.

William Grimes, "About Men: Venus Envy," from the magazine section of *The New York Times,* October 24, 1993. Copyright © 1993 by The New York Times Company. Reprinted by permission.

Acknowledgments and copyrights are continued at the back of the book on page 361, which constitutes an extension of the copyright page.

*To Alan
and to all
my students*

Contents

Alternate Contents

Reading and Thinking Strategies

Writing Strategies

Editing Strategies

Grammar Strategies

Preface

Writing the third edition of *A Writer's Workbook* has been a challenging and exciting experience for me. Guided by teachers' responses to the first two editions, I have tried to maintain a careful balance. I have attempted to keep features and selections that were much admired and to make suggested changes and additions that will make the book clearer and more effective for students and teachers.

In this edition, the integration of reading and writing has been emphasized. More readings have been added. The focus on literature has grown. More and more varied student writings have been added. Pedagogically, the book is meant to be dialogic, to present the concepts that cultures influence and change one another, that students learn from one another, and that teachers learn from their students. By reading, discussing, and writing, students gain experience in learning to question, to problematize issues that are critical to them, and to understand their own situations better.

The book is organized into five units, each dealing with a different aspect of life: "Focusing on Language," "Reflecting on Culture," "Considering Our Roles," "Concentrating on Work," and "Thinking about Roots." Each unit contains three chapters, each organized around a specific type of reading selection. The first chapter in each unit begins with a selection of journalistic writing—taken from a newspaper, magazine, or popular book and chosen because students have found it interesting, informative, and filled with ideas about American culture. The second chapter in each unit contains an excerpt from a textbook. These selections are from required or commonly paired courses for ESL students in colleges across the United States; they also introduce students to some aspect of American culture, such as language, education, gender, psychology, and sociology. The third chapter in each unit features a short story or an excerpt from a novel or autobiography. Three readings—two short stories and one personal essay—have been added to provide students with additional reading experiences related to the main themes of the units. The authors represented have written either about conflicts—about feeling like outsiders in society—or about needing to find ways to express themselves. There are selections by Ernest Hemingway, Nancy Duke S. Lay, Lensey Namioka, Pablo Casals, Kate Chopin, Han Suyin, Nahid Rachlin, and Willa Cather.

The book also contains more than 15 essays, 12 new to this edition, written by students from all over the world, thereby exposing students to a wide variety of writing styles and approaches.

Each chapter begins with "Prereading Activities." These activities provide occasions for students to interact while discussing and exploring the topic of the chapter. They also help students make predictions and organize their thoughts about the topic before they read that chapter's selection.

A new feature to this edition is the "Vocabulary Development" section, which precedes each reading and focuses on specific words in the reading to help students understand the selection and develop vocabulary-building strategies.

Following each reading, "Reading and Thinking Strategies" engages students in thinking about and discussing what they have read and the ideas the reading has generated. Following this is a "Journal" activity that focuses students' writing on themes and ideas related to the reading. This journal may be collected periodically or responded to frequently. Students can answer the questions presented or write about their personal responses to the various selections. The journal is useful for students as a source of ideas when they prepare to write longer essays on chapter themes.

The next section, "Writing Strategies," gives students the opportunity to write short responses, stories, and essays after reading each chapter selection. Although each chapter includes "Suggestions for Writing," encompassing a variety of rhetorical modes, the emphasis in the book is on description, narration, comparison, and persuasion—the most commonly taught modes in ESL writing courses. In this edition, a new writing strategy, "Writing about Literature," has been included to prepare students for the writing they will be doing in future classes.

Each chapter includes a "Getting Started" strategy to help students think about their writing topic, discuss it with a peer, and make notes before beginning to write. This is followed by a section on revising, and teachers need to encourage students to experiment with different revision techniques to discover which ones work best for them. After writing their first draft, it is recommended that students separate themselves from their writing by reading a student essay. Questions are provided to help them focus on the strong and weak features of that essay. They should then rewrite these questions and make them more appropriate for their own writing. Next they reread what they have written (on their own or with a classmate) and make decisions about how to improve their writing. After revising, students should share their essays with a classmate. These steps are designed to help students keep in mind the audience, purpose, and focus of each essay they write.

To assist students in understanding the differences between revision and editing, each chapter also contains "Editing Strategies" and related practice exercises. However, like most teacher-researchers, I am convinced that the best editing assignments involve students working on their own writing. After focusing on highlighted editing strategies, students can work alone or in pairs and apply what they have learned to their own writing. New to this edition are "Editing Your Own Work" questions to help students edit their essays. These questions are cumulative and include each new strategy as it is learned throughout the book. Using these question lists and focusing on their own particular problem areas, students learn to become better editors and, as a result, more self-sufficient writers.

Editing strategies are followed by "Grammar Strategies." In this edition, I have connected the editing and grammar strategies, as, for example, in pairing the editing strategy "Transitive and Intransitive Verbs" and the grammar strategy "Passive Verbs," or the editing strategy "Plurals" and the grammar strategy "Countables and Uncountables." No one student will need to do every exercise in the book. However, the wide variety of types and levels of activities should fulfill each student's individual needs. At the end of each "Grammar Strategies" section, questions are provided to enable students to review their own writing and focus on the strategy just presented.

As I revised *A Writer's Workbook,* I kept teachers' comments in mind. Most teachers agreed with the concept of an ESL writing textbook that is integrally connected to a wide variety of readings and of readings that are connected to writing and grammar strategies. I have tried to keep these ideas foremost throughout this revision process. I hope the book will meet the needs and expectations of teachers and students.

The process of revising a textbook is a collaborative experience involving the efforts and responses of many people. I want to express my gratitude to my friends, family, and colleagues, whose support and goodwill kept me going throughout the writing of this edition. I would particularly like to thank Linnea Tornquist of Kean College and Susan Ribner of Hunter College for the assistance and support they provided me in finding and securing a fine selection of student essays. I would also like to thank my own students for their willingness to share their writing with others. Indeed, my gratitude goes to the hundreds of students whose experiences and insights assisted me in understanding the complex process of learning to write and read in a new language.

I would like to thank the following reviewers and colleagues for their insights and suggestions: Linda Hirsch, Hostos Community College/CUNY; Susan Roberts, University of Connecticut–Hartford; Jana Zanetto, City College of San Francisco; Jessie M. Reppy, Kean College of New Jersey; Keming Liu, Medgar Evers College; Stephanie Vandrick, University of San Francisco; Bernice G. Kaufmann, Northeastern Illinois University; Susan Corey, California Lutheran University; Melissa Allen, English Language Institute, George Mason University; and Heidimarie Hayes Rambo, Kent State University.

I would also like to thank the following reviewers for their contributions to the earlier editions of *A Writer's Workbook:* Frank Pialorsi, Center for ESL, University of Arizona; Amy Sales, Boston University; Joanne Liebman, University of Arkansas–Little Rock; Craig Katz, ESL Program, Camden Community College; Ellen Lipp, California State University at Fresno; Janice Baldwin, Delaware County Community College; Carolyn Abels, Capital University; Karen Scriven, East Carolina University; and Jennifer McKenzie, University of Missouri–St. Louis.

Above all, I would like to express my deepest thanks to Naomi Silverman and Carl Whithaus, ESL editors, who contributed their intelligence, support, and patience to this project. I am deeply appreciative of the work of Erica Appel, senior project editor, who oversaw the production of *A Writer's Workbook* for the second time. In addition, Sandy Schecter, permissions associate, Jennifer Valentine, associate project editor, and Joe Ford, production supervisor, have made valuable contributions. Their vision and dedication have made this book elegant and well designed. I must thank Anthony A. D'Amico, art student at Kean College, for the beautiful illustrations that grace this book. And it is impossible for me to complete a project such as this without acknowledging the contribution of my husband, Alan Robbins—as Tony D'Amico's professor, as illustrator of one of the book's drawings, and for his gentle support, understanding, and love.

Trudy Smoke

A
WRITER'S
WORKBOOK

An Interactive Writing Text

Third Edition

Focusing on Language

CHAPTER ONE

Succeeding in School

PREREADING ACTIVITIES

1. As a class, discuss Haiti. Where is it located? What language do the people speak? What is the political situation in Haiti today?
2. If there are Haitian students in your class, they can serve as the experts about their country. If not, the class should decide what resources to use to find out information about the weather, food, religion, clothing, and family relationships of Haiti.
3. In small groups, discuss what it means to become "Americanized." What is positive about this and what is negative? Each group should prepare and present a short (three- to five-minute) presentation of its ideas to the class.
4. Who is Ruth Bader Ginsburg? Why is she considered "an American success story"?

VOCABULARY DEVELOPMENT

One way to learn a new vocabulary word is to try to discover its meaning by reading the word in the context of a sentence or a reading selection. The context gives you an idea of the meaning of the word. Look at the italicized words in the following sentences, and try to decide the meaning of the word based on the context of the sentence.

EXAMPLE

She lived in a *cramped* Brooklyn apartment, a far cry from the comfortable house they'd had in Haiti.

Now choose the definition that seems closest to the meaning of the word as it is used in the sentence.

a. agreeable   b. satisfactory   c. confined or tight

A far cry suggests that the apartment is different from the house, so the words *agreeable* and *satisfactory* can be eliminated. Alternative c, *Confined or tight,* seems to be the best choice.

1. She was learning a new language while enduring constant *taunts*. They cursed her in the cafeteria and threw food at her.

   a. insults   b. compliments   c. sweet words

2. She was speaking English, though not well enough to get into one of New York's *elite* public high schools. She had to settle for the neighborhood school.

   a. worst   b. choicest, most select   c. normal, average

3. It is possible that immigrant energy *reinvigorated* not just some schools but the city itself. "Without them, New York would have been a smaller place, a poorer place, a lot less vital and exciting," says Prof. Emanuel Tobier of New York University.

    a. gave new life   b. gave new problems   c. overpopulated

4. They restored the retail life of the city, starting a raft of small businesses—and doing the entry-level, bedpan-emptying jobs that nonimmigrants *spurn*.

    a. want   b. reject   c. seek

The Education of Berenice Belizaire

Joe Klein

Journalist Joe Klein wrote the following article for the August 9, 1993, issue of Newsweek *magazine. In it, he describes the success of a young woman who has immigrated to the United States from Haiti. Klein suggests that students who resist American culture may have the greatest chance of succeeding.*

When Berenice Belizaire arrived in New York from Haiti with her mother and sister in 1987, she was not very happy. She spoke no English. The family had to live in a cramped Brooklyn apartment, a far cry from the comfortable house they'd had in Haiti. Her mother, a nurse, worked long hours. School was torture. Berenice had always been a good student, but now she was learning a new language while enduring constant taunts from the Americans (both black and white). They cursed her in the cafeteria and threw food at her. Someone hit her sister in the head with a book. "Why can't we go home?" Berenice asked her mother.

Because home was too dangerous. The schools weren't always open anymore, and education—her mother insisted—was the most important thing. Her mother had always pushed her: memorize everything, she ordered. "I have a pretty good memory," Berenice admitted last week. Indeed, the other kids at school began to notice that Berenice always, somehow, knew the answers. "They started coming to me for help," she says. "They never called me a nerd."

Within two years Berenice was speaking English, though not well enough to get into one of New York's elite public high schools. She had to settle for a neighborhood school, James Madison—which is one of the magical American places, the alma mater of Ruth Bader Ginsburg among others, a school with a history of unlikely success stories. "I didn't realize what we had in Berenice at first," says math teacher Judith

Khan. "She was good at math, but she was quiet. And the things she didn't know! She applied for a summer program in Buffalo and asked me how to get there on the subway. But she always seemed to ask the right questions. She understood the big ideas. She could think on her feet. She could explain difficult problems so the other kids could understand them. Eventually, I realized: she wasn't just pushing for grades, she was hungry for *knowledge* . . . And you know, it never occurred to me that she also was doing it in English and history, all these other subjects that had to be much tougher for her than math."

She moved from third in her class to first during senior year. She was 4 selected as valedictorian, an honor she almost refused (still shy, she wouldn't allow her picture in the school's yearbook). She gave the speech, after some prodding—a modest address about the importance of hard work and how it's never too late to try hard: an immigrant's valedictory. Last week I caught up with Berenice at the Massachusetts Institute of Technology where she was jump-starting her college career. I asked her what she wanted to be doing in 10 years: "I want to build a famous computer, like IBM," she said. "I want my name to be part of it."

Berenice Belizaire's story is remarkable, but not unusual. The New 5 York City schools are bulging with overachieving immigrants. The burdens they place on a creaky, corroded system are often cited as an argument against liberal immigration policies, but teachers like Judith Khan don't seem to mind. "They're why I love teaching in Brooklyn," she says. "They have a drive in them we no longer seem to have. You see these kids, who aren't prepared academically and can barely speak the language, struggling so hard. They just sop it up. They're like little sponges. You see Berenice, who had none of the usual, preconceived racial barriers in her mind—you see her becoming friendly with the Russian kids, and learning chess from Po Ching [from Taiwan]. It is *so* exciting."

Dreamy Hothouse

Indeed, it is possible that immigrant energy reinvigorated not just 6 some schools (and more than a few teachers)—but *the city itself* in the 1980s. "Without them, New York would have been a smaller place, a poorer place, a lot less vital and exciting," says Prof. Emanuel Tobier of New York University. They restored the retail life of the city, starting a raft of small businesses—and doing the sorts of entry-level, bedpan-emptying jobs that nonimmigrants spurn. They added far more to the local economy than they removed; more important, they reminded enlightened New Yorkers that the city had always worked best as a vast, noisy, dreamy hothouse for the cultivation of new Americans.

The Haitians have followed the classic pattern. They have a signifi- 7 cantly higher work-force participation rate than the average in New

York. They have a lower rate of poverty. They have a higher rate of new-business formation and a lower rate of welfare dependency. Their median household income, at $28,853, is about $1,000 less than the city-wide median (but about $1,000 higher than Chinese immigrants, often seen as a "model" minority). They've also developed a traditional network of fraternal societies, newspapers and neighborhoods with solid—extended, rather than nuclear—families. "A big issue now is whether women who graduate from school should be allowed to live by themselves before they marry," says Lola Poisson, who counsels Haitian immigrants. "There's a lot of tension over that."

°improper, wrong
°standard of behavior

°drunk

Such perverse° propriety° cannot last long. Immigrants become 8 Americans very quickly. Some lose hope after years of menial labor; others lose discipline, inebriated° by freedom. "There's an interesting phenomenon," says Philip Kasinitz of Williams College. "When immigrant kids criticize each other for getting lazy or loose, they say, 'You're becoming American.'" (Belizaire said she and the Russians would tease each other that way at Madison.) It's ironic, Kasinitz adds. "Those who

°at a distance

work hardest to keep American culture at bay° have the best chance of becoming American success stories." If so, we may be fixed on the wrong issue. The question shouldn't be whether immigrants are ruining America, but whether America is ruining the immigrants.

Reading and Thinking Strategies

Discussion Activities

Analysis and Conclusions

1. Why did Belizaire's family leave Haiti? What in the Klein article tells you how the children felt about the move?

2. In what ways has Berenice Belizaire changed as a person from her early days in the United States? What might explain these changes?

3. According to Klein, in what ways have immigrants had a positive effect on New York and on the United States as a whole?

Writing and Point of View

1. What technique does Klein use in his introduction to make his readers want to read more? Was the introduction interesting to you? Why or why not?

2. Klein reports about Berenice Belizaire and her family. What specific details or phrases in the article tell his readers how he feels about the Belizaires?

3. Where in the essay does Klein make the transition from the specific story of Berenice to the general idea that immigrants have altered U.S. society? Whom does Klein quote to support his point of view?

Personal Response and Evaluation

1. In what ways has your memory helped or hindered your progress in English? In what subjects was memorization required in your home country? What techniques do you use to improve your memory?

2. What is the difference between "pushing for grades" and "being hungry for knowledge"?

3. Reread paragraph 7 of the Klein essay. What is the classic pattern for immigrants from your country when they come to the United States?

4. In what ways might students who become more "Americanized" also become more successful? In what ways might they have more problems in school? Why?

Interview

Two members of the class can interview each other trying to discover the story of each of your successes. Decide together what questions will lead you to uncover the types of experiences, educational and otherwise, that helped you learn English and enter college.

Write out the results of your interview to share with other members of your class. After listening to the various stories of the students in your class, list the factors that were most helpful in attaining their success.

Debate

Divide the class into two groups, one in favor of becoming more culturally "Americanized" and the other opposed. Debate the issues, using personal experiences and observations to support points of view. You might want to videotape or tape-record this debate and then review it and discuss what occurred.

Journal Writing

Keeping a journal will be a major part of your writing experience while you use this book. Your journal will be a place where ideas count much more than spelling or grammar. You may be able to use some of these ideas in other writing assignments; even more important, you will use them to get to know yourself better and to get to know your teacher. We will use dialogue journals in which you write to your teacher and he or she writes back to you. However, many students also keep private journals in which they write their private thoughts. Each chapter includes suggestions and questions to write about in your journal, but you may also decide to write about something else that is important to you. Sometimes the topics will simply point you in a direction, and you can explore as many or as few as you choose.

After reading about Berenice Belizaire and her family, think about your own experiences as a student in the United States. What thoughts come to your mind? What helped you succeed? What problems did you face? When you are ready, write down your thoughts. Do not worry about writing complete, grammatically correct sentences. Concentrate on expressing your ideas as completely as possible.

Writing Strategies

The Writing Biography

"Know yourself" is one of the basic premises of writing. The more you know and understand yourself as a writer, the better you will feel about expressing yourself in writing. The purpose of the following assignment is for you to think about yourself as a writer and to write your own "writing biography."

Because there is no neat, gradual way to learn to write and because progress *seems* so unpredictable and just plain slow, a major part of learning to write is learning to put up with this frustrating *process* itself.

PETER ELBOW

In essay form, write a "writing biography" about yourself in which you describe some of the experiences and people who have influenced your writing. Try to answer some of the following questions in your biography. Share these essays with your classmates.

1. What is your earliest memory about learning to write in your first language? How old were you?
2. What is your earliest memory about learning to write in English? How old were you?
3. What types of writing did you do in elementary school? How did you feel about writing when you were in elementary school? What did

your teachers do in elementary school that helped or did not help you learn to write?

4. What types of writing did you do in high school or in other schools you have attended? How did you feel about writing in those classes? What did your teachers do that helped or did not help you learn to write?

5. Do you write for any college classes other than this one? If so, which classes? What do you write for those classes?

6. Do you write letters, poems, stories, or do other kinds of writing for pleasure? What kind of writing do you prefer to do?

7. How do you feel about writing today?

8. What is the easiest part of writing for you?

9. What is the hardest part of writing for you?

10. What one aspect would you like to change about your writing?

Essay Strategies

The Paragraph

Part of learning to write in a new language is learning how readers of that language expect ideas to be organized. Most native speakers of English expect essay, text, and story writing to be divided into paragraphs. Each paragraph serves as a guide for the reader. It shows what the writer thinks is important, what belongs together, and where a new idea begins. Paragraphs help the reader digest writing, just as breaking up a meal into courses such as soup, salad, main dish, and dessert helps in the digestion of a meal. If all the food from a meal were piled on the table in front of you at once, you might not know where to begin to eat. When writers do not use paragraphs, readers often cannot understand the big blocks of sentences piled up in front of them. So a clear, considerate writer breaks up ideas into paragraphs.

A paragraph begins with an indented line. This makes it stand out from the rest of the text. A paragraph is not long, usually containing no more than 250 words, but you do not have to count the words. Simply use your judgment. When your focus or the idea you are discussing changes or when you want to divide a general concept into smaller parts, you should begin a new paragraph. A paragraph is a group of sentences related to a single subject.

A paragraph usually has a topic sentence or main idea that tells the reader what the paragraph is about. This topic sentence can appear anywhere in the paragraph. Sometimes it is implied, which means that it is not actually stated, but the reader can find it by inferring or reading into what the author has written.

A paragraph may have different purposes in a piece of writing. It may explain a concept introduced in a topic sentence. It may illustrate a point or give support to an argument. Each paragraph works together with the rest of the paragraphs in a letter, an essay, a story, or a book to help the reader understand the writer's point of view.

Fill in the following blanks with the seven characteristics of a paragraph discussed so far.

_____

_____

_____

_____

_____

_____

_____

☐ ☐ ☐

EXERCISE

Paragraphs make writing easier to read. They help the reader know how the writer thinks. The following piece of writing would be easier to read if it were divided into paragraphs. Read it with a classmate, and decide where new paragraphs should begin. Remember that each time you begin a totally new thought, you should indent for a new paragraph. Most writers agree that there should be three paragraphs in the following exercise.

The essay about Berenice Belizaire made me think about my family and what they expect of me. I am the first child in my family to go to college in the United States, so they think I should set a good example for my younger brothers and sisters. I have tried very hard to study and to do well in my courses although it was not easy at first. When I started college, I was nervous about English. I still made a lot of mistakes and did not understand everything my teachers said in class. Since I felt nervous about raising my hand, I usually did not ask questions, and I missed some important information. The best thing that happened to me in college happened when my biology teacher required each of us to join a study group. I found that I could ask my questions to the other students in my class, and some of them even knew the answers. We all share our notes, and that helps me, too. It also helps me to say the new words from biology out loud to the whole group. After I do that, I remember them better. Joining a study group has helped me become a successful student in college. As a result, I suggested to a few of the students in my anthropology class that we meet to discuss the class lectures and the reading. It seems to be helping them as much as me.

Essay Form

Paragraph Development

Learning to write in English involves more than just learning new vocabulary and grammatical structures. Part of learning to write is finding out the order in which readers expect ideas to be arranged.

Some researchers have stated that readers of English expect a straight line of development. In this kind of writing, the paragraph often begins with a statement of its main or most important idea; this is called the topic sentence. This main idea is divided into connected ideas that are developed further in the paragraphs that follow the first one. Although this is the traditional approach for most English speakers, it may be different from what you learned in your first language.

For example, Fan Shen, who was born in the People's Republic of China and is now living in the United States, wrote an article in 1989 about this difference. The article states:

In English composition, an essential rule for the logical organization of a piece of writing is the use of a "topic sentence." In Chinese composition "from surface to core" is an essential rule, a rule which means that one ought to reach a topic gradually and "systematically" instead of "abruptly."

□   □   □

EXERCISES

1. In some cultures, writing is organized differently from English. Discuss the answers to the following questions based on your first language or any other that you have studied other than English.

   a. In writing in your first language or any other language you have studied, do you divide your writing into paragraphs?
   b. If you do, how do you know when to begin a new paragraph?
   c. If you do not, how do you indicate to the reader that you are beginning a new thought?
   d. Is the idea of a topic sentence new to you? How are the ideas about a subject grouped in your language? What usually comes first, second, or last?

2. As part of focusing on paragraph structure, the class should divide

into small groups. Each group should look at paragraph 1 in Klein's essay. Copy the topic sentence of that paragraph here:

_____

_____

List the supporting details that tell more about the topic sentence or main idea:

_____

_____

_____

_____

_____

3. To help readers understand what they have written, writers connect their ideas from paragraph to paragraph. Answer the following questions about how Klein's essay is connected from sentence to sentence and from paragraph to paragraph.

a. Paragraph 2 begins with a fragment or incomplete sentence (see pages 248–50 for explanation). What is the fragment?

_____

How does this fragment connect to paragraph 1?

_____

Write a sentence in which you correct this fragment and also connect the ideas in paragraphs 1 and 2.

_____

_____

b. In the second sentence of paragraph 2, to what does *The schools* refer?

_____

c. In paragraph 3, Klein quotes a teacher as saying, "She applied for a summer program in Buffalo and asked me how to get there on the subway." To what does *there* refer?

_____

d. In paragraphs 5 and 6, Klein uses the word *they* repeatedly. To whom does *they* refer?

_____

e. In the second-to-last sentence in the concluding paragraph, Klein uses *we*. To whom is Klein referring?

_____

Suggestions for Writing

Give yourself time to think before you write. If you have any difficulty beginning your writing, look in your journal or at the "Getting Started" suggestion on page 14. When you do begin to write, keep your audience in mind. Try to make your writing interesting to your readers as well as to yourself.

1. In an essay, describe the most important ideas that you learned about yourself when you wrote your writing biography. Try to organize your writing so that it moves from your specific experience or experiences to general concepts about how students learn to write.

2. Write an essay in which you tell a story about someone who has had problems learning English or getting used to living in a new country. How did this person deal with the problems? What has this person learned from facing these problems?

3. Write an essay in which you compare your experiences living in a new country and learning a new language with Berenice Belizaire's experiences. Use the Klein article for information.

4. Some people think of success as the attainment of high grades, educational degrees, and good jobs. Write an essay in which you define the qualities that mean success to you. Explain why these qualities are meaningful to you.

5. Many ambitious parents push their children to succeed in school. Do you agree or disagree with the idea that pushing children helps them succeed? Support your point of view with your experiences, observations, and readings.

Research Project

> Write an essay in which you trace the immigration pattern of people from your country to the United States. Think about some of the following as you do research in your college or community library. Approximately how many immigrants from your country live in the United States? How many live in your community? Do people tend to live in the same neighborhoods? What is their median income? Their education level? Do people from your country tend to choose certain professions? What kind of community networks have they developed? (See paragraph 7 of the Klein article for other ideas.)

Getting Started

Talking to Get Ideas

> If you have any difficulty getting started, talk to a classmate about what you are planning to write. Begin by discussing each topic and the ideas on which a writer could focus. Take turns explaining to each other why you would or would not choose a particular topic; this will help you narrow down your choices.
>
> When you have reduced your choices to two or three possible topics, discuss your ideas for each topic. Then, together, choose the topic that interests you the most. Before you begin to write, together make a list of ideas that you will refer to as you write your essay. When you finish your first draft, share it with the same classmate.

Revising

> To give you some practice responding to an essay, it may be helpful to work with someone else's writing first. Working with a classmate, read the following student essay, "First Years of Migration."

A Student Essay

FIRST YEARS OF MIGRATION

When people arrive in a new country it is always hard for them to adopt   1
a new lifestyle. A new language, society, and culture can cause misunderstanding among the closest people, like parents and children. On the one hand, parents try to build a new life, study a new language, look for a job, and sometimes they do not even have enough time to pay attention to their children. On the other hand, when children go to a new

school they experience culture shock. They do not know the language, they do not understand their teachers, and they want to become popular in their new school among new classmates. They try to look and to behave like them and at this time they need their parents to be their closest friends, to share all their problems and happiness with them.

It is a hard time for both children and their parents. However, they 2 can get over these problems and still be one big, happy family only by understanding each other and having a lot of patience with each other.

I have a cousin named Igor. He is now twenty years old. When his fam- 3 ily decided to come to America for a better life, he was only five years old. Before they came to New York, my aunt and uncle knew that New York was a city of freedom, where many immigrants from different countries came and everybody could keep their traditions and speak their native language. So when they finally got here they thought they could keep their customs and language at home, but at work, for their own benefit in understanding other people, they would learn English.

It was the spring. New York met them with all its beauty, tenderness, 4 and grandeur. Everything seemed to work out until one day my cousin went to play in a garden with some children. When he returned home his eyes were full of tears, and when his mother asked him, "What happened, sweetheart?" he said to her with a sorrowful voice, "I do not understand anything. I do not know what language these children speak. I do not want to be here. I want to go back to my country and to my friends. I want to speak this language that we speak at home."

But after a while, every day Igor returned home having learned a new 5 English phrase. He was a very smart and nice kid. After one year he began to speak English fluently. When Igor got older, he began to forget the Russian language. His parents tried to teach him this language again, but it was too late. He did not even want to hear about it. He began to consider himself an American. He started to have only American friends, and his home and parents were the only parts that reminded him that he was not American but Russian. At this point, Igor's parents realized that every day their son was getting more and more separate from them. To resolve this problem and again become a happy family, they started to speak English at home, live an American type of life, and have American friends. The parents wanted to do anything just to be close to their son again.

In my opinion, it was a solution to the situation, and the family could 6 overcome it all together. But in their hearts the parents still remained Russian and they would like to speak Russian at home. But unfortunately it is impossible now because their children do not know Russian and they are afraid that conflict between the family members could begin again.

Irina Dolber, Russia

With a classmate, discuss Irina Dolber's essay by focusing on the following questions.

1. What is the main idea that holds together the entire piece of writing?
2. What specific words, phrases, and experiences reveal the writer's attitude toward learning English? Toward adapting to a new lifestyle?
3. What part of the essay did you like the most? Why?
4. What would you like to know that the writer does not include in the essay?
5. What advice would you give the writer for revising this essay?

Rewrite these five questions so that you can use them to help you as you read the first draft of your writing. Make any changes that will make your essay clearer and stronger. Share your revised essay with your partner.

Editing Strategies

Mechanics

Paper Format

When you hand in a paper to a teacher or to another student to read, make sure that it is neat and readable. To do this, you should follow these ten steps:

1. Use $8\frac{1}{2}$-by-11-inch paper, whether you are printing from a computer or writing by hand. Smaller pages get lost and are harder to read. (If you are printing on continuous computer paper, tear off the holes on the sides before handing it in.)
2. Use dark blue or black ink if you write by hand. Pencil smudges easily, and other colors can distract your readers.
3. If you use a word processor, double-space. If you write by hand and have large handwriting or if your paper has narrow rules, write on every other line.
4. Use 1-inch margins on all sides of your paper—top, bottom, left, and right. This is easy to do when you are writing by hand; margins are also easy to set on most word processing systems.
5. Put your name, date, and course number at the top of the first page unless your instructor requires that they be somewhere else.
6. Use a title, and center the title above the rest of the writing. Capitalize the first word and all major words in your title. Skip a line between the title and the first line of your writing.

7. Indent each paragraph about 1 inch, or five typed spaces.

8. Make sure that your capital letters are distinct from your lowercase letters. Also make sure that your *e*'s and *i*'s are distinguishable.

9. Make all your punctuation marks clear and distinct. Leave a space after each period. If you are using a word processor, leave two spaces between the period and the capital letter of the next sentence.

10. If you break a word at the end of the line, break it between syllables. Use the dictionary if you do not know where a syllable ends.

Editing Practice

Editing Other People's Writing

After revising their writing for content (see page 16), writers often edit their writing for errors. In the following draft, the author has made two formatting errors and five errors in verb tense. Find as many errors as you can and correct them. (If you have problems finding the verb tense errors, read pages 18–19) Answers are on page 355.

My earliest memory about learning english

I was about fifteen years old in Azerbaijan, my country, when I was starting to study English. I have spent a lot of time on it. I really wanted to know this language just for myself. I studied it in my elementary school, but it was too hard for me then. I have tried to study and do my homework by myself. Memorizing words and English grammar was awful for me. Then I was getting a tutor. That helped a lot. Now I know much more and I am trying to use English all the time.

Editing Your Own Writing

Reread an essay that you wrote for this chapter, asking yourself the following questions:

1. Did I format my paper correctly?
2. Did I start new paragraphs when necessary?
3. Did I use the past tenses correctly?

When you rewrite your essay, make any changes that will improve your writing.

Grammar Strategies

Verb Forms

Every verb in English except *be* has five forms:

1. The base form: *play, go*
2. The third person singular form (used in the present with *he, she,* or *it*): *plays, goes*
3. The past form: *played* (regular verbs), *went* (irregular verbs—form differs from one verb to another)
4. The present participle (progressive) form: *playing, going*
5. The past participle form: *played, gone*

Fill in the blanks with the five forms of each of the following verbs. (The first verb has been done for you.)

Base	Third person singular	Past	Present participle	Past participle
arrive	*arrives*	*arrived*	*arriving*	*arrived*
speak				
think				
work				
become				
write				
see				
do				
build				
ask				

Forms of the Past Tense

In English, we can express the past tense in five ways:

1. The *simple past* is used to describe an action that meets one of the following criteria:

   a. It occurred at a definite time in the past.
   b. It began in the past and ended in the past.
   c. It occurred repeatedly or habitually in the past.

She *lived* in New Jersey in 1989.
Trains *were* the fastest form of transportation.
People *paid* all their bills in cash. (They no longer do.)

2. The *past continuous (progressive)* is used in the following instances:

   a. To describe ongoing action occurring at or during a time in the past.
   b. To contrast two past events, one of which occurred while the other was still ongoing.

   She *was studying* English all day yesterday.
   I *was washing* my hair when he knocked on the door.

3. The *past perfect* is used to describe an action that occurred before another action in the past.

   He *had moved* to California three months before his sister moved there.

4. The *present perfect* is used to describe an action that began in the past and continues to the present and beyond.

   They *have lived* in a city all their lives.

5. The *present perfect continuous* is used to describe an ongoing or repeated action that began in the past and continues to the present and beyond.

   She *has been studying* French since 1990.

□   □   □

EXERCISES

1. A paragraph from "The Education of Berenice Belizaire" is reprinted here. Underline all the past tense verbs.

When Berenice Belizaire arrived in New York from Haiti with her mother and sister in 1987, she was not very happy. She spoke no English. The family had to live in a cramped Brooklyn apartment, a far cry from the comfortable house they'd had in Haiti. Her mother, a nurse, worked long hours. School was torture. Berenice had always been a good student, but now she was learning a new language while enduring constant taunts from the Americans (both black and white). They cursed her in the cafeteria and threw food at her. Someone hit her sister in the head with a book. "Why can't we go home?" Berenice asked her mother.

2. In which form of the past tense is each of the verbs you underlined?

3. Write a paragraph describing your first month in the United States. Share your paragraph with a classmate.

Question Form Using the Past Tense

When we create questions, we use question words such as *did, what, where, when, who, why,* and *how* and sometimes change the order of the words in the sentence.

1. In the simple past, a question is formed by changing a statement in the following way:

> She lived in New Jersey.
> BECOMES
> Did she live in New Jersey?
> OR
> Where did she live?

If the verb is *was* or *were,* we use these words to form the question and change the word order.

> Trains were the fastest form of transportation.
> BECOMES
> Were trains the fastest form of transportation?
> OR
> What was the fastest form of transportation? (When you ask the question, you do not know if the answer will be in the plural or the singular, so you use the singular in forming the question.)

2. The past continuous (progressive) uses *was* or *were* in the question form and changes the word order.

> She was studying English all day yesterday.
> BECOMES
> Was she studying English all day yesterday?
> OR
> What was she doing all day yesterday?

3. The past perfect tense uses *had* in the question form and changes the word order.

> He had moved to California three months before his sister moved there.
> BECOMES
> Had he moved to California three months before his sister moved there?
> OR
> How long had he lived in California before his sister moved there?

4. The present perfect uses *has* or *have* in the question form and changes the word order.

> They have lived in the city all their lives.
> BECOMES
> Have they lived in the city all their lives?
> OR
> How long have they lived in the city?
> OR
> Where have they lived all their lives?

5. The present perfect continuous uses *has* or *have* and *been* + the *-ing* form of the verb in the question and changes the word order from the order in the statement form.

> She has been studying French since 1990.
> BECOMES
> Has she been studying French since 1990?
> OR
> How long has she been studying French?
> OR
> What has she been doing since 1990?

□   □   □

EXERCISES   1. Make two questions for each of the following eight answers.

a. She attended high school in the United States.

Did _____

Where _____

b. The Belizaires believed in the importance of education.

Did _____

What _____

c. Her math teacher was Judith Kahn.
d. She was friendly with students from different parts of the world.
e. She had become a successful student before she attended college.
f. In her valedictory address, she spoke about hard work and the fact that it is never too late to try hard.
g. The United States has gained tremendously from the contributions of immigrants.
h. Immigrants have contributed by working hard, creating new businesses, and reinvigorating neighborhoods.

2. Reread Irina Dolber's essay on page 14. Notice how she uses the past tenses. Does she ever use the present tense? Explain when she uses the present and when she uses past tenses.

□ □ □

CHECKING YOUR OWN WORK

1. Read through your Writing Biography. Notice where you used the past tense. (It may be helpful to underline each instance.) Did you use the past tense when you described something that happened in the past or something that had already occurred? Did you use the correct form of the past tense each time? Were you consistent in putting all verbs in the past tense when you described something that happened in the past?
2. Read through other writing you have done. Focus on your use of the past tense. Did you use the correct form of the past tense each time? Were you consistent in putting all verbs in the past tense when you described something that happened in the past?
3. As an extra check, work with a classmate to make sure that you have used the past tense correctly in your writing.

CHAPTER TWO

Learning a Language

PREREADING ACTIVITIES

1. Do you feel more comfortable speaking, reading, or writing in English? Explain your choice.
2. In small groups, discuss specific methods that have helped you learn English and other methods that have not worked for you. Each group should prepare and present a short (three- to five-minute) presentation of its findings to the class.

VOCABULARY DEVELOPMENT

Look at each italicized word in the following sentences, and try to determine its meaning from the context of the sentence. Choose the definition that seems closest to the meaning of the word as it is used in the sentence.

1. It is not necessary to be in a classroom to learn a second language. One simply *utilizes* it in the social contexts in which one finds oneself to fulfill the functions necessary to communication in the context.

   a. organizes   b. uses   c. reads

2. One should not first plan the *utterance* in one's native language and then translate.

   a. reading   b. ideas   c. spoken words

3. Learning better meant learning the language more *authentically:* "When you are in a country, you get everything, . . . not only grammar and vocabulary. . . . It's mixed up more."

   a. genuinely   b. slowly   c. technically

4. Finally, being mentally active means acting upon or *transforming* what one has received or asked about: "I just don't take it as it comes. I change it in my mind. There's always movement."

   a. changing   b. remembering   c. understanding

How to Be a Successful Language Learner

Anita L. Wenden

Anita L. Wenden teaches English as a second language at York College in Queens, New York. She has been interested in finding out the strategies that successful students use to learn English. The following selection includes the results of interviews with adult ESL learners at Columbia University in New York City. The selection is a description of her research and is not written in narrative form. Notice the kinds of language that Wenden uses and the ways that she connects her ideas throughout the selection. Keep in mind that different types of writing are used for different purposes.

°clear

A group of 25 adults who had lived in the United States for no longer   1
than two years and who were enrolled part time (5 hours a week) in the advanced level classes of the American Language Program at Columbia University were selected and interviewed. . . . Fourteen of the twenty-five learners made explicit° statements about how best to approach language learning. Five of the statements stressed the importance of using the language, i.e. especially of speaking and listening. Four pointed to the need to learn about the language, especially grammar and vocabulary. Three others emphasized the role of personal factors.

Group 1: Use the Language

°situations

1. *Learn the natural way.* This statement means that it is not necessary   2
to be in a classroom to learn a second language. One simply utilizes it in the social contexts° in which one finds oneself to fulfill the functions necessary to communication in the context. Moreover, while opportunities to use the language should not be avoided, this does not mean that learners should force themselves to use it. Stating his view on using new words, a young Israeli who stressed the importance of "living the language" explained: "I don't think I have to use it. If it happens to me to use it, I use it. I don't force myself to use a word, 'cause if it's compulsive, it's not natural." Describing his stay with a British family, Miguel says: "Everything was natural. The relationship [with my landlord] was as with a family. We watched TV and talked about what we saw." And later referring to his courses in the Business School at Columbia University: "I took two courses in business—microeconomics and accounting. . . . I read, studied, listened to lectures and took notes in English. I thought about the meaning of the subject. I did not think about the language. I was trying to learn the natural way."

2. *Practice.* This second theme stresses the *necessity* of using the language *as often as possible.* There is a note of intensity not present in the   3

preceding theme, e.g. "I tried this way not only to study very hard, but to take every opportunity (to speak) . . ."; "I tell myself . . . if you are here you must speak"; "You have to do everything in English . . ."; "Practice. That's the secret." Learners varied on what the result of intensive practice would be. For some practice was necessary or one would forget or lose one's sense of English. Others felt that with practice one would learn "automatically," "get accustomed to speaking," "understand better," and/or "learn to think in English."

3. *Think in your second language.* This third theme emphasizes the need to focus directly on the meaning of the communication when using the language. One should not first plan the utterance in one's native language and then translate. Says Laszlo, "Even when someone asks me a question, I concentrate on the meaning. I don't plan what I have to say. I try to eliminate my native language so the idea and word are almost simultaneous.° This is the best way not to think in your native language. You must think in the language you are learning." Ilse's view is similar. Reflecting upon a listening strategy she had used during her first month in the United States, she says: "[It's] also very important to get the sound and keep it, then to transfer everything into thinking." 4

°occurring at the same time

Generally, it was felt that thinking in the second language would enable one to learn better: "I thought the less we think, speak, read Portuguese, the better we can get in English . . ." And, more specifically, it was felt there was a kind of reciprocal° relationship between using the language and thinking in the language: "You hear it, you speak it, you learn to think in the language. . . . If you have to think in English, you speak better." 5

°two-way

4. *Live and study in an environment where the target language is spoken.* For most learners this guideline meant that one should be in the country where the target language was the main or official language of communication. And so, if one wanted to learn English, for example, one should go to the United States or Britain. On the other hand, one learner decided it might be even better to go to a country where neither his native language nor the target language was the main language of communication but where one could expect to meet speakers of the target language. He felt that it would be easier to become a part of a community of [target language] speakers living abroad (in his case, Americans) than it was to do so in their country of origin. 6

Learners had different reasons for stressing this guideline. For some, living in a target language community provided one with the opportunity to practice: "You learn to speak English when you learn here because you have to practice, . . . because everywhere you have to speak English and have to listen. . . . I think if you don't go to the place, you don't learn the language." 7

Others, such as Ryuichi, a Japanese businessman, felt that if his "hearing is a little better" it is because "now, he understands America." So 8 even if he can't understand some words, he can guess. "It's not related [to] the improvement of language." In other words, being in the target language country, one could better understand the culture and once that happened one would better understand the language.

For Ilse, however, "It's not important to know the culture. But when you are in the culture it's easier to learn and when everything is in this language, then it's better. You learn it better, . . . not easier." Learning better meant learning the language more authentically: "When you are in a country, you get everything, . . . not only grammar and vocabulary. . . . It's mixed up more." 9

5. *Don't worry about mistakes.* Of course most learners wanted to learn to speak accurately, but learners who made this statement believed that excessive concern about accuracy would get in the way of using the language. "If you don't speak and if you don't write because of your mistakes, you'll have to wait twenty years before you say something. It's better to talk." Asked what advice he would give a friend coming to study English Oshi said, "Speak as much as you can . . . [and] don't care about mistakes." Or (Oshi again), "Just say it. Never be concerned about English structure." 10

Group 2: Learn about the Language

1. *Learn grammar and vocabulary.* Learners who made this statement considered grammar and vocabulary fundamental to successful learning for they are the building blocks of English: "I'm watching my English by learning more vocabulary. . . . English consists of words and I think I should learn more vocabulary." Or, "Grammar background is important to learn. Without grammar background you can't improve. There are some limitations." One learner spelled out these limitations: "If I don't pay attention to constructions, I may translate all the words, but I don't know what they're talking about." 11

2. *Take a formal course.* Learners had different reasons for recommending the taking of a formal course. For some it is the "best way" because "it's systematic." One proceeds "step by step from easy to hard" and in that way does not "miss some basic material" (which was usually grammar, vocabulary and in some cases the "right pronunciation"). 12

Taking a course was also a means of ensuring° that one learned correct English: 13

°making sure

> The course gives me the right base. . . . If you learn to play tennis or to use a weapon, if you don't have the right base to use it, you make mistakes all the time and afterwards you get to making mistakes and you'll never be good cause someone who makes mistakes sticks to them. They'll never get rid of them. Anyway, someone who wants to learn the language has to take a course for the direction.

3. *Learn from mistakes.* This view on mistakes is different from the view 14

presented in the previous category in that it emphasizes the importance of feedback as a way to learn, i.e. mistakes brought to one's attention should be reflected on so that they may be avoided in the future. In some cases feedback comes from friends or a teacher: "When I make a mistake [my friends] correct me. It is a good way to learn from those mistakes." Or "the best way is to write the sentence and let the teacher correct you." And, in others, one becomes aware of one's mistakes oneself. One simply speaks out and contrasts what one has said with what native speakers say and notes the differences. Of this strategy, Jairo says: "I think it's a good way to learn . . . though what one says may not always be right. But, if I don't speak out my mistakes I'll never learn. . . . I'll never find out the right way." Alternately, in the very act of speaking out one becomes aware of one's mistakes. Says Oshi: "Don't care about mistakes, grammar or rules of English. Speak according to the order of your thinking; it will be wrong. You will notice it is different [from English]. Then I'll think according to the English way. I'll speak naturally English. I can change the order of thinking."

4. *Be mentally active.* This statement stressed the need for deliberate, 15 conscious effort on the part of the learner. For Jose, this means paying a lot of attention: "It's very important that you have attention. Without attention, I couldn't understand." Laszlo adds a note of intensity° to the same notion when he says, "My mind is always open to accept information about the language. . . . I always concentrate because I have to learn." Moreover, when one doesn't understand, it is important to ask: "This is the best way to learn—ask always." Finally, being mentally active means acting upon or transforming what one has received or asked about: "I just don't take it as it comes. I change it in my mind. There's always movement."

°force, strength

Group 3: Personal Factors Are Important

1. *The emotional aspect is important.* It is understood that *feelings* have a 16 strong influence on language learning and that they must be taken into account. "I think one problem for me and perhaps everyone learning a language, you have to be stimulated to learn." In some cases, feelings can facilitate° learning: "If the discussion is interesting, one's mind is awake and one is open to learn—even unconsciously." And in others learning is inhibited unless feelings are overcome: "I was not ashamed to ask. That was the main point. I had to overcome this shame or fear."

°make easier

2. *Self-concept can also facilitate or inhibit learning.* Cida reports, "My theory was similar to the theory I had working with adults. They become like children when they're in school . . .; they regress. I decided when it happened to me I wouldn't worry. But still it wasn't easy to endure and live through it." And so, referring to her landlady, she acknowledges, "She treated me like a child—she only made me regress further."

3. *Aptitude° for learning is a third personal factor considered necessary for* 18 *learning.* Says Ryuichi, "I think the improvement of language is due to

°natural ability

some inheritance. . . . I think the most important thing is our personal ability to learn English. In my case, I have no personal ability, so I think it will take a long time. . . . There is no good way to speed up my learning."

Reading and Thinking Strategies

Discussion Activities

Analysis and Conclusions

1. Which of the three groups is helped most by attending language classes? Which is helped least?
2. What types of situations would help the students in group 1 learn the most? Think of specific activities in which students could participate.
3. Which of the factors mentioned in group 3 is inborn? Which of the factors can be changed?
4. Explain the following statement made by a student in group 2: "If I don't pay attention to constructions, I may translate all the words, but I don't know what they're talking about."

Writing and Point of View

1. What is the purpose of the words in italics at the beginning of each of the numbered paragraphs?
2. Reread the article without reading the students' quotations. In what ways do you think the article is improved by including the quotations?
3. What is Wenden's point of view about learning languages? How did you know this as a reader?

Personal Response and Evaluation

1. Which category best describes you as a language learner? Explain your choice.
2. Miguel expressed his attitude toward learning new words as follows: "I don't think I have to use . . . a word, 'cause if it's compulsive, it's not natural." Do you agree? How do you learn new words? The word *compulsive* does not make sense in this sentence. What word do you think Miguel meant to use? Have you ever used the wrong word? What happened?
3. Students in group 1 believe that it is important to use language in a natural way. How often and in what situations do you use English outside of school? Do you have any friends with whom you speak only

English? If so, how did you meet? What has been your experience taking courses only in English?

4. According to students in group 2, the most important material in a language course includes grammar, vocabulary, and "right pronunciation." What else do you want to learn in your English classes?

5. Students in group 2 find it helpful if someone corrects them when they make mistakes. How do you feel about this? Is there ever a time when you would prefer not to be corrected?

Journal Writing

The story depends upon every one of us to come into being. It needs us all, needs our remembering, understanding, and creating what we have heard together to keep on coming into being.

TRINH T. MINH-HA, *Woman, Native, Other*

After reading the Wenden article, think about your own experiences learning English. Write in your journal about something in the Wenden selection that corresponded to your experience learning English. Describe that experience.

Extra Reading

Learning from Natural Language Labs
Nancy Duke S. Lay

Nancy Duke S. Lay is a professor of English at City College, City University of New York. Lay teaches ESL courses and has done research into the way students learn a new language. Her essay describes her own experience learning new languages when she was a girl growing up in the Philippines.

°visited often

In 1945, the store my father owned in Leyte [a city in the Philippines] was frequented° by a majority of the Americans and other foreigners in town because it carried many otherwise unavailable imported goods. Of course, there was also the local community. Most of them were from the middle and upper classes of society. This did not mean that the lower status group did not frequent the store. They did, but not often because they could not afford the prices. Thus, my father's store was known as the meeting place of a certain "elite." Because of this, most of the people who came to the store spoke English, and English became the medium of communication 90% of the time. Even the local people working as employees there had to be able to speak some English.

We, the children of my father, had the advantage of participating in a "living" language lab even before such a term existed. In fact, I never even heard of a language lab until I came to graduate school in New York many years later. However, at my father's store, my language skills—whether English or the Filipino dialect—automatically got exercised as we practiced these languages in a very "natural setting," with "real" people.

The anxiety and stress that resulted from speaking another language slowly disappeared as we tried to communicate with people who came into the store. Even the Filipino customers spoke to us in English with some Filipino words inserted at times. There were also opportunities to practice Fookienese, the local dialect of the Chinese community, and any other dialect that the customers happened to speak. In general, the °welcoming   customers were kind, hospitable,° and helpful to us in our attempts to learn English. Although they were not necessarily ideal people to model the various languages, they were ideal in the sense that they were native speakers of those languages. Thinking back now, I cannot imagine any setting better than this one.

I remember one time when a foreign ship docked at the Tacloban harbor and a group of Taiwanese sailors came ashore. As children, we were always curious and excited when "new visitors" arrived. How often do we meet "people from other lands"? On this occasion, we managed to use our newly learned "Mandarin" in order to communicate with these visitors. It was always fun.

°brothers and sisters   My father encouraged me and my siblings° to spend time at the store. During the academic year, we always helped out after school. This was true of all the families in town who were engaged in commerce, but my brothers and sisters were disciplined so that working in the store became partly our responsibility as early as I could remember.

°soldiers   Ours was a small town grocery store. Behind the store was the sea. There was a bar where hard liquor was served and the American GIs° frequented it. There were legs of smoked Chinese ham hanging from the ceiling. In 1947, a fire broke out across the street. Unfortunately, the wind reversed its direction and fire swept across and gulped down the store.

I remember how my father and mother hurriedly took all of us out through the back door onto a barge that was docked at the wharf. As the barge moved towards the ocean, we saw our store burn and collapse into debris. This was Christmas Day. Our family was about to have Christmas dinner. The night had turned into a nightmare! The next day when my father went back to the site, all that was left were burnt ashes and a metal safe. My father almost gave up his business after the fire of 1947. He planned to take the whole family back to China.

A few months later, using the small amount of insurance money 8 which he had received and the money my mother had managed to save over the years, my father rented another building and started his business all over again. He had lost virtually everything. However, he was determined to save his family of eight from poverty. Since he was a trusted customer, the wholesale companies were willing to help my father get started by giving him credit for certain goods. He worked night and day to rebuild the business he had lost.

The newly rented store was a little smaller than the previous one. On 9 the left, shelves were stacked with varieties of liquor—Martini, Gordon Dry Gin. There were also two glass cases where imported chocolate was displayed—M&M's, Whitman, etc. Only the rich and affluent Filipino and foreign customers could afford these expensive items. In the middle aisle, imported delicious apples and oranges could be seen in square wooden containers. There was also a glass case where imported cigarettes were kept—Philip Morris, Camel, Chesterfield, and Kool. Aside from the usual canned goods, my father's store was unique in its gourmet selection of imported jams, jellies, and peanut butter combined with a display of traditional Filipino mango jams. On top of one shelf that used to display the imported Jacob cream crackers were now the local MYSan cream crackers.

No grocery store is complete without a freezer or refrigerator. The 10 coolers in my father's store were used to store fresh butter, frozen meats, cooked ham, eggs, cheese, and, later, Magnolia ice cream. On the second floor, it was very crowded. Every space was filled with cartons and boxes of goods. It looked like a little warehouse with boxes on top of boxes, some open, some half open. Around one corner were the sleeping quarters for the employees. Space was tight, so only basic furniture was available—a wooden bed and a wooden crate° used as a desk. On top of the bed hung a mosquito net made of cheesecloth. The top of the net was pulled together by its four corners where strings were attached and tied to a nail on the wall. During the day, the net was pulled up, and at night it showered down onto the square bed where a tireless body lay resting.

°box

This store moved to another location nearby ten years later after my 11 father bought a new piece of land (150 square meters) and built a building of his own. This more modern store has glass walls all around, and there is only one entrance/exit compared to the multientrances of the previous store. The mezzanine has become a storage area. In addition, there is an office space and an apartment on the third floor. The rooftop is flat. One can see a large part of the city from the roof since there are no neighboring buildings to block the view. At night, the ocean breeze is delightful!

Although nowadays more grocery stores have been established in my 12 city, my father's store has become "an institution" to most foreign visitors. Some remember "the good old days," and the special personal contact the store offered its customers. Despite modern technology and improvements, the store continues to deal with customers on a one-to-one basis—thus maintaining the uniqueness of a small country-style store.

My most recent visit was in the summer of 1991. The store remains a 13 haven for customers to shop and "chat" in. Instead of going to the local bank, for example, the German Redemptorist priest brings in heavy bags of coins collected in church to change into bills; another young man visiting from California comes in with his chauffeur, only to be told by his middle-aged driver that his father used to shop here. The man is too young to remember anything. An American couple with their five-year-old boy steps into the store asking, "Are these fig bars fresh?" A Japanese engineer with an interpreter is looking for Evian "mineral water."

Discussion Activities

1. Which of the learning styles described in the Wenden article is closest to the one described by Lay?
2. What eliminated the stress and anxiety that are often associated with learning a new language?
3. What part of this essay meant the most to you? Why?

Writing Strategies

Essay Form

Writing a Process Essay

When you write about a process, you are making clear to your readers the steps that are involved in doing something, in coming to a decision, or in experiencing something. Try some of the writing strategies described in the following five steps as you organize your process writing.

1. *Look around* and carefully observe the specific details of the way you or other people behave while going through the process you are writing about. If you are learning English, use your memory. Think about the step-by-step details of the process before you begin to write.

2. *Define* or narrow your subject. Some writers use the dictionary or other source book to help them define the process they wish to

describe. Others narrow the process down after step 1, once they have recognized the detail that will be needed in the final essay.

3. *Describe* in detail the steps that are needed to understand the process or pattern. Readers see the picture through your words, so make them clear and direct. What specific steps did Wenden describe that helped her students learn English? How do the specific details add to the overall effectiveness of the essay?

4. *Analyze* the parts or steps of the pattern or process you are explaining. Then tell how these steps work together. Tell the reader about the history and the future of your subject. What could you include about your personal history to help the reader understand your language learning process? How does knowing something about you help your readers understand your experiences?

5. *Evaluate* the reasons why the pattern or process you are explaining is important to the reader. What could you write that convinces your readers that the issue you are explaining is important to them?

You will not need to use all five steps in every process essay that you write, but keeping them in mind can help you write a clear and effective essay.

Some of the words and phrases that are used in writing a process essay are *first, second, third, as soon as, when, as, next, now, then, before, after,* and *finally.* These words describe the order in which an activity is accomplished; they also connect or make transitions from one idea to the next.

□   □   □

EXERCISES

1. In the following essay, a student describes one way of learning English. After reading the description, underline each occurrence of the transition words and phrases just listed.

The students in Professor Wenden's class talked about many things that helped them learn English. But for me, I agree with the students who say that you have to "live and study in an environment where the target language is spoken."

I studied English for four years in my country, and I could hardly say anything. Even though I could read, I could not hear the words in my head. Then I moved to the United States. As I sat on the airplane, I began to hear people talking English around me. It sounded like noise, but once in a while I could make out a word. I felt afraid about what would happen when the plane landed.

As soon as I arrived in the United States, I enrolled in a language class. I went to school five days a week. First of all, I listened carefully to my teachers. Then, even though it was hard for me, I talked in class when I could. Next, I did my homework every night, and I always watched the television news. After a while, I could understand some of the news stories pretty well. Then, once in a while, I tried to ask questions when I was outside in a store or on the bus. Later, when I got more confident, I made phone calls to ask for information or to order something by mail. That was very hard for me. When I felt I could understand many words, I got a part-time job where I had to speak English. I learned a lot there.

Finally, I made some friends, and I speak some English with them every day. Now I also attend college, and I can understand about 80% of what my teachers say. I still have a long way to go, but I have made a lot of progress.

2. Note the steps involved in accomplishing each of the following goals.

   a. The steps you took to find, apply for, and get accepted at your present school
   b. The steps you took to register for this semester at your school
   c. The steps you took to get a driver's license, a green card, or a social security card
   d. The steps you took to find your present apartment or house

3. Choose one of the tasks in Exercise 2, and write an essay following the description and model of the process essay. Use some of the words and phrases listed in the section titled "Essay Form."

Suggestions for Writing

1. Write an essay in which you describe, step by step, the way you have learned English. What types of activities helped you the most? Which

have been most difficult for you? What have you learned about your-self through your experiences learning English?

2. Write an essay in which you describe the most difficult thing you have ever learned how to do. Explain step by step how you learned and what difficulties you faced. What did you learn about yourself through this experience?

3. Write an essay in which you compare your experiences learning English with those of one of the students described in the Wenden article or those of Nancy Lay. Use the selections for information.

4. Many people say that learning a new language is easier for children than it is for adults. Do you agree or disagree? Explain your point of view, telling about yourself and people you have known or read about. Try to convince your audience.

5. Write an essay in which you compare your first language with English. What are some of the similarities and differences? Be sure to mention word order, plurals, questions, and tenses.

Group Project

After deciding which of Wenden's three groups best describes you as a language learner, work with two or three other students who learn similarly. Your goal is to write an essay describing and explaining your learning style. Describe the situations that are most helpful for you to learn the language and then explain what aspects of the language you focus on and what "advice" you give yourself to learn the most. Give examples from your own language-learning experiences to illustrate your points. Share your essays with the entire class.

Getting Started

Freewriting

It is like fishing. But I do not wait very long, for there is always a nibble—and this is where receptivity comes in. To get started, I will accept anything that occurs to me. Something always occurs, of course, to any of us. We can't keep from thinking.

WILLIAM STAFFORD, *A Way of Writing*

This will be one of the simplest yet probably most productive exercises in this book. Freewriting is a way of getting yourself to write. The technique is easy. Take out a pen or pencil and a blank piece of paper. Note the time and start writing. Write for ten minutes. Do not think about spelling, grammar, punctuation, or organization. Just keep writing. Do not stop even if the only thing you can write is "I have nothing to write about." You will not have to hand this paper in. Freewriting is simply for you; it is a way for you to loosen up your hand and your mind.

Many people say that freewriting helps them get over writing blocks, times when they feel they just cannot write. It is a technique that you can use at any time. All you need is paper, a pen, and ten minutes. So anytime you want to practice your writing, freewrite. Eventually, you may find that freewriting will help you produce ideas that you can use in your formal writing.

☐ ☐ ☐

EXERCISES

1. Before you begin to freewrite, reread some of your journal entries. These may give you ideas. You may also find it enjoyable to see how much progress you are making in your writing.
2. Choose a reading selection from this book and then freewrite. The reading may stimulate your thinking and give you some interesting ideas.

Revising

As practice in learning to revise an essay, it may be helpful to work with someone else's writing first. Working with a classmate, read the following first draft of a student essay.

A Student Essay

There are many languages in the world. In the United States, there are many people who came from other countries, so many people speak different languages here. Those are different from each other very much, but there are similarities, too. My first language is Korean. It is really different from English. Of course, there are some similarities between them, but they are mostly very different. 1

When I came to the United States, I was afraid of people because I didn't know how to speak English. I couldn't read the signs around me in English. It was hard to learn English in the beginning because it's very different from Korean. For example, the subject comes first in English and also in Korean, but the verb comes at the end of the sentence in Korean, not right after the subject like it does in English. 2

In Korean, there are no such things as articles. That is the reason I often forget to put articles in sentences. In questions, Korean has more ways to say than in English. When people ask questions as negatives in English it is negative. No matter what people say, the answer has to be "no," but in Korean it could be "yes" or "no." Making plurals of nouns is 3 very similar as English. In Korean, we put one letter as "s" in English but in Korean that's not really important. When people write, it matters. But when people talk, they often don't use it.

Each language is unique, although there may be some similarities be- 4 tween them. English and Korean are very important to me. There are some differences and similarities between them, but both are important to communication, and I am glad that I could learn English and Korean.

Sohyung Kim, South Korea

With a partner, discuss Sohyung Kim's first draft, asking the following questions:

1. What is the main idea that holds together the entire piece of writing?
2. What specific words or ideas in the first paragraph make you want to read more?
3. What are the supporting details—facts, observations, and experiences that support the main points?
4. What in the final paragraph tells you as a reader that the piece of writing is complete?
5. What one idea will remain with you after reading this essay? Why did you choose this particular idea?

When you finish discussing Kim's essay, reread your own essay. Keep in mind that your writing is not in its final form. With your partner, discuss your writing using the same five questions you used when discussing Kim's. Then rewrite your essay, keeping your partner's suggestions in mind. Share your revision with your partner.

Editing Strategies

Mechanics

Final Sentence Punctuation

Every sentence ending is signaled with a mark. A *period* is the most common indicator to the reader that a sentence has ended. A period is used to end a sentence that makes a statement or gives a command.

When is a *question mark* used? It is used at the end of a direct question. It is not used after an indirect question.

An *exclamation point* is used to express strong feeling. It can be placed after a word or a phrase or at the end of a sentence. However, writers should be careful not to overuse the exclamation point and not to use more than one at a time!

The word that follows the period, question mark, or exclamation point begins with a capital letter. Make sure that your reader always knows where your sentences begin and end.

The Apostrophe

The apostrophe creates an editing problem for many writers. In the following sentences, underline the words that have an apostrophe ('). Then examine the sentences to decide how it is used.

1. I don't think I have to use it.
2. I don't force myself to use a word 'cause it's not natural.
3. Mistakes brought to one's attention should be reflected on.
4. Anita Wenden's study is about language acquisition.

An apostrophe can be used in two ways:

1. It can be used in contractions to show that part of a word is missing.
2. It can be used to show possession, that something belongs to someone.

The apostrophe in sentences 1 and 2 is used to show _____.

The apostrophe in sentences 3 and 4 is used to show _____.

Note: Contractions are found mostly in dialogue and informal writing. The uncontracted forms are usually used in formal writing and speech.

□ □ □

EXERCISES

1. In each of the following sentences, the apostrophe is used to indicate that part of a word is missing. In the blank, fill in the complete word. The first has been done for you.

____*is*____ a. That's the secret.

_____ b. I'll never learn the right way.

_____ c. I wouldn't worry about trying to be perfect.

_____ d. She'd rather practice with real people.

_____ e. He'd spoken English with his friends for many years.

_____ f. It's been said that practice makes perfect.

2. The second use for the apostrophe is to show possession or association, that is, to show that something belongs to or is associated with someone. Fill in the blanks showing the possessive form.

a. the research that belongs to Wenden   <u>*Wenden's research*</u>

b. the friend of Ryuichi   _____

c. the experiences of language learners   _____

d. the needs of the business   _____

3. In the following paragraph, fill in the nine missing apostrophes.

Anita Wendens research involved asking for students opinions about how best to approach language learning. Some students preferred using the language naturally so they dont have to force themselves to use artificial forms and words. One student said hes open-minded about learning. He believes theres always movement if one doesnt try too hard. Cidas experience with her landlady illustrates that its possible to get too much help. Researchers find out important information when they try to get learners perceptions of their experiences.

4. Review any writing you've done recently. Look at your use of apostrophes. Did you use them correctly and appropriately? Then check your use of final sentence punctuation.

Editing Practice

Editing Other People's Writing

After revising for content, writers need to edit their writing for errors. The following paragraph is an unedited draft summarizing some of the main points from the Wenden selection. Find as many errors in format, tense, and final sentence punctuation as you can, and correct them. (If you have problems with the present tense errors, see pages 40–43.) Answers are on page 355.

Becoming a successful language learner

Twenty-five students from Columbia University have talked about their experiences learning English. They think that students needs to use English in a natural way? They should practice and try to think in the new language as much as possible. A lot of students were thinking that they should be in an English-speaking country to learn English!! Some students had said that it is important to learn the grammar and vocabulary. They think people learned from making mistakes. Personal factors such as personality and aptitude for learning is also important. I am learned a lot from reading this article.

Editing Your Own Writing

Reread an essay that you wrote for this chapter, asking yourself the following questions:

1. Did I format my paper correctly?
2. Did I start new paragraphs when necessary?
3. Did I use final sentence punctuation and apostrophes correctly?
4. Did I use the past tenses correctly?

When you rewrite your essay, make any changes that will improve your writing.

Grammar Strategies

Forms of the Present Tense

In English, we can express the present tense in four ways, with slightly different meanings.

1. The *simple present* is used to describe the following:

   a. *Habitual or routine activities.* Adverbs of frequency, such as *usually, each day,* and *always* (see page 44 for a more complete list), sometimes are used with simple present tense.

   Sometimes I *stay* up as late as 2 A.M. doing homework.
   I usually *do* my homework before I *watch* television.

b. *States of being.* Verbs that refer to sensory perceptions, emotional states, conditions, judgments, and states of being are called *stative* verbs and are almost always in the simple present tense unless they are describing the past.

> They *want* me to be number one.
> I *love* my parents very much.
> I just *feel* like taking a break.
> She *is* a lawyer.

c. *What is going on* in scientific experiments and other types of research, on television or radio, and in newspaper headlines.

> She *puts* the chemical in the tube and *heats* it slowly.
> The pitcher *throws* a curve ball at the batter.
> "Fires *rage* in California, *threaten* many homes"

2. The *present continuous (progressive)* is used to describe actions that are happening right now or at the moment of speaking. Some expressions that are used with the present continuous tense are *now, right now, at this moment,* and *at present.* (Certain verbs are not used in the present continuous tense; see page 45 for a list of these verbs.)

> I *am studying* for my math test.

3. The *present perfect* is used to describe an action that began in the past and continues to the present and beyond. (See page 19 for uses of this tense to describe the past.)

> They *have lived* in a city all their lives.

4. The *present perfect continuous* is used to describe an ongoing action that began in the past and continues to the present and beyond.

> She *has been studying* French since 1990.

Question Form Using the Present Tense

When we create questions, we use question words such as *do, does, what, where, when, who, why,* and *how* and sometimes change the order of the words in the sentence.

1. In the simple present, a question is formed by changing a statement in the following way:

Sometimes I stay up as late as 2 A.M. doing homework.
BECOMES
Does he stay up until 2 A.M. doing homework?
OR
How late does he stay up?
OR
What does he do until 2 A.M.?

If the verb *am, is,* or *are* is used, we use these words to form the question and change the word order.

She is a lawyer.
BECOMES
Is she a lawyer?
OR
What is her profession?

2. The present continuous uses *am, is,* or *are* in the question form and changes the word order.

They are studying English right now.
BECOMES
Are they studying English right now?
OR
What are they studying right now?
OR
What are they doing right now?

3. The present perfect uses *has* or *have* in the question form and changes the word order.

They have lived in a city all their lives.
BECOMES
Have they lived in a city all their lives?
OR
How long have they lived in a city?

4. The present perfect continuous uses *has* or *have* and *been* + the *-ing* form of the verb in the question and changes the word order.

She has been studying French since 1990.
BECOMES
Has she been studying French since 1990?
OR
How long has she been studying French?

OR

What has she been doing since 1990?

□   □   □

EXERCISES

1. Make two questions for each of the following eight answers about the Wenden selection.

   a. Wenden thinks that researchers can learn from doing interviews.

      Does _____

      How _____

   b. One of the themes focuses on using the language in a natural way.

      Does _____

      What _____

   c. Wenden is trying to understand what helps her students learn.
   d. Some learners think that grammar and vocabulary are the building blocks of English.
   e. Students have learned from their mistakes.
   f. Some students are living in the United States just to practice the language.
   g. Ilse has been listening to get the sounds of English and transfer them into her thinking.
   h. Many have learned by going to school and using English every day.

2. An excerpt from "How to Be a Successful Language Learner" is reprinted here. Underline all the present tense verbs.

This view on mistakes is different from the view presented in the previous category in that it emphasizes the importance of feedback as a way to learn, i.e. mistakes brought to one's attention should be reflected on so that they may be avoided in the future. In some cases feedback comes from friends or a teacher: "When I make a mistake [my friends] correct me. It is a good way to learn from those mistakes." Or "the best way is to write the sentence and let the teacher correct you." And, in others, one becomes aware of one's mistakes oneself. One simply speaks out and contrasts what one has said with what native speakers say and notes the differences.

3. When is the final *s* used in each of the present tense verbs you underlined? What is the subject of each of these verbs?

Adverbs of Frequency

Adverbs of frequency are used to tell how often something happens or someone does something. On a continuum from the most often to the least, adverbs might be arranged this way:

always → generally → usually → frequently → often → occasionally → sometimes → seldom → rarely → never

Another adverb of frequency, *ever,* which means "at any time," is often used in questions.

□   □   □

EXERCISES

1. Interview a member of your class, asking the following questions. Write down the answers so that you will be able to use them later.

   a. What subjects do your teachers generally ask you to write about in your classes?
   b. What subjects do you usually prefer to write about in your classes?
   c. Do your teachers generally give you a choice of several subjects to write about or only one?
   d. Do you ever find it difficult to get ideas when you start to write? If you do, what do you usually do to help you get going?
   e. Do you ever talk to your classmates before you start to write?
   f. When you write, what do you usually concentrate on?
   g. Outside of school, when do you usually write in English?
   h. Do you usually do your homework at home or in school?
   i. Do you ever do your homework on the way to school?
   j. Do you sometimes find it difficult to understand your teachers in your classes? If you do, what do you generally do to help you understand what is going on in class?

2. Reread your answers to the questions in Exercise 1, and discuss with the student you have interviewed any areas about which you are confused. Then write an essay describing the student you interviewed, using his or her answers from Exercise 1 and writing in the third person, for example, *Dora often goes to the library to read books, and she regularly uses these ideas when writing in her journal.* . . . Check your verb endings and tenses.

Verbs Not Used in Continuous Tenses

Certain verbs are not usually used in the continuous tenses (present continuous, past continuous, future continuous, present perfect continuous, and so on). Here is a list of these verbs:

appear	hate	need	seem
appreciate	have	own	smell
be	hear	possess	sound
believe	know	prefer	taste
cost	like	recognize	understand
dislike	love	remember	want
feel	mean	see	

These verbs can be divided into three basic categories:

1. *Words that relate to feelings.* For example, "I hate you" or "I love you" is treated as a permanent state of being, not just a present-moment feeling, whereas "I am feeling sick today" is correct because the verb is expressing a temporary state of being.
2. *Words that relate to ownership or possession.* For example, "I own a green convertible" or "I have a house in the country" is regarded as permanent, whereas "I am having some people over for dinner tonight" is correct because the verb does not express a permanent state of being.
3. *Words that relate to perception.* For example, "I see a blue sky above me" or "I smell the potatoes burning" is not treated as a continuous action, whereas "I am hearing Bach for the first time" is correct, since it expresses a perception that takes place at the moment the sentence is spoken and refers to an event that takes place over a period of time.

□ □ □

EXERCISE   In the following text, choose the simple present or the present continuous tense. If either tense is possible, discuss the difference in meaning created by the tense you choose. Some verbs you might use are *study, describe, want, come, help, learn, try, explain, say,* and *need.* You may choose other verbs; there are many correct possibilities. Experiment to see how changing the verb or its tense can change the meaning of a sentence.

Linguistic reseachers such as Anita Wenden _____ to know

more about the way people _____ languages. They

_____ to find out by talking to their own students, who

_____ from different parts of the world and _____

different languages. Students _____ three different ways that

_____ them learn English. Some _____ they

_____ to talk in a natural environment with real people in

real situations. Some of these students _____ in the United

States so that they can practice English. Others _____ with

American families, and some _____ for companies in which

they can speak English. Another group _____ that going to

school is the best method. They _____ classes and _____

after school. The third group _____ that the student's per-

sonality _____ a big difference. These students

_____ to learn English even though they _____

that people _____ a special ability to learn a new language.

What do you think?

This text would be easier to read if it were divided into paragraphs.
Read it with a classmate, and decide where new paragraphs should begin. Mark each new paragraph with the symbol ¶. Most writers agree that
there should be three paragraphs. If you have any difficulty with this, review "The Paragraph" on pages 9–10.

Reread Sohyung Kim's essay on page 36. Notice her uses of present
and past tenses. When does she use each? Why?

◻ ◻ ◻

**CHECKING
YOUR OWN
WORK**

1. Read through each essay you wrote for this chapter. Look at the
   verbs in the essay. (It may be helpful to underline them lightly.) Did
   you use the correct forms of the present tenses? Did you use the correct forms of each of the verbs? Is there an *s* ending on all present
   tense verbs in the third person singular (*he, she, it*)? Did you use any
   verbs in continuous tenses that are not usually used in these tenses?
2. As an extra check, work with a classmate to make sure that you have
   used the present tense correctly in your writing.

CHAPTER THREE

Struggling to Communicate

PREREADING ACTIVITIES

1. The story you will read in this chapter is by Ernest Hemingway. Based on what you know about him or his writing, what do you expect to find in the story?
2. Discuss some of the differences you have noticed in living in two different cultures.
3. If you or anyone you know has been sick in the United States, did you have any problems in getting help, getting medicine, or communicating to someone what was wrong?

VOCABULARY DEVELOPMENT

One way to learn new words is to learn the different forms that a word can take. In English, a word can be a noun, a verb, an adjective, or an adverb. Not all words take all forms, but many words have more than one form. Fill in the blanks (if no word exists, no blank appears in the column.) The first row has been done for you.

Noun	Verb	Adjective	Adverb
difference	differ	different	differently
_____		miserable	_____
instruction	_____	_____	_____
_____	_____	prescribed	
_____	exist	_____	
_____	_____	_____	evidently
_____	commence		

A Day's Wait
Ernest Hemingway

Ernest Hemingway (1899–1961) was an American writer who often wrote about relationships. The story "A Day's Wait" is about one day in the life of a father and his young son who is suffering from the flu and a mysterious fear.

He came into the room to shut the windows while we were still in bed 1
and I saw he looked ill. He was shivering, his face was white, and
he walked slowly as though it ached to move.

"What's the matter, Schatz?" 2

"I've got a headache." 3

"You better go to bed." 4

"No. I'm all right." 5

"You go to bed. I'll see you when I'm dressed." 6

But when I came downstairs he was dressed, sitting by the fire, look- 7
ing a very sick and miserable boy of nine years. When I put my hand on
his forehead I knew he had a fever.

"You go up to bed," I said, "you're sick." 8

"I'm all right," he said. 9

When the doctor came he took the boy's temperature. 10

"What is it?" I asked him. 11

"One hundred and two." 12

Downstairs, the doctor left three different medicines in different col- 13
ored capsules with instructions for giving them. One was to bring down
the fever, another a purgative,° the third to overcome an acid condition.
The germs of influenza can only exist in an acid condition, he explained. He seemed to know all about influenza and said there was nothing to worry about if the fever did not go above one hundred and four
degrees. This was a light epidemic of flu and there was no danger if you
avoided pneumonia.

Back in the room I wrote the boy's temperature down and made a 14
note of the time to give the various capsules.

"Do you want me to read to you?" 15

"All right. If you want to," said the boy. His face was very white and 16
there were dark areas under his eyes. He lay still in the bed and seemed
very detached from what was going on.

I read aloud from Howard Pyle's *Book of Pirates;* but I could see he was 17
not following what I was reading.

"How do you feel, Schatz?" I asked him. 18

"Just the same, so far," he said. 19

I sat at the foot of the bed and read to myself while I waited for it to 20
be time to give another capsule. It would have been natural for him to
go to sleep, but when I looked up he was looking at the foot of the bed,
looking very strangely.

"Why don't you try to go to sleep? I'll wake you up for the medicine." 21

"I'd rather stay awake." 22

After a while he said to me, "You don't have to stay in here with me, 23
Papa, if it bothers you."

"It doesn't bother me." 24

"No, I mean you don't have to stay if it's going to bother you." 25

°laxative, cleanser of the
bowels

I thought perhaps he was a little lightheaded and after giving him the 26
prescribed capsules at eleven o'clock I went out for a while.

°partly frozen rain

It was a bright, cold day, the ground covered with a sleet° that had 27
frozen so that it seemed as if all the bare trees, the bushes, the cut brush
and all the grass and the bare ground had been varnished with ice. I

°dog often used for
 hunting

°slid

took the young Irish setter° for a little walk up the road and along a
frozen creek, but it was difficult to stand or walk on the glassy surface
and the red dog slipped and slithered° and I fell twice, hard, once dropping my gun and having it slide away over the ice.

°drove out of hiding
°flock or group
°a type of wild bird

We flushed° a covey° of quail° under a high clay bank with overhang- 28
ing brush and I killed two as they went out of sight over the top of the
bank. Some of the covey lit in trees, but most of them scattered into
brush piles and it was necessary to jump on the ice-coated mounds of
brush several times before they would flush. Coming out while you were
poised unsteadily on the icy, springy brush they made difficult shooting
and I killed two, missed five, and started back pleased to have found a
covey close to the house and happy there were so many left to find on
another day.

At the house they said the boy had refused to let any one come into 29
the room.

"You can't come in," he said. "You mustn't get what I have." 30

I went up to him and found him in exactly the position I had left him, 31
white-faced, but with the tops of his cheeks flushed by the fever, staring
still, as he had stared, at the foot of the bed.

I took his temperature. 32

"What is it?" 33

"Something like a hundred," I said. It was one hundred and two and 34
four tenths.

"It was a hundred and two," he said. 35

"Who said so?" 36

"The doctor." 37

"Your temperature is all right," I said. "It's nothing to worry about." 38

"I don't worry," he said, "but I can't keep from thinking." 39

"Don't think," I said. "Just take it easy." 40

"I'm taking it easy," he said and looked straight ahead. He was evi- 41
dently holding tight onto himself about something.

"Take this with water." 42

"Do you think it will do any good?" 43

"Of course it will." 44

I sat down and opened the Pirate book and commenced to read, but 45
I could see he was not following, so I stopped.

"About what time do you think I'm going to die?" he asked. 46

"What?" 47

"About how long will it be before I die?" 48

"You aren't going to die. What's the matter with you?" 49

"Oh, yes, I am. I heard him say a hundred and two."   50

"People don't die with a fever of one hundred and two. That's a silly   51
way to talk."

"I know they do. At school in France the boys told me you can't live   52
with forty-four degrees. I've got a hundred and two."

He had been waiting to die all day, ever since nine o'clock in the   53
morning.

"You poor Schatz," I said. "Poor old Schatz. It's like miles and kilo-   54
meters. You aren't going to die. That's a different thermometer. On that
thermometer thirty-seven is normal. On this kind it's ninety-eight."

"Are you sure?"   55

"Absolutely," I said. "It's like miles and kilometers. You know, like how   56
many kilometers we make when we do seventy miles in the car?"

"Oh," he said.   57

°limp   But his gaze at the foot of the bed relaxed slowly. The hold over him-   58
self relaxed too, finally, and the next day it was very slack° and he cried
easily at little things that were of no importance.

Reading and Thinking Strategies

Discussion Activities

Analysis and Conclusions

1. What is the relationship between the boy and his father? Did you
   think it was odd that the boy's mother did not figure in the story?

2. Why do you think Schatz didn't just tell his father what he was afraid
   of? Why wouldn't he want his father to know that he was afraid? What
   does this say about the father? About the son?

3. Why does the boy suggest that his father leave?

4. Does Hemingway help you picture the boy and the father? How did
   you see them? Describe what the father looks like. Describe what the
   boy looks like. When you read, do you usually picture the characters
   inside your head? Does it help you if the author describes the characters carefully, or do you prefer to use your imagination?

Writing and Point of View

1. For the first half of the story, we do not know who the narrator (teller
   of the story) is; in other words, we do not know from whose point of
   view the story is being told. When you began reading the story, who
   did you think "I" was? What clues did you have?

2. When Schatz asks his father if "it" will bother him, what is "it"?

3. Fiction creates a mood or a feeling. What is the mood of this story? What elements or parts of the story create this mood? Some things to think about are these: In what season does the story take place? Where does it take place—the city or the country? What does the father leave the house to do? What might Hemingway's purpose be for including the hunting scene in the middle of the story? Are the boy and the father alone in the house? Do we meet any other characters?

Personal Response and Evaluation

1. If you were Schatz's father or mother, how would you have handled the situation?
2. Have you had any similar experience?
3. If Schatz were a girl, how would the story change? Why?
4. Why does the father go hunting?

Response Paragraph

1. After reading "A Day's Wait," write a paragraph describing how the story made you feel and what personal memories it brought to your mind. Share your paragraph with a classmate.
2. Write a paragraph explaining how Shatz's confusion about the temperature corresponds to some confusion you have felt because of cultural differences. Share your paragraph with others in a small group.

Journal Writing

First, I do not sit down at my desk to put into verse something that is already clear in my mind. If it were clear in my mind, I should have no incentive or need to write about it. . . . We do not write to be understood; we write in order to understand.

C. DAY LEWIS, *The Poetic Image*

Writing in a journal, whether it is shared or kept for yourself, is powerful. It is a means of touching on feelings and experiences hidden inside yourself. Lewis writes that we write in order to understand. What do you understand about this story or yourself as a result of writing?

"A Day's Wait" is about a fundamental fear in life, the fear of dying. It is about a boy's unexpressed fear and in some ways his unexpressed love as well. Have you ever felt afraid? Have you ever thought about dying?

Writing Strategies

Essay Strategies

Describing a Place

When you write a description of a place, you are trying to paint a picture with words. As you prepare to write, look at the place in person, in a photograph, or in your mind. Make notes about what makes this place interesting, unique, or worth describing. In your notes, describe shapes and sizes and the colors, textures, and designs of the place. Think about how these contribute to the feeling of the place. Compare the place to other places you have seen or read about.

Refer to your notes when you write about the place. In your writing, be sure to include enough details so that your readers will be able to imagine the place. Make sure your readers understand why you want them to know in detail about this place.

Notice how Ernest Hemingway's clear and vivid picture emphasizes the coldness of a winter day in the country in "A Day's Wait."

It was a bright, cold day, the ground covered with a sleet that had frozen so that it seemed as if all the bare trees, the bushes, the cut brush and all the grass and the bare ground had been varnished with ice. I took the young Irish setter for a little walk up the road and along a frozen creek, but it was difficult to stand or walk on the glassy surface and the red dog slipped and slithered and I fell twice, hard, once dropping my gun and having it slide away over the ice.

1. What picture forms in your mind as you read this paragraph?
2. If you have never seen ice, what does Hemingway compare it to that will help you picture this wintry day?

If Hemingway's paragraph were rewritten to include warmer images, the story might change.

It was a sunny spring day, the ground alive with wildflowers that had just opened so that it seemed as if all the daisies, the chamomile, the clover, and the grass had been filled with new life. I took the young Irish setter for a little walk up the road and along the green path, but it was difficult to keep the dog from rushing ahead. I fell twice against the soft ground, dropping my gun and having it slide off into the deep, new grass.

Reread the story, substituting this paragraph for Hemingway's version. Does the mood of the story change? Try doing this with another story. Rewrite a paragraph using the author's style but changing the images to create a different mood. How does it affect you as a reader?

In Nancy Duke S. Lay's essay in Chapter Two, she writes:

The newly rented store was a little smaller than the previous one. On the left, shelves were stacked with varieties of liquor—Martini, Gordon Dry Gin. There were also two glass cases where imported chocolate was displayed—M&M's, Whitman, etc. Only the rich and affluent Filipino and foreign customers could afford these expensive items. In the middle aisle, imported delicious apples and oranges could be seen in square wooden containers. There was also a glass case where imported cigarettes were kept—Philip Morris, Camel, Chesterfield, and Kool. Aside from the usual canned goods, my father's store was unique in its gourmet selection of imported jams, jellies, and peanut butter combined with a display of traditional Filipino mango jams. On top of one shelf that used to display the imported Jacob cream crackers were now the local MYSan cream crackers.

No grocery store is complete without a freezer or refrigerator. The coolers in my father's store were used to store fresh butter, frozen meats, cooked ham, eggs, cheese, and, later, Magnolia ice cream. On the second floor, it was very crowded. Every space was filled with cartons and boxes of goods. It looked like a little warehouse with boxes on top of boxes, some open, some half open. Around one corner were the sleeping quarters for the employees. Space was tight, so only basic furniture was available—a wooden bed and a wooden crate used as a desk. On top of the bed hung a mosquito net made of cheesecloth. The top of the net was pulled together by its four corners where strings were attached and tied to a nail on the wall. During the day, the net was pulled up, and at night it showered down onto the square bed where a tireless body lay resting.

1. What picture forms in your mind as you read this description?
2. What do you think are Lay's feelings about the store? What words and phrases stand out for you?

A student from Afghanistan, Zelimin Sarwary, writes about a visit to the home of a family friend, Nasema:

The dining room was in a square shape about 18 feet wide. Nasema, as was customary, had no dining table or cabinet in her dining room. Instead of a cabinet for china wares, the dining room had four shelves which Nasema decorated with antique things such as ancient spoons, plates, glasses, teapots, cups, china, and so on. The decoration of the dining room made my mother enjoy Nasema's delicious home-cooked meals even more. Because Nasema had no dining table, she had to use a cloth on the floor and place the food on it.

There were three bedrooms of equal size, one white, one pink, and one light green. Nasema and her children slept on the soft comfortable cotton mats, the "toshaks," that the Afghan people sleep on. The colors are sometimes coordinated with the walls. The bathroom was large and was without a shower. Seldom did Nasema wash herself and her children at home. Regularly they went to a "hammom" or sauna because it was warm and more comfortable than home where there were not so many people.

The simple hammom Nasema used held about four hundred people. It had five different rooms for different purposes. The very first room was used by those who paid money to the cashier and their clothes were kept there. The second was used for changing clothes. It had about twenty benches. Each bench seated about ten people. In the third room, people washed their bodies. It had two white and black stone "Dake Done" or communal bath tubs, one for hot water and the other for cold water. Against the wall, there were two cubicles. For some reason, the people called those two cubicles the "Bride's House." They had only cold water. People usually went there at the very end and took a cold shower. After that, they went to the dressing room to get dressed. There were a few masseuses for the customers. The women's hammom was separated from the men's but up to five-year-old boys were allowed to go with their mothers. People in Afghanistan believe that up to five-year-old boys are not mature enough to think about sex.

After the hammom, Nasema and my mother stayed up half the night talking about the Soviet invasion of Afghanistan. They both cried. Night passed and the following morning came.

1. What picture forms in your mind as you read this descriptive essay?
2. What do you know about Nasema and Afghanistan from reading this essay? What words and phrases stand out for you?

□   □   □

EXERCISES

1. Write two descriptions of a room that you know well—your living room, kitchen, or bedroom, for example. Write a short description and then a detailed description. Share both with a classmate. Discuss the differences and how you decide how much detail to include in your writing.
2. Write two descriptions of a room from your past—your fifth grade classroom or your old bedroom, for example. Follow the same steps as in Exercise 1.

Essay Form

Dialogue

When you read or write stories or essays, plays or film scripts, you should be aware of the way people talk to each other. Writers try to make the conversation or spoken interchanges between people realistic, interesting, and illustrative. Illustrative dialogue means that what the person says should indicate something about the person's personality or character. It should reveal the relationship of the people talking.

In "A Day's Wait," Hemingway writes:

"You go up to bed," I said, "you're sick."
"I'm all right," he said.

Dialogue is also a way of presenting actions or providing information that moves the story along.

"People don't die with a fever of one hundred and two. That's a silly way to talk."

"I know they do. At school in France the boys told me you can't live with forty-four degrees. I've got a hundred and two."

He had been waiting to die all day, ever since nine o'clock in the morning.

"You poor Schatz," I said. "Poor old Schatz. It's like miles and kilometers. You aren't going to die. That's a different thermometer. On that thermometer thirty-seven is normal. On this kind it's ninety-eight."

What can a reader guess about the relationship of the two individuals? What does this suggest about what Hemingway wants his readers to feel?

□ □ □

EXERCISES

"What's the matter, Schatz?"
"I've got a headache."
"You better go to bed."
"No. I'm all right."
"You go to bed. I'll see you when I'm dressed."

1. After reading this excerpt from the Hemingway story, discuss the following questions.

   a. Who is talking, and how do you, as a reader, know this?
   b. How would you describe the relationship of these people? Who has the power in this conversation?
   c. What pictures of these people did you form as you read this? What do they look like and sound like to you as reader?

2. Look at the stories in Chapters 6, 9, 12, and 15. Choose one interchange of dialogue—three or four lines in each of these stories—and ask yourself the same questions as in Exercise 1. Discuss your answers.

Direct Speech

Using direct speech, quotations that occur in articles we read and write, is a little different from using dialogue in a story or a play. The purpose, however, is similar. The author tries to show the readers an individual's personality, character, or relationship to others through the vocabulary and expressions that the person uses. Using direct speech also reveals opinions and actions, so writers usually use quotations when describing a politician, a famous person, or a particular individual's activities. In the article on Berenice Belizaire, (see page 4) Joe Klein quotes Belizaire several times.

"Why can't we go home?" Berenice asked her mother.
"I have a pretty good memory," Berenice admitted last week.
"They started coming to me for help," she says. "They never called me a nerd."

"I want to build a famous computer, like IBM," she said. "I want my name to be part of it."

He could have written these same ideas in indirect speech (see pages 295–97 for more information on this) as follows:

Berenice asked her mother why they couldn't go home.
Berenice admitted that she had a pretty good memory.
She said that students started going to her for help and never called her a nerd.
She said that she wants to build a famous computer and wants her name to be a part of it.

Why do you think Klein decided to quote Berenice herself? Read the article, substituting the rewritten lines. How do they change the article? Which version do you prefer? Why?

□   □   □

EXERCISE

Read through several other selections in the book looking for quotations. Choose three or four examples to discuss with your class. Why do you think the author chose the particular quotation? What does it indicate about the speaker?

Suggestions for Writing

Before you begin to write, you may want to review your journal or any other writing you have done for this chapter. Try clustering to help you get ideas, as described in the next section, "Getting Started." Always spend some time thinking before you begin to write.

1. Write a description of a place that you do not like. Use words and phrases that convey your feelings to your reader.

2. Write a description of a place that you enjoy thinking about. Use words and phrases that convey your feelings to your reader.

3. Read Alevtina Musheyeva's essay "A Dilemma" (below), about the city of Tashkent. Then write an essay describing a place that you know well from your past. Use many sensory details so that your reader can experience the place as fully as possible. What historical sites are there to visit? What modern conveniences make it a comfortable place to visit? What entertainment would enable a visitor to have fun? What natural attractions—beaches, parks, mountains—make it a special place to visit? Use this essay to convince your reader of the pleasures and excitement of traveling to and visiting this place.

4. Write an essay describing an imaginary city of the future. What special conveniences make this an interesting city to live in? What entertainment would enable an inhabitant to have fun? What unusual nat-

ural attractions make it a special place? What inventions of the future make this an especially exciting place in which to live?

A Student Essay

A DILEMMA

You have a dilemma? You don't know where to spend your vacation and money? Stop thinking about it and hurry to visit my home city: Tashkent. 1

Tashkent is the capital of Uzbekistan. It is a part of Middle Asia. Tashkent is 3000 years old. It's the most ancient city in all of Middle Asia. In Tashkent, the climate is very pleasant, particularly in spring and late fall. People in my city are very kind, generous, and friendly. 2

Tashkent is a really exciting place to visit. There are a lot of sightseeing adventures there for tourists. My city is full of fashionable, luxurious hotels, and beautiful buildings in *mosaic style.* Also there are many bars, restaurants, theaters, cinemas, and various stores and shops. 3

Recently, developers built a skyscraper. It is the second tallest building in the former Soviet Union. At the top of that skyscraper there are two restaurants with views all over the city. It is very romantic to spend your evening there near the open window with fresh air. 4

Besides the skyscraper, there is a very big theater. It is the most famous "Palace of People's Friendship." All famous and big stars perform there. The structure of the palace is similar to the twin towers in New York. 5

Tashkent is very famous for its fantastic subway. The Tashkent subway stations are made of marble and look like palaces. The Tashkent subway is a place where you meet your date and travel to different stations astonished by the dazzlingly beautiful architecture of the subway palaces. 6

Uzbekistan is rich in oil, coal, copper, and building materials. Tashkent trades with all the countries of the world. Tashkent even has reciprocal friendship relations with Seattle, Washington. 7

Uzbekistan is also the chief cotton-growing area in the former Soviet Union and the third in the world. If you have a chance to go to the cotton field, don't miss it; try by yourself to separate the cotton from the shell. In the past, people did everything with their own hands. It was the hardest work among all other work, but now people have created special machines to do their work more easily. But it is still fun to go there and try it with your own hands. 8

Tashkent has gone through a lot of cultural changes. In the earlier years, when the shah was ruling, my city was totally different. For example, one change was in the way that people were clothed. Women used to cover their faces with special covers. Men had to be separated from 9 women. Women didn't go to work. They stayed at home and took care of their families.

In recent years the situation has changed. Now women are equal with men. They can do everything they want. They are free to choose their own style of dress. And women can take any position equally with men. 10

If you decide to visit Tashkent, don't miss the marriage ritual because it's a very interesting process. In the past, when a couple got married, they didn't know each other before the day of the wedding. It was the rule for everybody. But in contrast, now if a couple want to get married, they spend a lot of time together before the wedding. You can see now that time changes everything. 11

I think that I forgot something else, something important. If you want to taste the natural flavor of fruits and vegetables, go to my city and get them; don't deprive yourself. Delight yourself. I can't describe everything because I can't find the words for it. It is really an amazing city to visit. 12

I could write a lot about my city. But I think that it is better to see it once than to hear about it many times. And even if it doesn't look perfect on paper, it's perfect to see it by yourself, with your own eyes. And I can guarantee you will have fun and you won't regret your choice. 13

Alevtina Musheyeva, Uzbekistan

Getting Started

Clustering

Sometimes even though we have ideas about a subject, we cannot seem to write them down. The blank page fills us with fear. One technique that may help you overcome this problem is clustering. It is a simple but effective method to get started writing.

First, begin with a blank notebook page. In the middle of the page, write your nucleus term (the key concept you will be writing about) and circle it. (In our example, the nucleus term is *favorite room.*) Then write down any other words that occur to you; circle these words and draw arrows connecting your original word to them.

Write the words down quickly, as they occur to you. Connect words where you think they belong together. When something new occurs to you, go back to the nucleus and draw a new arrow and circle. You can have as many circles as you have ideas. Don't try to make sense, and don't worry if the clustering doesn't seem to be going anywhere. If you temporarily run out of ideas, doodle a little bit by drawing your circles or arrows darker. Keep clustering until you get a sense of what you are going to write. Then stop clustering, read the ideas in the circles, and start to write.

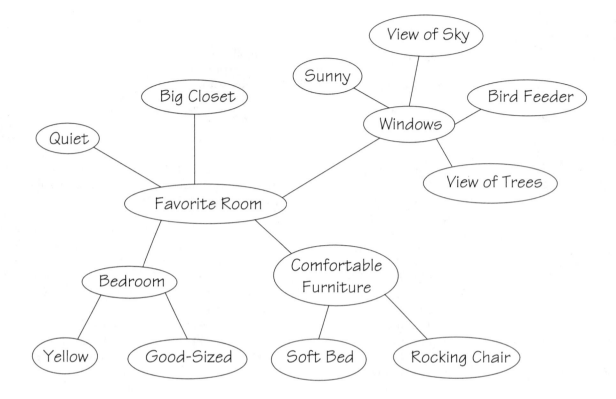

There is no right or wrong way to form clusters. When you start to write, the words will come and begin to take over; the writing will come easily. Don't stop yourself. Let it happen and see what occurs in your writing.

□   □   □

EXERCISES

1. Begin with a clean page. Write the word *home* in the middle of the page, and circle it. Let your mind begin to make connections. You may want to close your eyes. When a word comes to you, write it on the page, circle it, and draw an arrow to it from your nucleus or from its connecting word. Let yourself go, and do not judge or even really think about what you are writing. You will know when to stop when you feel a strong urge to write, when you suddenly know what you want to say. Then glance at your word clusters, and begin writing on a new page. Write until you feel that you have written out all your ideas. You may want to look at your clustering again to see if you had any ideas that you did not develop. Then read what you have written, and spend a few minutes making any changes that you think will improve the piece of writing.
2. Do the same with the term *favorite room* or *dream house*.

Revising

When you have finished writing your essay, separate yourself from your writing by reading the following student essay.

A Student Essay

A SPECIAL PLACE

It is not easy to choose a place that is meaningful for me. Life consists of 1
many different steps having different meanings. Everybody recalls special moments and special places, each one of which is placed in a specific time of life.

Many people recall the "special place" from their childhood. Some- 2
one else may have a "special place" from adolescence. Many others are still "looking" for the special place in their life. None of these three cases applies to me. My "special place" has always been the same since the day I was born. It is my home and family. I understand that the family is not a "place," but I cannot see my house without my family inside.

When I talk about my home, I refer to the house we have in Rome, 3
Italy. I spent more than twenty years of my life there before I came to the United States. Twenty years is a very long period of time in anyone's life, and certainly it's long enough to build strong feelings for the house and the location. I do not miss the house in Rome physically because I also have a very nice house here in the United States. I miss it for sentimental reasons because the house in Rome still has a "special place" in my heart.

I would like to give a general description of the house. First of all, I 4
should make a technical correction because the house is really an apartment. It is on the third floor of a modern building in the southern part of Rome. From this location, it takes about fifteen minutes to drive to the center of the city where all the famous monuments of Rome are— the Colosseum, the Roman Forum, Vatican City, Trevi Fountain, etc. Rome always has a very good public transportation system which allows people to reach any place in the city by taking the bus, the tram, or the subway.

The apartment is not very big, but it is large enough to satisfy all our 5
family's needs. It consists of a kitchen, bathroom, dining room and living room combination, the bedrooms, and a large room at the entrance. The appearance is different from American houses. The style is typically Italian with marble and ceramic floors, brick walls, wallpaper, and ceramic walls in the kitchen and bathroom. Also, there are two large balconies outside of the kitchen and the dining room. The kitchen's balcony is situated over the driveway, which connects the main entrance of

the building to the street, and the other balcony faces a secondary road. It is possible to see the ruins of the Roman Aqueduct from this balcony. The building is located in a quiet area because there is not much traffic in the streets nearby.

I always felt very secure and free in the apartment in Rome. I was able to relax immediately after entering it and feel some kind of immunity from the outside world. I already mentioned that I spent all my youth in Rome. This period is very important in anyone's life. Anything that happens during this time leaves strong and deep impressions which we carry with us for the rest of our days. The apartment in Rome has been important to me in this way. I physically grew up in the apartment and became an adult there. In that place I built and shaped part of my personality between happy and very sad moments. I cannot forget all the problems my parents had paying for the apartment since both of them were fighting health problems. Keeping the apartment represents the results of many sacrifices which I felt in my heart, in my head, and in my entire body. This is another reason why I love the apartment in Rome. These negative aspects make me express positive feelings because my entire family worked hard and rationally to keep the apartment. No one in my family can forget all the energy that each one of us spent physically and mentally for it. That is why we all consider the apartment our special place. As a matter of fact, even though the whole family lives in the United States, we still have the apartment in Rome completely furnished and with all the necessary things. We never talk about selling it because it is not possible to sell a part of our life and our soul that we call "the apartment in Rome—our special place."

6

Gianni Bergesio, Italy

With a partner, answer the following questions about Gianni Bergesio's writing. (It is useful to write out your answers.)

1. What specific words and phrases tell the reader what Bergesio feels about his "special place"?
2. What words and phrases connect paragraph 1 to the next paragraph and so on?
3. What specific descriptive phrases create a "picture" of Bergesio's apartment?
4. What did you like best about this essay?
5. What did you want to know more about when you read the essay?

Next revise the same five questions to fit the essay you are working on. Exchange a draft of the essay with a partner. After reading your classmate's essay, write the answers to the questions, and discuss them with your classmate.

Keeping your classmate's comments in mind, revise your own essay. Then share your revised essay with the same classmate.

Editing Strategies

Mechanics

Quotation Marks

Read the following excerpt from "A Day's Wait," and underline all the words that are enclosed by quotation marks, including words in this sentence.

Back in the room I wrote the boy's temperature down and made a note of the time to give the various capsules.

"Do you want me to read to you?"

"All right. If you want to," said the boy. His face was very white and there were dark areas under his eyes. He lay still in the bed and seemed very detached from what was going on.

I read aloud from Howard Pyle's *Book of Pirates*; but I could see he was not following what I was reading.

"How do you feel, Schatz?" I asked him.

"Just the same, so far," he said.

Look closely at what you have underlined; then answer the following questions.

1. Do question marks belong inside or outside quotation marks?

   _____

2. If you end a quotation and then identify who said it, does the quotation end with a period or with a comma?_____

3. In what tense are the quotations in the excerpt written?_____

4. In what tense is the story written?_____

5. Why are the story and the quotations written in different

   tenses?_____

6. In the directions, there are quotation marks around "A Day's Wait."

   What do those quotation marks indicate to the reader? Why do the

   words begin with capital letters?_____

7. One use for quotation marks is for the names of short stories. What

   is another use for quotation marks?_____

Look at the quotations you selected for the exercises on dialogue and direct speech in the "Writing Strategies" section of this chapter. Notice how quotation marks are used by the various authors.

Using Dialogue and Quotations

When writing a story, each time a new speaker speaks, begin a new paragraph.

"Do you want me to read to you?"
"All right. If you want to," said the boy.

When you include a quotation in an essay or an article, you do not have to begin a new paragraph for the quotation. It can be included in the paragraph.

Her mother had always pushed her: memorize everything, she ordered. "I have a pretty good memory," Berenice admitted last week. Indeed, the other kids at school began to notice that Berenice always, somehow, knew the answers. "They started coming to me for help," she says. "They never called me a nerd."

Reread some of the writing you have done recently. How have you used dialogue and direct speech in your writing? Have you punctuated it correctly? Does it reveal something about the people speaking? If you are writing a story, does it move the story along? Does it provide new information?

Editing Practice

Editing Other People's Writing

The following paragraph is a first draft that has not yet been edited for errors. Find as many errors in format, tense, final sentence punctuation, and pronouns as you can, and correct them. (If you have problems with pronoun errors, see pages 64–68.) Answers are on page 355.

A BAD COMMUNICATION

I am wanting to tell you the story about my visit to the hospital in the United States. One year ago I came to this country with my parents, my husband, and my nine-month-old son. Last month my mother had got a bad stomach problem and she was deciding to go to the hospital. When we got there, the nurse asked her for information about himself. My mother got so confused!! She was told the nurse the wrong street number. No, she is gave you our address in San Salvador, I shouted. Her mother finally was seeing the doctor. After several tests, the doctor said that she had eating too fast and his stomach was upset. We was all relieved. She felt much better the next day. Now we all are trying to eat our food slowly and chew them carefully?

Editing Your Own Writing

Reread an essay that you wrote for this chapter, asking yourself the following questions:

1. Did I format my paper correctly?
2. Did I start new paragraphs when necessary?
3. Did I use final sentence punctuation and apostrophes correctly?
4. Did I use the past tenses correctly?
5. Did I use the present tenses correctly? Do my subjects and verbs agree?
6. Did I use quotation marks correctly?

When you rewrite your essay, make any changes that will improve your writing.

Grammar Strategies

Pronouns

Pronouns are used to substitute for specific nouns (I, you, him) or as determiners before nouns (*my* book, *their* car). To determine which pro-

Pronoun Chart

Subject	Object	Possessive		Reflexive
I	me	my*	mine	myself
you	you	your*	yours	yourself
she	her	her*	hers	herself
he	him	his*	his	himself
it	it	its*	—	itself
we	us	our*	ours	ourselves
you	you	your*	yours	yourselves
they	them	their*	theirs	themselves

*These words are not used alone. They are possessive adjectives and are followed by nouns or subject words.

noun to use, you need to know its referent, the noun to which it refers. For example, in the sentence before this one, to what does *it* refer?

_____

We use the *subject* form of the pronoun in the following sentences from "A Day's Wait":

> *He* came into the room to shut the windows while *we* were still in bed and *I* saw *he* looked ill.
> "*I*'m all right," *he* said.
> *We* flushed a covey of quail . . .

Fill in the blanks with two of your own sentences that use the subject form of the pronoun.

_____

_____

We use the *object* form of the pronoun in the following sentences:

> "What is it?" I asked *him.*
> "Do you want me to read to *you?*" (Notice that *you* can be used as a subject or an object pronoun.)
> After a while he said to *me,* "You don't have to stay in here with *me,* Papa, if it bothers *you.*"

Fill in the blanks with two of your own sentences that use the subject form of the pronoun.

_____

_____

We use the *possessive determiner* form, the adjective form, in the following sentences from "A Day's Wait":

He was shivering, *his* face was white, and he walked slowly as though it ached to move.
When I put *my* hand on *his* forehead, I knew he had a fever.
"*Your* temperature is all right," I said.

Fill in the blanks with two of your own sentences that use the possessive adjective form.

_____

_____

We use the *possessive noun* form of the pronoun in the following sentences about "A Day's Wait":

I told the doctor that the boy was *mine.*
I read him the book, and he wanted to hold it. After all, it was *his.*
We had owned and lived in the house for all nine years of the boy's life. It was *ours* free and clear.

Fill in the blanks with two of your own sentences that use the possessive noun form of the pronoun.

_____

_____

We use the *reflexive* form of the pronoun in the following sentences from "A Day's Wait":

I sat at the foot of the bed and read to *myself* while I waited for it to be time to give another capsule.
He was evidently holding tight onto *himself* about something.

Fill in the blanks with two of your own sentences that use the reflexive form of the pronoun.

_____

_____

◻   ◻   ◻

EXERCISE   The pronouns have been left out of the following sentences. On the basis of what you know about sentence structure, fill in the appropriate pronouns.

1. The father read the story to the boy. _____ read _____ to

   _____ slowly and clearly, but the boy didn't seem interested in

   _____.

2. People often worry when _____ get sick. _____ wonder when

   _____ health will return and when _____ will feel more like

   _____ again.

3. The father thought to _____ that _____ son seemed unusually

   upset, but _____ didn't occur to _____ that the boy was afraid

   of dying.

4. When children get sick, _____ sometimes run high temperatures.

   _____ parents get very nervous, so _____ call for medical help.

Pronoun Rules

1. Pronouns take the place of nouns. Pronouns must refer clearly to the nouns they replace (their *antecedents*).

   Ernest Hemingway was born in Illinois in 1899; *he* died in 1961. *He* won the Pulitzer Prize in 1953 for *his* book *The Old Man and the Sea.*

   Make sure that each character or topic in your story or essay is clear before you use a pronoun to refer to it.

2. Pronouns should not shift point of view unnecessarily.

He was awarded the Nobel Prize for Literature the following year. *You* know that he is widely read all over the world. In his novels, he often fictionalized his experiences living in various parts of the world, including Spain, Cuba, and France.

Who is "you"? Unless there is a good reason to use *you*, it can be confusing to the reader. Rewrite the sentence to make it clearer.

_____

3. Pronouns must agree in number with the word or words they replace.

Hemingway enjoyed hunting and fishing, and *it* is reflected in his writing.

What is "it"? *Hunting* and *fishing* are two activities, but *it* is singular. Rewrite the sentence to make it clearer.

_____

4. Indefinite pronouns *(anybody, anyone, each, either, everybody, everyone, everything, neither, no one, someone, something)* refer to nonspecific persons or things. They are treated as *singular* forms in written English, even though they seem to have plural meanings.

Everyone who reads Hemingway has a different opinion of his writing. *Anyone* who has read his books is likely to recommend them.

□ □ □

EXERCISE

A fable is a fictitious story that is meant to teach a lesson called a moral. The following is a famous fable told by Akiba Ben Joseph, a great scholar and head of the school for rabbis in Palestine in the first century. Fill in the appropriate pronouns. Answers are on page 355.

Once upon a time there was a smart young man who decided to trick a wise old man. _____ caught a little bird and held _____ in one hand behind _____ back. The boy approached the wise man and said, "Sir, _____ have a question for _____. _____ want to see how very wise _____ are. _____ am holding a bird in _____ hand. Is _____ alive, or is _____ dead?"

The boy thought that if the man said the bird was dead, _____ would open _____ hand to reveal the live bird, but if the man said the bird was alive, _____ would crush the bird, killing

_____ . The old man stared into the boy's eyes for a long time. Then _____ said, "The answer, my friend, is in _____ hands."

What is the moral of this fable?

CHECKING YOUR OWN WORK

☐ ☐ ☐

1. Read through each essay you wrote for this chapter. Look at the pronouns in the essay. (It may be helpful to underline them lightly.) Is it clear which nouns each of the pronouns replaces? Do the pronouns always agree with their antecedents? Do pronouns shift point of view only when necessary? Do the pronouns always agree with their antecedents in number? Are indefinite pronouns followed by a singular pronoun and a singular form of the verb?
2. Repeat check 1 with other writing that you have done recently.
3. As an added check, work with a classmate to make sure that you have used pronouns correctly in your writing.

Reflecting on Culture

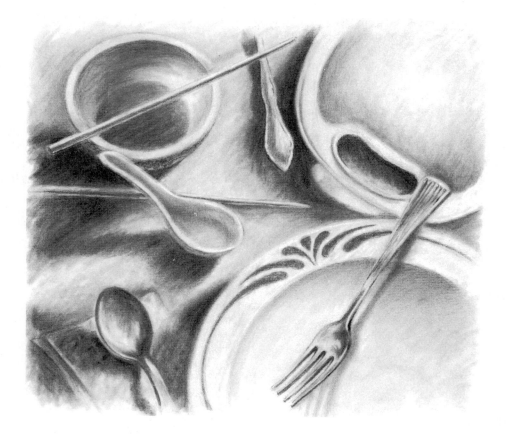

Chapter Four: Fashioning Differences

Journalist Grimes reflects on female and male attitudes toward fashion as he describes his "people-watching" experiences on New York's subways.

Chapter Five: Contrasting College Systems

Althen compares the American college system to other systems in the world and discusses some of the problems faced by newcomers to the system.

Chapter Six: Learning from One Another

Namioka tells the story of a Chinese family having difficulty understanding the eating customs of people in the United States.

CHAPTER FOUR

Fashioning Differences

PREREADING ACTIVITIES

1. Does fashion matter to you? Do people today care too much about wearing "fashionable" clothes or the "right" clothes?
2. How do you decide what clothes to wear to school, to work, or for relaxing?
3. Is fashion more important to men or to women today? What age group seems to care most about fashion? Why?

VOCABULARY DEVELOPMENT

Context clues—the words, phrases, and sentences surrounding a new word or idea—can often help you discover meaning. Certain words from the world of fashion are italicized in the following sentences. See how many you can understand by examining the sentence or phrase in which each is contained. Then choose the definition that seems closest to the meaning of the word as it is used in the sentence.

1. She also wore the satisfied expression of a woman who was pretty certain she was the chief *ornament* on that particular subway car.

   a. a beautiful object   b. a difficult problem   c. an ordinary person

2. From a far corner of the car, a second *fashion plate* appeared.

   a. person who dresses well   b. person who cooks well   c. person who serves beautiful food

3. Men may not understand women's fashion very well, but they care, deeply. In a vague sort of way they recognize that the *plumage display* is largely for their benefit.

   a. elephant-like exhibit   b. monkey-like behavior   c. birdlike feathery beauty

4. No wonder, then, that a woman who dresses with *flair* makes a big impression.

   a. sense of style   b. feeling of embarrassment   c. concern about problems

5. A *chic* scarf knotted around the neck, a snappy bracelet, an unexpected color combination will do it.

   a. small chicken   b. something stylish   c. something silly

73

Venus Envy

William Grimes

William Grimes wrote "Venus Envy" for the "About Men" column of the New York Times Magazine *for October 24, 1993. In his essay, Grimes contrasts the extraordinary effort women make to be fashionable with the minimal, almost passive stance of men. Grimes sees men as fashion spectators who enjoy watching women play the fashion game.*

Given the opportunity to switch places with women, most men would politely decline, for two reasons. The first is childbirth. The second is women's fashion. It's too hard.

Women reinvent themselves every day. And they face an intimidatingly° large field of choices. Consider the skirt (if, in fact, it's going to be a skirt and not slacks, or leggings with some sort of loose outer garment, or those culotte things that look like a skirt). It can hit at the shoe, the ankle, midcalf, just below the knee, just above the knee or onward and upward to midthigh.

°frighteningly

The look can be mannish, mannish-womanish, womanish-mannish, boyish, girlish or androgynous. . . .

That's not the end of it, either. Shoes, earrings, bracelets, scarves and purses can make or break a look.

When the alarm clock goes off, it's a miracle that modern woman does not simply lie there, stunned, and curse her fate.

But women don't seem to regard fashion as a punishment. Not only do they achieve fluency in its rich, complex language, they actually seem to enjoy it. Many of them have enough energy left over, after tackling their own fashion problems, to give helpful advice to their boyfriends or husbands.

Men do the minimum. They get a fix on the uniform that's accepted in whatever environment fate has thrown them, then produce an approximation. In a devil-may-care° mood, they may play a wild card, but even then the herd instinct prevails. That's why, in executive offices across America, several hundred thousand raging individualists wear Mickey Mouse watches.

°careless

Women inhabit a different country. They go to a different school. While men attend State U. and major in accounting, women go to top Ivy League universities and write dissertations on Provençal metrics or quantum mechanics. Men play checkers, women play chess.

The stakes of the game are high.

On a recent subway ride, I noticed a young woman reading a magazine. She had a clear statement to make, a look that the fashion magazines call "low-maintenance beauty": jeans, an expensive-looking white

^omeasured

T-shirt rolled up a carefully calibrated°turn or two at the sleeves, blond hair pulled back in a ponytail, minimal but artfully applied makeup. She also wore the satisfied expression of a woman who was pretty certain she was the chief ornament on that particular subway car.

But as the train pulled into Times Square, Miss Subways picked up dis- 11 turbing fashion signals. From a far corner of the car, a second fashion plate appeared—a young woman wearing a close-fitting black leather skirt that hit a few inches below the knee, a very wide black belt that cross-laced in the back and a lightweight, pea green cashmere sweater with the sleeves pushed up to the elbows. Around her neck, a small cameo hung from a black ribbon.

^ohunting dog
 pointing out
 game for a hunter

Miss Subways reacted like a setter on point.° The fashion package be- 12 fore her was at once a puzzle, a threat and an opportunity. She studied with the slack-jawed intensity of a commodity trader eyeing the big board. Was this a fashion disaster, or a brilliant stroke? If the latter, would a wholesale revision of one's own approach be in order? The mental wheels were turning so fast that they were throwing off sparks.

^ostronger

Men just don't care that much. They may in a general sort of way rec- 13 ognize that colleague A is a snappy dresser. As a practical matter, they may ask colleague B where he bought his shoes. They may indulge in a few moments of sullen reflection when confronted with a man the same age whose suit advertises a more robust° earning power.

But men do not usually see fashion as a literary vocabulary that can 14 be shaped into poetry, or as a ticket to a fantasy destination. The captions in men's fashion magazines tend to stress utility, versatility, quality. The layouts and descriptions in women's magazines propose a whole new life. This approach is alien to men, who do not see fashion as a thrilling opportunity to play with image and identity, or as an art form

^ohidden message

energized by the running subtext° of pleasure, sex and power.

If that sounds extreme, consider a recent film, *The Temp*, in which 15 Lara Flynn Boyle is sent by a secretarial agency to work for Timothy Hutton, a rising young exec. The first camera shot of Boyle points straight down to the floor and lingers on her shoe.

It's not just any shoe. For a frozen moment, the camera focuses on a 16 black, pointy-toed sling-back job with laces. It's a wicked shoe, a witch's

^otemporary worker

shoe. It says, eloquently, that the new temp° is a force to be reckoned with. She knows the corporate dress code, and without exactly breaking any rules, she has introduced a disturbing new element. She has mastered the language and made it work for her. Not bad. What man's shoe could produce an effect like that?

Hutton, by the way, reacts as any man would, with admiration. There 17 is the instant flash of sexual attraction, of course. But also the silent awarding of points that takes place whenever a man comes face to face with an original fashion statement.

Men may not understand women's fashion very well, but they care, 18 deeply. In a vague sort of way they recognize that the plumage display is largely for their benefit. And believe me, they appreciate it. They also respect the mastery of a hellishly complex subject. Sportswear, day wear, evening wear—each represents a formidable body of knowledge. Underwear and makeup come close to being major disciplines in their own right.

No wonder, then, that a woman who dresses with flair makes a big im- 19 pression. It doesn't have to be a major fashion offensive, either. A chic scarf knotted around the neck, a snappy bracelet, an unexpected color combination will do it. Something that hints at a sense of fashion and, more important, an individual sense of style, which suggests all sorts of positive things: visual sensitivity, a creative engagement with one's surroundings, a distinctive way of looking at things. A good fashion sense is like a good sense of humor, or a clever, fresh way of phrasing things.

It's all the more impressive for being a kind of high-wire act, with the 20 ever-present possibility of absolute failure. At this year's [1993] Academy Awards, Diane Keaton stepped out on the stage in granny glasses, a huge cream overcoat and a large white beret. The look was somewhere between Emmett Kelly° and Annie Hall,° and it was deeply unnerving. This was the fatal miscalculation of someone who jumps off the high dive without noticing that the swimming pool is empty.

°clown known for baggy clothing
°movie character known for baggy clothing

°appears suddenly

No wonder men tend to shy away from the fashion game. The risk of 21 making a mistake, of looking silly, looms° too large. They are happy, for once, to step back and take the passive role of spectator. But they do know enough to cheer when they see the game played well.

Reading and Thinking Strategies

Discussion Activities

Analysis and Conclusions

1. To what does the word *Venus* refer? Does it have a male or female connotation? What psychological term is the title "Venus Envy" playing with?

2. Grimes states that women's fashion is "too hard." What examples does he provide to prove his point?

3. Grimes states that women face an "intimidatingly large field of choices" each day when they get dressed. What does he tell his readers about types of skirts to support this idea? About kinds of looks?

4. According to Grimes, are men or women more individualistic? What examples does Grimes provide to support his point of view?

5. What does Grimes mean by "low-maintenance beauty"?

Writing and Point of View

1. What is the tone or feeling of this essay? Is it angry, humorous, silly, serious, for example? Support your answer by citing words and phrases in the article.

2. Make a list of words in the article that refer specifically to clothes. Which of these refer to men's clothes? Which to women's clothes? What does this tell you about the focus of the article?

3. Read the description of "Miss Subways," the young woman reading the magazine, the description of the "fashion plate," and the description of Diane Keaton. In what order does Grimes present information? On what does he focus in each description?

4. Paragraph 9 is one sentence long: "The stakes of the game are high." Where else in the article does he refer to "the game"? How does this idea hold the essay together? What game does he mean?

Personal Response and Evaluation

1. Is it true that men watch women and women watch women when it comes to fashion? Explain your answer.

2. In what ways are attitudes toward clothing and fashion in the United States different from attitudes in your native country?

3. Do men really do the minimum when it comes to fashion? Why or why not? Give examples from your own observations and experiences.

Journal Writing

It should be beautiful, and powerful, but it should also *work*. It should have something in it that enlightens; something in it that opens the door and points the way. Something in it that suggests what the conflicts are, what the problems are.

TONI MORRISON, "Rootedness: The Ancestor as Foundation"

Write in your journal about fashion and what it means to you. How might the Morrison quotation explain some people's attitude toward fashion?

Writing Strategies

Essay Strategies

Specific Details

Writers use specific details to tell about experiences that they have had or observations that they have made in their own lives, that other people they know have had, and that they have read about or seen in movies or on television. Writers often use direct quotations (see page 55) or detailed descriptions to make these specific details come alive for the reader.

☐ ☐ ☐

EXERCISES

1. Reread Grimes's article, looking for specific details about the people he has observed. What details stand out for you? Which details are the most vivid? Which ones confused you?
2. Reread Klein's essay in Chapter One, looking for specific details about Berenice Belizaire's life.
3. Reread the Wenden selection in Chapter Two, looking for specific details about how students learn a second language.
   How do these details bring the writing alive for you as a reader?

Generalizations

Writers often use ideas or statements that emphasize the extensive or general qualities of a subject. These statements are broad and somewhat imprecise, so writers must be careful not to use *always* or *never* when they write such general statements. If they do, readers will think that the writers are exaggerating. When using generalizations, writers need to support them with specific details to convince readers that their sweeping statements are logical and realistic.

☐ ☐ ☐

EXERCISES

1. Reread the Grimes selection, looking for general statements about how women and men view fashion. Every time you find such a general statement, look for the specific details he used to support his idea.
2. Reread the Klein article in Chapter One, looking for generalizations Klein made about immigrants in the United States. On what evidence did Klein base his generalizations?
3. Reread the Wenden article in Chapter Two, looking for generalizations about how students learn English. On what evidence did she base her generalizations?

In each case, what kinds of generalizations did the writer use—specific descriptive details, stories, quotations from authorities, or facts? Was the support strong enough to convince you of the writer's generalizations?

Essay Form

Description of a Person

When you write a description of a person, you are trying to draw a picture of a person with words. In "Venus Envy," William Grimes describes two young women on the subway train.

On a recent subway ride, I noticed a young woman reading a magazine. She had a clear statement to make, a look that the fashion magazines call "low-maintenance beauty": jeans, an expensive-looking white T-shirt rolled up a carefully calibrated turn or two at the sleeves, blond hair pulled back in a ponytail, minimal but artfully applied makeup. She also wore the satisfied expression of a woman who was pretty certain she was the chief ornament on that particular subway car.

But as the train pulled into Times Square, Miss Subways picked up disturbing fashion signals. From a far corner of the car, a second fashion plate appeared—a young woman wearing a close-fitting black leather skirt that hit a few inches below the knee, a very wide black belt that cross-laced in the back and a lightweight, pea green cashmere sweater with the sleeves pushed up to the elbows. Around her neck, a small cameo hung from a black ribbon.

Miss Subways reacted like a setter on point.

In this detailed description, we can almost see these young women. In addition to telling his readers about the way the young women are dressed, Grimes tells us what he thinks they are feeling and how their clothing reflects women's and men's attitudes toward fashion.

In Chapter One, Joe Klein writes about Berenice Belizaire:

When Berenice Belizaire arrived in New York from Haiti with her mother and sister in 1987, she was not very happy. She spoke no English. . . . Within two years Berenice was speaking English, though not well enough to get into one of New York's elite public high schools. . . . "I didn't realize what we had in Berenice at first," says math teacher Judith Khan. "She was good at math, but she was quiet. . . . But she always seemed to ask the right questions. She understood the big ideas. She could think on her feet. She could explain difficult problems so the other kids could understand them." . . . She moved from third in her class to first during senior year. She was selected as valedictorian.

Klein does not describe Belizaire physically, but he tells his readers about her through her actions and through the eyes of the people around her.

Description makes us feel something about a person. Through our choice of words, we can make a person seem interesting or dull, kindly or hostile. It is up to us as writers to choose the words that best convey what we are trying to express.

When you write about a person, the following five steps will help you think about and organize your writing.

1. *Observe* and reflect on the person before you start to write. Make notes about the stories that tell you something about the person's character and behavior patterns.

2. *Describe* the person so that your reader can visualize him or her clearly. Use picture words that are specific and vivid. Avoid words like *nice, cute, sweet,* and *great.* Show your reader how the person looks, sounds, moves, and smells.

3. *Analyze* the person's weaknesses and strengths, and explain how they make the person unique and interesting to know.

4. *Tell a story* about the person that may include a quote or several short quotes from a conversation. What makes this person special? Do not avoid conflicts or problems. They show the person as real and believable.

5. *Evaluate* why you have chosen to write about this person and why a reader should want to read about the person. Why is this person important to you and to others?

Keep these steps in mind when you describe a person in your next piece of writing.

Suggestions for Writing

Before you begin to write, choose one of the topics listed here. Discuss some of your ideas about this subject with a classmate, or try freewriting (see page 81) to help you find ideas. You may also decide to review your journal for ideas. Always spend some time thinking before you start to write.

1. Write a description of a person whose appearance you especially admire. Explain in detail how the person looks and what the person is wearing. Use words and phrases that convey your feelings to your reader.

2. Write a description of a person whose appearance you do not approve of or like. Explain in detail how the person looks and what the person is wearing. Use words and phrases that convey your feelings to your reader.

3. Write a description of some special clothing worn by people in your home country. Explain why this type of clothing is significant to your culture.

4. Look at students in your college cafeteria. Write an essay describing the typical dress of men and women in your school. What did you learn about "fashion" in your school from this experience?

5. After listening to some of the essays your classmates have written, write an essay in which you compare your findings about fashion and clothing with William Grimes's ideas. Reread his essay before you write. Reread your journal entry. What have you learned about your own values toward fashion and clothing?

Extra Projects

1. Bring to class two pictures from magazines, one showing a man and the other showing a woman. Write an essay describing one of the pictures in detail. Display the pictures in your classroom. Read your essay aloud to the class. See if students can decide which picture is being described. As a class, discuss the significance of the clothing worn by the people in the pictures. Why did you choose these pictures? What do they tell you about the culture of the people depicted? What do these pictures tell you about the roles of men and women?

2. Go to the library and look for information on clothing in another historical period. Write an essay describing the clothing of the time you have researched. Bring pictures if possible. Read your essay aloud to the class. As a class, discuss the different periods chosen by the group. Why did you choose that period? What did you learn about the clothing worn then? What does the clothing tell you about the culture? What does it tell you about the roles of men and women?

Getting Started

Focused Freewriting

Begin your freewriting by writing at the top of a blank sheet of paper the name of the person about whom you are going to write. If you do not know the name, use an imaginary name or title. (Notice how Grimes refers to a young stranger as "Miss Subways.") Then write down any ideas, words, or phrases that come to your mind about this person. Write for 10 to 15 minutes without stopping. Do not worry about writing complete ideas, stories, or descriptions. Just write down any thought that occurs to you about the person. You can fill in the details later. (It may help, before you begin freewriting, to look at a picture of the person about whom you are going to write.)

Revising

When you have finished writing your own essay, separate yourself from your writing by reading the following student essay.

A Student Essay

MY FATHER

Like most immigrants, my family has had to build a new life by working 1 hard. Watching my father as he does this shows me what it means to be strong. He is 5 feet 9 inches tall, has light brown skin color, short black-and-white hair, and brown eyes, and weighs roughly 180 pounds. My father is now 59 years old, and I am truly one of his secret admirers.

The first of seven children, my father was born in Haiti in a town 20 2 miles away from the capital of the country. He then proceeded to Port-au-Prince, the capital of Haiti, for his schooling, which he finished before he left the city.

My father became a minister at about the age of 30 or 31. From that 3 time on, he went through some traumatic experiences in his life. At the age of 32, he was married to a woman and had two children with her. A year and a half later, his wife was suddenly attacked by a sickness. She succumbed to the sickness and died. There was no indication what caused the sickness or even the name of the sickness.

Two years after the death of my father's first wife, my father married 4 my mother. She conceived seven children with him, which gives him a total of nine children. The first two were sons. They are now married and have children of their own. They are now living with their wives, three blocks from our house.

My father went through a lot in Haiti, and finally my whole family 5 moved to the United States. My father has always played a very important role in my life. If it weren't for him, I don't think I would be sitting here in school writing about him. My father is a very diligent man. He works 12 hours every day to support the family. Sometimes when there is an extra expense such as the gas bill, the electric bill, or the telephone bill, he has even worked on Saturdays to make the extra money to pay the bills.

My father works every day except Sunday. He works in the summer as 6 well as in the winter. He wakes up at 5 o'clock in the morning and goes to wait for the bus, which is two blocks away from where he lives. Sometimes when it's really cold, below zero, I feel like crying thinking about my father waiting in the cold weather to catch a bus. It is even worse when he has finished working inside in the heat, and he is exhausted, tired, hungry, and yet he must go back through the same process again.

He has shown me what it means to be strong, and one day I want to 7
be the strong one. One day, I will make sure that all his hard working
will stop. That's a promise.

Nickso Marcellus, Haiti

Answer the following questions about this student's writing. (It is useful to write out the answers.)

1. What in Marcellus's introduction makes you want to read more?
2. What is the main idea that holds the entire piece of writing together?
3. What supporting details—facts, observations, and experiences—
   stand out for you?
4. What details help you understand, see, and feel the events in
   Marcellus's father's life?
5. What in the ending lets the reader know the piece is completed?

Editing Strategies

Mechanics

Plurals

One common problem in editing writing and looking for surface errors is recognizing plural forms. Test your knowledge of plurals in the
next paragraph by circling and correcting each singular noun that
should really be a plural. There are 23 missing plurals. Can you find
them all?

Fashion is one of the biggest industry in the United State today.

Thousand of man and woman make their living in the fashion industry.

Unfortunately, there are few high-paying job and many low-paying job in

fashion. The designer make lots of money creating clothing for millions

of person. Highly paid model pose for picture in magazine and newspa-

per. They perform in fashion show. But the garment are made by poor

person, often immigrant. They sew in factory all over the world and get

paid very little money for their hard work. Despite the many problem of

such employment, these job provide work and money for many man,

woman, and child in the world.

Turn to page 356 to check your answers. If you made more than two mistakes, review the following rules.

regular plurals

The regular plural of a word is usually formed by adding -*s* to the singular form. The article about fashion has many examples of regular plurals.

Singular	*Plural*
reason	reasons
skirt	skirts
shoe	shoes

Can you find three more examples of regular plurals in the article? List them with the singular forms on the left.

_____   _____

_____   _____

_____   _____

special plurals

Many words follow special rules to form their plurals.

Words that end in a consonant (*b, c, d, f, g,* etc.) plus *y* form their plurals by changing the *y* to *i* and adding -*es.*

body	bodies
country	countries
baby	_____
library	_____
university	_____
family	_____
agency	_____

Words that end in a vowel (*a, e, i, o, u*) plus *y* form their plurals by adding -*s.*

journey   journeys

attorney   _____

ashtray   _____

boy   _____

highway   _____

Words that end in *s, sh, ch, ss, zz,* or *x* usually form their plurals by adding *-es.*

plus   pluses   mattress   _____

brush   brushes   wish   _____

inch   inches   watch   _____

dress   dresses   business   _____

fizz   fizzes   buzz   _____

wax   waxes   tax   _____

Words that end in one *z* usually double the *z* and add *-es.*

quiz   quizzes   whiz   _____

Words that end in *o* usually form their plurals by adding *-es.*

tomato   tomatoes   hero   _____

veto   vetoes   mosquito   _____

Many words that end in *f* or *fe* form their plurals by changing the *f* to *v* and adding *-es.*

scarf   scarves   housewife   _____

knife   knives   yourself   _____

leaf	leaves	life	_____
calf	calves	half	_____

There are some exceptions to this rule, however.

roof	roofs
belief	beliefs

irregular plurals

Some words have irregular plurals. This means that the plurals have special forms and do not use the regular *-s* form we have already learned. Here are some examples of irregular plurals:

man	men	woman	women
child	children	foot	feet
tooth	teeth	goose	geese
mouse	mice	ox	oxen

Here are some other words with special plurals:

Singular	*Plural*
crisis	crises (crucial turning point in politics, story, play, or everyday life)
criterion	criteria (standard or rule to judge something by)
axis	axes (fixed or center line about which things are arranged, as in a graph or on a globe)
medium	media (means or agency; instrument of communication)

false plurals

Some words that end in *s* are not plural. These words are treated as singular in sentences. They are followed by the singular form of the verb, as you can see in the following examples.

news	No news is good news. The news is broadcast at 6 o'clock.
measles	Measles is a highly contagious disease, and many children get sick from it.
mumps	Even though it is usually not a serious sickness for children, mumps is often dangerous for adult males.
politics	Politics refers to the science of government.

uninflected plurals

There are also a few words, mostly the names of animals, for which the plural form is the same as the singular form.

sheep	One sheep always gets lost from the flock.
	There are thousands of sheep in New Zealand.
fish	The shiny silver fish is swimming downstream.
	They saw hundreds of fish in the aquarium.
deer	The deer is a very graceful animal.
	Many deer live in the woods.
moose	The moose is a large animal that looks like a deer.
	Moose have large antlers.

□   □   □

EXERCISE   In the following paragraph, there are 19 missing plurals. Using what you have just practiced, make the corrections.

William Grimes is like many man and woman who like to watch other on bus, train, and airplane. People watching is one of the most enjoyable hobby a person can have. However, some individual do not like to be watched too closely, so you must be discreet. But there are so many thing to see! It's like going to the theater. I have seen young girl putting on their makeup and brushing their hair without even looking at their neighbor sitting around them. They can miss their stop or get lost on their way to the movie, their job, or class while they retie their scarf, put mascara on their eyelash, or wipe lipstick off their tooth. And as we watch, our life become intertwined so easily!

Commonly Confused Words

cloth/clothes

Read the following paragraph, noticing the use of *cloth* and *clothes*.

Cloth is a piece of fabric. You make *clothes* out of *cloth*. *Cloth* is not singular for *clothes*. *Clothes* are the items that we put on our bodies when we dress. Men's and women's *clothes* are very different in some parts of the world. In Iran, for example, women wear very different *clothes* from those that men wear. In the United States, by contrast, some *clothes* that men and women wear are very similar.

Fill in each of the following blanks with *cloth* or *clothes*.

1. I bought some _____ to make some _____.

2. A designer buys beautiful _____ to put together a new line of

   _____.

3. Because there was no door, the heavy dark _____ hung in front of

   the _____ closet.

Write two more sentences using these words.

Editing Practice

Editing Other People's Writing

The following paragraph is a first draft that has not been edited for errors. Find as many errors in tense, pronouns, plurals, and countable or uncountable nouns as you can. (If you have problems finding countable/uncountable noun errors, see pages 89–92.) Answers are on page 356.

Each morning, Henry get up at 6 o'clock and prepare to go to work. After taking a shower, he is combing her hairs and put on her shirt, pant, and tie. He shave every other day because his skins are delicate and his beards are thin. This morning he was shaving in the steamy shower. Then he blow his hairs with one of the hair dryer in his closet. He put on hair mousse because they are smelling nice and fresh. He brush his tooth with an electric toothbrush because he is thinking it saved time. He boils waters and makes coffees for his family. They are eating cereals or toasts together, and then they all ran off to their different bus.

Editing Your Own Writing

Reread an essay that you wrote for this chapter, asking yourself the following questions:

1. Did I format my paper correctly?
2. Did I start new paragraphs when necessary?
3. Did I use final sentence punctuation and apostrophes correctly?

4. Did I use the past tenses correctly?

5. Did I use the present tenses correctly? Do my subjects and verbs agree?

6. Did I use quotation marks correctly?

7. Did I use pronouns correctly? Do the pronouns agree with their antecedents?

8. Did I form plurals correctly?

When you rewrite your essay, make any changes that will improve your writing.

Grammar Strategies

Countable and Uncountable Nouns

Countable Nouns

Countable nouns describe things we can count. For example, we can count students: one student, two students, and so on. Plurals are formed by adding *-s* or by following special rules such as those listed on pages 84–87.

1. In the singular form, countable nouns are preceded by articles (*the, a* or *an*) or the word *one.*

    the student
    a student, an individual
    one student

When we use *the,* we refer to a specific thing that our listener or reader knows about.

The book that we use in English class has a green cover.

When we use *a* or *an,* we refer to a general thing.

I want to put *a* book on the chair so the baby can reach the table.

2. In the plural form, countable nouns with no article express a general meaning.

People often use *computers* for writing.

3. Countable nouns with *the* express a specific meaning.

   The computers in my school lab are networked.

4. In the plural form, countable nouns answer the question "How many?" They are preceded by quantifiers such as *a certain number of, a few, a lot of, a majority of, a minority of, a number of, a percentage of, all, almost all, almost no, enough, hardly any, many, no, too few, too many,* and *two* (or any greater number).

   a certain number of people
   a few dresses
   a number of individuals
   almost all women
   many scarves

5. The word *any* is used with plural nouns in questions and after negative verbs. *Some* or the quantifiers in rule 4 are used in positive statements.

   Do you have *any* dresses on sale? Yes, I have *some* dresses on sale.
   Do you have *any* pants on sale? No, I don't have *any* pants on sale.

Uncountable Nouns

Uncountable nouns describe things we cannot count. They fit into specific categories, including these:

Mass items: advice, clothing, equipment, furniture, grammar, hair, homework, housework, information, jewelry, merchandise, money, traffic, vocabulary

Liquids: blood, coffee, juice, milk, soda, tea

Powders: flour, pepper, rice, salt, sand, sugar

Gases: air, fog, hydrogen, oxygen, pollution, smog, smoke, steam

Specific types of food: bread, cereal, fruit, meat, soup, toast

Abstract ideas: anger, beauty, courage, education, entertainment, experience, fashion, freedom, fun, happiness, hate, health, honesty, intelligence, justice, knowledge, love, peace, pride, recreation, success, time, truth, violence, wealth

Subjects of study: accounting, anthropology, biology, chemistry, economics, mathematics, medicine, physics, sociology

Diseases: arthritis, cancer, influenza, measles, mumps, pneumonia

Games and sports: baseball, checkers, chess, football, golf, tennis

Natural forces: electricity, gravity, heat, humidity, moonlight, rain, snow, sunlight, thunder, weather, wind

1. We do not use *a* or *an* with uncountable nouns.
2. Uncountable nouns have *no* plural form.
3. Uncountable nouns are used with the third person singular (*he, she, it*) verb form (ending in *s*).

> Fashion is an interesting subject.
> Water plays an important role in proper diet.
> Love makes the world go round.
> Her vocabulary seems excellent.
> The new furniture looks beautiful in the living room.

4. Uncountable nouns with no article express a general meaning.

> Coffee grows well in Colombia.
> Sugar tastes sweet.

5. When we use *the* with an uncountable, we refer to a specific and clearly identified thing that our listener or reader knows about.

> *The* coffee that is sold in my neighborhood is fresh and tasty.
> I dropped *the* coffee on my research paper.
> *The* sugar that is less refined is brown.
> He passed *the* sugar to his friend.

6. Uncountable nouns answer the question "How much?" They are preceded by quantifiers such as *a good deal of, a large amount of, a small amount of, a large degree of, a little, a lot of, enough, hardly any, most, no, not enough, not much, only a little, some, too little,* and *too much.*

> a large amount of information
> a lot of soup
> hardly any food
> too little love
> too much violence

7. The word *any* is used with uncountable nouns in questions and with negative answers. *Some* or the quantifiers in rule 6 are used in positive answers.

> Do you have *any* money?
> No, I don't have *any.* I have *no* money.
> Yes, I have *some.*

Note: Some words in English can be used as either countables or uncountables.

His hair is too long.
I found a hair in my soup.
I don't drink coffee anymore.
Please give me a coffee and two sugars.
Experience is necessary to get a job nowadays.
I didn't have any good experiences when I tried to become a model.

Some uncountable ideas can be expressed using countable words.

Uncountable	*Countable*
water	five bottles of water
clothing	a coat, ten shirts, a pair of socks
furniture	a couch, two couches, four tables
information	a fact, two ideas, three opinions
homework	three assignments
housework	washing dishes, mopping floors
laundry	two loads of laundry

□   □   □

EXERCISES

1. Choose the correct word from the choices given.

    a. Many people in the United States think that time _____ money.
       (is/are)

    b. The tastiest soup _____ to cook for a long time.
       (need/needs)

    c. Furniture _____ a lot these days.
       (cost/costs)

    d. The couches _____ on sale this weekend.
       (are/is)

    e. Clothing _____ much to William Grimes.
       (mean/means)

    f. Men's pants _____ little from year to year.
       (change/changes)

    g. Violence _____ as the number one problem in the United
       (rate/rates)
       States today.

    h. Murder _____ a brutal crime.
       (is/are)

    i. I put _____ soup in the bowl.
       (almost all/almost no)

j. _____ students registered for your course.
(A number of/A good deal of)

k. The designer had _____ models in the show.
(too many/too much)

l. _____ people came to the show.
(Quite a few/Only a little)

m. I told _____ the students about the test.
(all/a good deal of)

n. _____ clothing is sold directly to consumers by the manufac-
(Some/a few)

turers.

o. The car engine produces _____ smoke.
(too much/too many)

p. There was _____ snow last winter.
(a lot of/a number of)

2. Using the uncountable and countable nouns in the lists, fill in the blanks in the following sentences.

   a. I did lots of _____ for my math class.

   b. My husband washed two _____ of

   _____ in the machine when he came home from

   work.

   c. The bride and groom bought new _____ for their

   apartment.

   d. Watching the news on television provides most people with

   _____ about what is going on in the world.

   e. The hall closet was filled with _____ and

   _____. It was so full that some of the

   _____ fell on the floor.

3. In the following paragraph, fill in each blank with a verb that makes sense to you as a reader. Think about countables and uncountables when you decide if verbs need an *-s* ending or not.

Life _____ confusing when students first _____ college. Although academic freedom _____ students to choose some of their own courses, placement tests _____ them from taking some of their favorite courses. Those first weeks, homework in each class _____ due every day. New students _____ lots of questions, but fear _____ them back from asking them the first few days. A tremendous amount of information _____ available if students _____ where to find it. Signs _____ all over the college walls. The best advice _____ not to give up. Success _____ with perseverence.

4. Reread one of the selections in this book that you have enjoyed. Notice how the author used countables and uncountables in the writing. Notice the verbs that refer to these words.

□   □   □

CHECKING YOUR OWN WORK

1. Read through each essay you wrote for this chapter. Look at the nouns in the essay. (It may be helpful to underline them lightly.) Are there any uncountable nouns? Make sure that they do not have *s* endings. Are they followed by the singular form of the verb? Does the essay contain countable nouns? If they are being used in the plural sense, do they have plural endings? Are they followed by the plural form of the verb?
2. Check other writing that you have done recently to make sure that uncountable and countable nouns are used correctly.
3. As an added check, work with a classmate to make sure that you have used countables and uncountables correctly in your writing.

CHAPTER FIVE

Contrasting College Systems

PREREADING ACTIVITIES

1. Spend about five minutes writing the answer to the question "What is an American?" Discuss your answers in class.
2. As a class, talk about your experiences with teachers in the United States and in any other country in which you have attended school. Discuss some of the differences in teaching styles that you have observed.
3. Read the Vocabulary Development section; then discuss the differences in educational systems in your home countries.

VOCABULARY DEVELOPMENT

Education in the United States starts with *nursery school* for children under the age of 5. At 5, pupils attend *kindergarten* and so enter *elementary school,* also referred to as *primary* ("first-level") *education.* After five or six years, they move on to *middle school* or *junior high school,* which lasts three years, and then to three or four years of *high school;* these years are also known as *secondary* ("second-level") *education. Higher education* (college or university) can also be referred to as *post-secondary* or *tertiary* ("third-level") *education.*

A *matriculant* is a student who *matriculates* at college, that is, who has been officially accepted as a candidate for a degree. A *nonmatriculant* has been accepted only provisionally and must complete a particular number of credits with passing grades to qualify for *matriculation.*

The middle item in a ranked series of values or numbers is known as the *median.* In the series 10, 9, 9, 7, 6, 6, 5, the median is 7. (The median differs from the *average,* which for this series of numbers would be 7.42857 . . .)

American Ways: Education

Gary Althen

Gary Althen has been the foreign-student advisor at the University of Iowa for many years. He has also lived and worked in Peru and Malaysia. This excerpt is from his book American Ways: A Guide for Foreigners in the United States. *In this book, Althen uses the term* American *to refer to a citizen of the United States. Although he is aware that there are differences among people, he tries to describe general patterns of behavior in his book.*

"**A**nybody can get into college in the USA," it was common to hear 1
Malaysians say. They were referring to the fact that at least some
American post-secondary educational institutions have rather low ad-
missions standards. Applicants who had no possibility of entering a
Malaysian university could get into one in the States. Malaysians who remarked on the easy accessibility of American colleges and universities
were comparing the American system unfavorably to that of the British,
who once ruled Malaysia and who provided the model for Malaysia's educational system. Under the British approach, difficult school-leaving
examinations are used to limit the number of people given places in
post-secondary schools° and to assure that the people who got those
places were well qualified to be students.

°schools beyond high
school

On the other hand, these Malaysians would observe, "You 2
[Americans] put men on the moon. So there must be something right
about your system."

Many people interested in education get trapped into trying to an- 3
swer the question, "Which is the better educational system, the
American, the British, or some other?" That question cannot be answered. A more appropriate question is, "What are the advantages and
disadvantages of the American educational system?"

Access to Education

The American educational system is based on the idea that as many 4
people as possible should have access to as much education as possible.
This fact alone distinguishes the U.S. system from most others, since in
most others the objective is as much to screen people out as it is to keep
them in. The U.S. system has no standardized examinations whose results systematically prevent students from going on to higher levels of
study, as the British and many other systems do. Through secondary
school and sometimes in post-secondary institutions as well, the
American system tries to accommodate students even if their academic
aspirations° and aptitudes° are not high, even if they are physically (and
in some cases mentally) handicapped, and even if their native language
is not English.

°hopes
°natural abilities

The idea that as many people as possible should have as much edu- 5
cation as possible is, of course, an outcome of the Americans' assumptions about equality among people. These assumptions do not mean
that everyone has an equal opportunity to enter Harvard, Stanford, or
other highly competitive post-secondary institutions. Admission to such
institutions is generally restricted to the most academically able. The less
able can usually matriculate in a post-secondary institution, as the
Malaysians observed, but one of lower quality.

As of March 1982, only 3 percent of all Americans aged 25 or more 6
had completed less than five years of elementary school. Seventy-one

percent of those 25 or more had completed four years of high school or gone beyond that, and 17.7 percent had completed four or more years of post-secondary education. The median number of school years completed was 12.6. The number of tertiary (that is, post-secondary) students per 100,000 inhabitants was 5355. Some contrasts: The number of tertiary students per 100,000 in the population was 4006 in Canada. In no other country, according to UNESCO° data, was the number of post-secondary students above 2700 per 100,000. Korea had 2696 tertiary students per 100,000 inhabitants; Japan, 2030; the USSR, 1970; Argentina, 1890; Hong Kong, 1353; Malaysia, 472; and Ethiopia, 48.

°The United Nations Educational, Scientific, and Cultural Organization, founded in 1946 to "advance mutual knowledge and understanding of peoples"

Naturally, an educational system that retains as many people as the American system does is likely to enroll a broader range of students than a system that seeks to educate only the few who seem especially suited for academic work. In the American system, academic rigor tends to come later than it does in most other systems. In many instances, American students do not face truly demanding educational requirements until they seek a graduate (that is, post-baccalaureate) degree. Many other systems place heavy demands on students as early as their primary years—though college may be far less demanding, as is the case in Japan. . . . 7

Student-Teacher Relationships

Differing ideas about formality and respect frequently complicate relationships between American professors and students from abroad, especially Asian students (and most especially female Asian students). The professors generally prefer informal relationships (sometimes, but not always, including use of first names rather than titles and family names) and minimal acknowledgment of status differences. Many foreign students are accustomed to more formal relationships and sometimes have difficulty bringing themselves to speak to their teachers at all, let alone address them by their given names. 8

The characteristics of student-teacher relationships on American campuses vary somewhat, depending on whether the students involved are undergraduate or graduate students, and depending on the size and nature of the school. Graduate students typically have more intense relationships with their professors than undergraduates do; at smaller schools student-teacher relationships are typically even less formal than they are at larger schools. 9

To say that student-teacher relationships are informal is not to say that there are no recognized status differences between the two groups. There are. But students may show their difference only in subtle ways, mainly in the vocabulary and tone of voice they use when speaking to teachers. Much of their behavior around teachers may seem to foreign students to be disrespectful. American students will eat in class, read newspapers, and assume quite informal postures. Teachers might not 10 enjoy such behavior, but they tolerate it. Students, after all, are individuals who are entitled to decide for themselves how they are going to act.

American teachers generally expect students to ask them questions or 11 even challenge what they say. Teachers do not generally assume they know all there is to know about a subject. Nor do they assume that they invariably explain things clearly. Students who want clarification or additional information are expected to ask for it during the class, just after class ends, or in the teacher's office at the times the teacher has announced as "office hours." Students who do not ask questions may be considered uninterested or uncommitted.

While most teachers welcome students' questions and comments 12 about the material being covered in the course, they do not welcome student efforts to negotiate for higher grades. Teachers normally believe that they have an acceptable system for determining grades, and, unless it seems possible that a mistake has been made, teachers respond very negatively to students who try to talk them into raising a grade. Some foreign students, particularly ones from countries where negotiating is a habit, severely damage their reputation in teachers' eyes by trying to bargain for better grades.

Plagiarism

To plagiarize is to represent someone else's academic work—in the 13 form of writing or ideas—as one's own. The Americans' belief in the value of the individual and the sanctity° of the individual's property extends to ideas. Ideas belong to people; they are a form of property. Scholars' writings and ideas are considered their property. Students and other scholars are not supposed to use those ideas in their own writing without acknowledging where the ideas came from. To leave out the acknowledgment and thereby convey the impression that another's words are one's own is "plagiarism."

°sacredness

Foreign students are sometimes accused of plagiarizing the works of 14 other people. It is probably the case that much of the plagiarism foreign students commit (usually by copying the words of another writer into a paper they themselves are writing and failing to include a footnote saying who originally wrote the words) is committed out of misunderstanding rather than out of dishonesty. To American scholars the notion of "intellectual property" is perfectly clear and sensible. It is obvious to them when an idea has been "stolen." And stealing ideas is a cardinal sin° in the American academic world.

°serious wrongdoing

Many foreign students do not share the Americans' conceptions 15 about individuality, private property, and the ownership of ideas. They see no wrong in copying relevant, well-expressed ideas into a paper they are writing. But their faculty will see it as quite wrong, and foreign students need to know that and behave accordingly.

Reading and Thinking Strategies

Discussion Activities

Analysis and Conclusions

1. According to Althen, what is the difference between the American and British approaches to higher education?

2. What examples of highly competitive postsecondary institutions does the author include? How do people get admitted to these schools?

3. From your own observation, what behaviors do teachers in the United States seem to value in students? What does this tell you about the culture in the United States? From your observation, what behaviors do teachers in other countries in which you have studied value in students? What does this tell you about the culture in those countries?

4. In many classrooms in the United States today, the teacher is from one culture and the students are from many different cultures and countries. What effects might this have on the classroom? What suggestions do you have to help people in the classroom get to know each other better?

5. Why is plagiarism a problem for many foreign students?

Writing and Point of View

1. Althen includes two quotations in this selection. What is the purpose of these quotations?

2. What statistics does Althen include in the selection? What point is he trying to prove with these statistics?

3. What audience do you think Althen is writing this for? If you were writing this to help teachers in the United States understand students from different cultures, what changes would you make in the selection?

4. What is Althen's point of view about student-teacher relationships? Does he state his point of view? Why do you think this is so? What is the purpose of this piece of writing?

Personal Response and Evaluation

1. What problems are created by the American system of higher education? What advantages does this system offer?

2. What problems are created by the British system of higher education? What advantages does this system offer?

3. What does the phrase "equal opportunity" mean? In your experience,

is there equal opportunity in higher education in the United States? Explain your answer.

4. Althen states that American teachers often prefer informal relationships with their students. Have you found this to be true? If so, why do you think this is the case?

5. Althen states that students from some cultures have difficulty asking questions in class. Have you found this to be true? If so, what can these students do so that their teachers know that they are interested and involved in the class?

6. The words of a language are only part of what you learn when you live in a new country and learn a new language. What cultural differences have you observed?

Group Activity

After reading and discussing the Althen article, as a group project, make a list of suggestions that will help a student become successful in college in the United States. When you have completed this list, you may want to share it with other classes and compare your ideas with the students in those classes.

Journal Writing

A primary reason for my success in the classroom was that I couldn't forget that schooling was changing me and separating me from the life I enjoyed before becoming a student.

RICHARD RODRIGUEZ, *Hunger of Memory*

Write in your journal about your experiences learning English. Think about the Rodriguez quote. Has it been easy for you? What kinds of problems have you had? Have you discovered anything about yourself by learning a new language? Do you like English? Do you feel or act differently when you speak English?

Writing Strategies

Essay Strategies

The Formal Essay

Although you will learn about many types of essays and styles of writing as you write in your college classes, it is important to know what is meant by the traditional or formal essay. Readers have particular expectations when they read an essay. To meet these expectations, writers begin by learning the structure of the traditional essay.

Simply put, an essay is a series of paragraphs written on one theme. Traditionally, the main idea for the essay is found in the first paragraph, which is called the introduction. The main idea for an essay is called the thesis statement. The supporting points and details of the essay are found in the body paragraphs that follow the introduction.

Each of the developmental or body paragraphs contains a topic sentence that tells the main idea for that paragraph. The rest of the paragraph is made up of ideas or details that tell more about the main idea. These paragraphs may have different purposes, depending on the topic of the essay. A particular paragraph may describe, define, tell a relevant story, provide evidence to argue a point, compare and contrast, or analyze an issue. A writer often begins a new paragraph with a transition that connects the paragraph to the one that preceded it in order to help the reader follow the writer's train of thought.

The traditional essay ends with a concluding paragraph. In this paragraph, the writer ties together the important points that have been made in the essay. The conclusion lets the reader know that the writer has thought the topic through and believes that the ideas presented in the essay are complete.

Conclusions are usually short and may include a brief summary of the main points of the essay. Most writers agree that new ideas should not be presented in the conclusion, although a related story or idea might pull the theme of the essay together effectively.

Keep this standard structure in mind when you write your next essay.

In the preceding paragraphs, circle the words *introduction, main idea, thesis statement, body paragraphs, topic sentence,* and *conclusion.* Then answer the following questions on the basis of the information in those paragraphs.

1. What is the first paragraph of an essay called? _____

_____

2. What is the main idea for the whole essay called? _____

_____

3. What do the body paragraphs contain? _____

_____

4. What is the main idea for each body paragraph called? _____

5. What is the final paragraph in the essay called? _____

_____

6. What is the purpose of the final paragraph? _____

_____

A diagram of a formal essay follows. (Remember that this is a sample essay form; not all formal essays contain five paragraphs.)

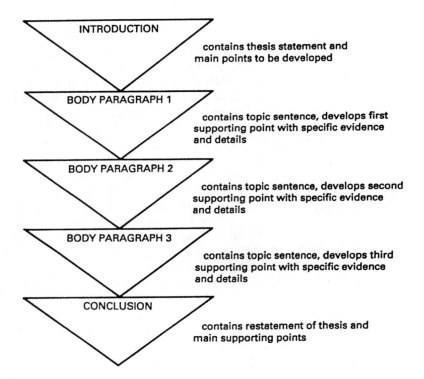

INTRODUCTION
contains thesis statement and main points to be developed

BODY PARAGRAPH 1
contains topic sentence, develops first supporting point with specific evidence and details

BODY PARAGRAPH 2
contains topic sentence, develops second supporting point with specific evidence and details

BODY PARAGRAPH 3
contains topic sentence, develops third supporting point with specific evidence and details

CONCLUSION
contains restatement of thesis and main supporting points

Although this approach to writing is quite formal and traditional, it is the type of writing required in many college first-year writing courses. It is useful to know these terms, and it is also good discipline for the writer to organize his or her ideas to fit this model. However, remember that this is just one model of writing.

□   □   □

EXERCISE   Reread one of your own essays with a classmate. Underline the main idea or thesis statement for the entire paper. Then underline the topic sentence or main idea for each paragraph. Discuss the supporting details and decide the purpose of each. After discussing your writing, you may decide to rewrite parts of your essay to clarify your main idea or supporting details.

Essay Form

The Introduction

A formal essay usually begins with an introductory paragraph. Generally, the introduction serves several purposes:

1. To capture the reader's interest
2. To state the thesis of the essay
3. To introduce the major ideas that will be developed in the body of the essay

The introduction is useful to the writer as well as to the reader. It helps the writer plan the rest of the essay. If the introduction is well structured, the writer knows what the rest of the essay will contain. There are several ways to write an introduction to a formal essay.

1. *General statement.* One type of introduction starts with a general statement: "Fourteen of the twenty-five learners made explicit statements about how best to learn." The essay then becomes more specific: "Five of the statements stressed the importance of using the language." In this type of introduction, the writer takes the reader from the general to the specific.

2. *Anecdote.* Another way to begin an essay is with an anecdote or a brief story:

   When Berenice Belizaire arrived in New York from Haiti with her mother and sister in 1987, she was not very happy. She spoke no English. The family had to live in a cramped Brooklyn apartment, a far cry from the comfortable house they'd had in Haiti. Her mother, a nurse, worked long hours. School was torture. Berenice had always been a good student, but now she was learning a new language while enduring constant taunts from the Americans (both black and white). They cursed her in the cafeteria and threw food at her. Someone hit her sister in the head with a book. "Why can't we go home?" Berenice asked her mother.

   This is a very good way to capture readers' interest. It is often used by newspaper and magazine writers.

3. *Question.* The introduction might ask a question that will be answered in the body of the essay: "Are women really more intuitive than men?"

This is another technique that can create a great deal of reader interest.

4. *Quotation.* An introduction can contain a quotation: "'Anybody can get into college in the USA,' it was common to hear Malaysians say." Be sure to use quotation marks if you are using the exact words spoken or written by someone.

5. *Definition.* Some writers define in their introduction a word or phrase that they will use throughout their writing to help readers grasp their ideas. "To plagiarize is to represent someone else's academic work—in the form of writing—as one's own."

When you write, you can use one of these types of introductions or a combination of several of them. You may even create your own method of introduction. Your overall goal is to engage your reader, to make your reader want to continue reading what you have written.

□ □ □

EXERCISES

1. What are five ways of writing an introduction? What is the overall goal of the introduction?
2. Read introductions from any of the selections in this book. What kinds of introductions have the various writers used? Is textbook material introduced differently from journalistic writing?
3. You will find many excellent pieces of student writing throughout this book. Select two that you especially like. Look at their introductions. Why do they work for you? Try rewriting one of the introductions using a different approach. How does it change the effect of the essay for you?
4. Using one of the approaches described in this chapter, rewrite the introduction to an essay you have written. Then read the original and the rewritten essay. Which do you prefer? Why?

Suggestions for Writing

Before you begin to write, try brainstorming with a small group, as described in the next section, "Getting Started." You may also want to look in your journal for ideas. When you do begin to write, keep your audience in mind. Try to make your writing interesting to your readers as well as to yourself.

1. Write an essay in which you discuss the purpose of a college education. Should it be to help someone qualify for a job? Should it be to increase someone's general knowledge?
2. Write an essay comparing the system of higher education in another

country in which you were a student with the higher education system in the United States. Explain which one you prefer, and give reasons for your choice.

3. Write an essay in which you describe an effective teaching style and explain why you think that teaching style helps students.

4. Write an essay to other ESL students in your school who are trying to become successful in a U.S. college, advising them what they should do to improve their chance for success in college.

5. In an essay, explain the problems you have seen in the system of higher education in another country or in the United States and give some suggestions for improvement. Explain how your suggestions would improve the present system.

Getting Started

Small Group Brainstorming

Meet in a small group to discuss possible topics for writing. Each person should have a notebook open to an empty page. As you are talking together, brainstorm by jotting down every idea or word that makes you think about the topic of your essay. After several minutes of talking, each of you should have a list of ideas and words.

As you brainstorm in the group, ask each other *who, what, where, when, why,* and *how* questions about schools, teachers, and students. When each person has enough ideas, read through your list of ideas and words and add any details that you will develop later in your writing.

Revising

Writing is a personal experience, but it is also a communicative activity. One way to find out how your writing communicates your ideas is to share it with a peer. Practice doing the following revising activity using the two drafts of Mohibur Rob's essay in this section. When you finish discussing the revisions in Rob's essay, share with a classmate an essay that you have written in two drafts. Discuss the changes you made. You may decide to make other changes. You may add or delete ideas. You may want to move or remove sentences or paragraphs. You may decide that other words express your meaning better.

Rewrite the following questions to use with your writing, and write the replies on a piece of paper that you will refer to when you revise.

1. What differences do you find in the first paragraph in the two drafts? Which version do you prefer? Why?

2. What specific details does the writer use?

3. What generalizations does the writer include?

4. Does the draft have a clear ending so that the reader knows that the piece is completed?

5. Which version do you prefer? Why? Would you recommend that Rob make any other changes?

Write your revision, and share it with your partner.

A Student Essay (First Draft)

Teaching is the basic way to educate the student. It differs from country 1
to country. My native country is Bangladesh, and its teaching method and education system is much different from the United States of America. Here are a few comparisons between the two countries.

The basic teaching system of Bangladesh is very different from the 2
United States of America. In Bangladesh, teachers lecture in the class and ask the students to follow the lecture and memorize the book. To get the good grade, students should write what the teacher lectures in class and whatever is written in the book. If some students have different opinions than the teacher, they will not get good grades in the examination. But in America when teachers lecture in class, students take notes, study different books, and draw their own opinions. These opinions could differ from the teacher's opinion and conception. As long as the students can prove their logic, they will get good grades. In this way, students in America develop their own opinion and ideas.

The examination system of both countries is also very different. In 3
Bangladesh, most of the schools and colleges have two major examinations throughout the year. One is midterm and the other is final examinations. The formats of the examinations are also different. Students have to write five or six essay questions in the examination. But in America, there is a semester system and there are many examinations throughout the year or semester. There are three formats of the examination. One is multiple-choice questions, another is true-false questions, and the third one is essay type questions. These examinations are cumulative.

In Bangladesh, teachers are respected like parents. Students respect 4
the teachers and obey their words. Students must pay attention when a teacher teaches the class. If teachers find someone who is not paying attention, that student will be punished by standing on the chair, standing in front of the class, or the teacher can throw that student out from that class. In the elementary class, the teachers can beat the student. All students must be in the class as long as the teacher is present in the class. If someone wants to go out of the class, that student needs permission from the teacher. In the United States of America, beating students or

punishing in front of the class is not possible. Students can go out from the class whenever they want to, and they don't need permission from the teacher. Students treat the teacher like a friend, not a parent. They also respect the teachers.

As a matter of fact, there are many differences in the teaching systems 5 between the two countries. Both countries have their own ways of teaching methods and educational systems, depending on economic, social, and cultural positions.

Mohibur Rob, Bangladesh

A Student Essay (Revised)

Although most educators agree that teaching is the basic way to educate 1 a student, teaching itself differs from country to country. For instance, my native country is Bangladesh, and its teaching method and educational system are much different from those of the United States of America. In this essay, I will discuss a few differences between the two countries.

The basic teaching system of Bangladesh is very different from that 2 used in the United States of America. In Bangladesh, teachers lecture in the class and ask the students to follow their lectures and memorize the books. To get a good grade, students should be able to write exactly what the teacher lectures in class and whatever is written in the book. If some students have different opinions from the teacher and they express these, they will not get good grades in their examinations. But in America it is different. When teachers lecture in class, students take notes, study different books, and draw their own opinions. These opinions could differ from the teacher's opinion and conception. As long as the students can prove their logic, they will still get good grades. In this way, students in America are encouraged to develop their own opinions and ideas.

The examination system of both countries is also very different. In 3 Bangladesh, most of the schools and colleges have only two major examinations each year: midterms and final examinations. Not only is this different from America, but also the formats of the examinations are different. Students have to write five or six essay questions in the examination. However, in America, there is a semester system, and there are many examinations throughout the two semesters each year. There are three basic formats for examinations: multiple-choice questions, true-false questions, and essay questions. Some teachers create combinations of these three types of examinations, too. The examinations are cumulative, and a student's grade is based on an average of the various tests.

Classroom behavior is different in the two countries as well. In 4 Bangladesh, teachers are respected like parents. Students respect the teachers and obey their words. Students must pay attention when a teacher teaches the class. If teachers find someone who is not paying attention, that student will be punished by being made to stand on a chair or stand in front of the class, or the teacher can throw that student out of the class. In the elementary classes, teachers can beat students. All students must be in the class as long as the teacher is present. If someone wants to go out of the class, that student needs permission from the teacher. In the United States of America, beating students or punishing them in front of the class is not possible. Students can leave the class whenever they want to, and they don't need permission from the teacher. Students treat the teacher like a friend, not a parent. They also respect the teachers, but in a different way, not through fear.

As a matter of fact, there are many differences in the teaching systems 5
of the two countries. I have focused on only a few of these. Both countries have their own teaching methods and educational systems. Each country's system seems to work for its particular population.

Mohibur Rob, Bangladesh

Editing Strategies

Mechanics

Use of the Definite Article

the

Read the following paragraph from *Language Two* by Heidi Dulay, Marina Burt, and Stephen Krashen, noticing how the word *the* is used with country names.

Over a billion people in the world speak more than one language fluently. In the Philippines, for example, many people must speak three languages if they are to engage fully in their community's social affairs. They must speak the national language, Pilipino; one of the eighty-seven local vernaculars; and English or Spanish. In small countries, such as the Netherlands or Israel, most children are required to study at least one foreign language in school, and sometimes several. Most adults in the Netherlands speak German, French, and English in addition to Dutch. Even in the United States, whose inhabitants are notoriously unconcerned about languages other than English, about 10% of the residents usually speak at least one language in addition to English in the course of their daily lives. Throughout much of the world, being able to speak at least two languages, and sometimes three or four, is necessary to function in society.

Find four country names in the excerpt you just read. Copy them in the spaces provided below. If *the* comes before the country name, copy it too. The first one has been done for you.

the Philippines _____   _____

_____   _____

Notice that some place names occur with *the* and some do not.
The does not occur with names of continents:

Australia   Africa
South America   Europe

In general, *the* does not occur with country names:

France   Turkey   Uzbekistan
Japan   Chile   Sri Lanka

unless the name of the country refers to a political union or association:

the United Arab Republic   the British Commonwealth

or unless it uses common nouns plus a proper noun with an *of* phrase:

the Dominion of Canada   the Kingdom of Thailand

or unless it is plural:

the West Indies   the United States   the Bahamas

In general, *the* does not occur with names of cities:

New York   Paris   Tashkent
Bangkok   Caracas   Jaffa

The is used with names of mountain ranges:

the Himalayas   the Alps   the Appalachians

but not with the name of a single mountain or volcano:

Bear Mountain   Mount Everest   Kilauea

The is used with most bodies of water:

the Pacific Ocean	the Red Sea
the Mississippi River	the Gulf of Mexico

but it is not used with lakes and bays:

Lake Erie   Hudson Bay

unless it uses an *of* phrase:

the Bay of Bengal

or unless they are plural:

the Great Lakes   the Finger Lakes

The is used with deserts, forests, canals, and peninsulas:

the Sahara	the Black Forest	the Suez Canal
the Gobi Desert	the Iberian Peninsula	

The is used with the names of geographic areas and points on the globe:

the Northwest	the Midwest
the South Pole	the equator

The is not used with names of languages:

Mandarin   Arabic   Spanish   Korean

unless you follow the name with the word *language:*

the English language   the Russian language

The is used to refer to people's nationalities:

the Italians   the Japanese   the Ethiopians

In general, *the* is used with names of public institutions and buildings but not churches:

the Plaza Hotel	the Museum of Natural History
the Louvre	the Taj Mahal
the Forbidden City	St. Patrick's Cathedral

In general, *the* is used with the names of schools if they contain an *of* phrase or if c*ollege, high school,* or *university* precedes the name:

the College of Charleston the Colorado School of Mines
the High School of Art and Design the University of California

but not when the descriptor follows the name:

Lincoln High School Kingsborough Community College
Marymount College Harvard University

In general, *the* is used with the names of ships:

the *Intrepid* the *Maine*

The is used with the names of newspapers but not magazines unless it is part of the name itself:

the *Los Angeles Times* *Newsweek*
the *Washington Post* *The New Yorker*

In general, *the* is used for celestial objects:

the universe the galaxy the stars
the planets the sun the moon
the Milky Way

but not for the names of planets:

Venus Mars

These are some of the rules for using *the* with place names and languages. Apply these rules to the following sentences. Write *the* in the space if it is needed; otherwise, leave the space blank.

1. _____ English is the primary language spoken in _____

   Australia, which is located between _____ Indian Ocean and

   _____ Pacific Ocean.

2. The enormous landmass extending from _____ Russia in _____

   north to _____ Iran in _____ south and eastward via _____

Afghanistan and _____ Pakistan to _____ northern India and

_____ Bangladesh is home to people who speak primarily Indo-

European languages.

3. The Malayo-Polynesian language family includes tongues spoken in

_____ Indonesia, _____ Madagascar, _____ Philippines, and

other islands as far east as _____ Hawaii.

4. The Sino-Tibetan group is the second largest language family in

number of speakers; the major languages in this group are _____

Burmese, dialects of _____ Chinese, _____ Thai, and _____

Tibetan. However, the majority of speakers in this group speak

_____ Mandarin and _____ Cantonese.

5. Some important language families are found on the continent of

_____ Africa and throughout _____ Middle East.

□ □ □

EXERCISE   Use the rules you have just learned to correct the six *the* errors in the
following paragraph. In some cases you will need to delete *the,* and in
others you must add *the.*

My best friend moved to the New Jersey from the Philippines three
years ago. Now she lives in the Hoboken, and she can see Hudson River
and the boat that travels up to the Bear Mountain each day. She has
learned to speak the English, and she plans to travel to the Canada next
year as an exchange student.

Editing Practice

Editing Other People's Writing

The following paragraph is a draft that has not been edited for errors.
Find as many errors in the use of the definite article and verb forms as

you can, and correct them. (If you have problems with the definite article, review pages 108–11.) Answers are on page 356.

Flying over Pacific Ocean from California to United States' most distant state, Hawaii, is exciting. I have visited Hawaiian Islands last year to celebrate my twenty-first birthday. More than twenty islands makes up Hawaiian group. Hawaii has nickname, "Aloha State"—*aloha* mean "greetings" in Hawaiian language. People live on seven of eight main islands. Hawaii covers 4,021 square miles and is a biggest island. It is built by volcanoes. The Mauna Kea and the Mauna Loa are the highest volcanoes in Hawaiian group. The Honolulu is capital and largest city and is located on island of Oahu. Hawaii is most beautiful place I has ever seen. I recommend that you are visiting there soon.

Editing Your Own Writing

Reread the essay that you wrote for this chapter, asking yourself the following questions:

1. Did I format my paper correctly?
2. Did I start new paragraphs when necessary?
3. Did I use final sentence punctuation and apostrophes correctly?
4. Did I use the past tenses correctly?
5. Did I use the present tenses correctly? Do my subjects and verbs agree?
6. Did I use quotation marks correctly?
7. Did I use pronouns correctly? Do the pronouns agree?
8. Did I form plurals correctly?
9. Did I use *the* correctly?

When you rewrite your essay, make any changes that will improve your writing.

Grammar Strategies

Understanding Determiners

A determiner is a type of word that occurs before a noun. One type of determiner is an article. There are two articles in English:

a (or *an*) and *the*. The following are some other types of determiners:

Possessives: *my, your, his, her, its, our, their,* and *'s* at the end of a word, as in *Irene's book* (see pages 65–66 for more on possessives)

Demonstratives: *this, that, these, those*

Quantifiers: *no, each, every, any, a few, some, several, much, most, many, lots of, all*

Used before a noun, these words give information about the noun:

a class	the class	my class	every class
several classes	this class	those classes	many classes

Nearly all *singular countable nouns* (see page 89) are preceded by a determiner. Look at the following sentences based on information from the Althen selection at the start of this chapter, and underline each noun that is preceded by a determiner.

1. Malaysians who remarked on the easy accessibility of American colleges and universities were comparing the American system unfavorably to that of the British.

2. The American educational system is based on the idea that as many people as possible should have access to as much education as possible.

3. This fact alone distinguishes the U.S. system from most others.

Plural countable nouns do not have to have determiners. If the idea is general, you do not need to use a determiner. If the idea is specific, pointing to a particular instance, person, or idea, a determiner is required. Look at the following sentences based on information from the Althen selection, and underline each plural countable noun. Notice whether it is preceded by a determiner or not.

1. "Anybody can get into college in the USA," it was common to hear Malaysians say.

2. On the other hand, these Malaysians would observe, "You Americans put men on the moon."

3. Differing ideas about formality and respect frequently complicate relationships between American professors and students from abroad.

4. Many foreign students are accustomed to more formal relationships and sometimes have difficulty bringing themselves to speak to their teachers at all, let alone address them by their given names.

Uncountable nouns do not have to have determiners. Just as for plural countable nouns, if the idea is general, you do not need to use a determiner. If the idea is specific, pointing to a particular instance, person, or idea, a determiner is required. Look at the following sentences from the Althen selection, and underline each plural countable noun. Notice whether it is preceded by a determiner or not.

1. Students who want clarification or additional information are expected to ask for it during the class.

2. While most teachers welcome students' questions and comments about the material being covered in the course, they do not welcome student efforts to negotiate for higher grades.

3. It is probably the case that much of the plagiarism foreign students commit is committed out of misunderstanding rather than out of dishonesty.

Deciding When to Use a Determiner

When a plural countable noun or an uncountable noun refers to something specific, it must have a determiner. If it refers to something general, no determiner is required. Look at the following sentences:

1. a. Students often worry about succeeding in school.
   b. The students in my school often worry about succeeding in their science courses.
2. a. Schools need to provide students with information about educational expectations.
   b. The schools in my state need to provide all the entering students with the necessary information about their expectations.
3. a. Plagiarism can lead to serious consequences.
   b. In my college, the consequence for the plagiarism of a writer's exact words and ideas can be very serious.

□ □ □

EXERCISE

Read each sentence, and add determiners where they are needed. Try to vary the determiners you use.

1. Teacher told us name on first day of class.

2. Students got together to interview each other.

3. We asked for each other's names, names of countries, how long we had been in country, and how long we had spoken English.

4. Student I worked with told me about background.

5. I told about language, job, and goals I had for future.

Moving from the General to the Specific

Look at these following pairs of sentences. Note that the first sentence in each pair, referring to a nonspecific item, uses *a* (*an*) or *some;* the second sentence, which makes that item specific, uses *the.*

I saw *a* movie last night. *The* movie was about a monster.

She read *an* interesting book. *The* book was so fascinating that she read until 1 o'clock in the morning.

We read *some* good stories in my English class. *The* stories were about people who had overcome difficulties and had succeeded.

We went to see *a* basketball game last night. *The* game went into overtime, and our team won *the* game by two points.

☐ ☐ ☐

EXERCISE

Write three pairs of sentences using *a/an* or *some* in the first sentence and *the* in the second sentence.

1. _____

_____

2. _____

_____

3. _____

_____

Special Use of *the*

Answer the following questions as in the example.

Where do you take a shower?
I take a shower in the bathroom.

1. Where do you cook dinner?
2. Where do you wash your hair?
3. Where do you read a book?
4. Where do you have a picnic?
5. Where do you walk your dog?
6. Where do you watch television?
7. Where do you take a nap?
8. Where do you get your teeth cared for?

We write "in the bathroom" even if there are several bathrooms in the house. We write "in the park" or "on the beach" even if we are referring to a specific park or beach. We write "in the hospital" or "at the dentist's" even though we are referring to a specific hospital or dentist. However, there are a few expressions for which we do not use *the;* for example,

I go to school (to class, to bed, to work, to church).

□　□　□

EXERCISES

1. The following is the first draft of an essay. Find as many errors in the use of *a/an* and *the* as you can. Correct the errors. Answers are on page 356.

In my class last week, we had to interview the student in our class. A student I interviewed came to United States from Poland. Her name is Irina, and she wants to become the nurse. She is majoring in the nursing in college, but she wants to take the courses in the psychology too. First, she has to take the courses in the English. Irina studies very hard, and she also likes to play a violin and read the books. Her favorite books are the mysteries, especially ones about the hospitals and the medicine. We had the good conversation, and I am happy to be in the class with Irina.

2. Reread one of the selections in this book that you have enjoyed. Notice the determiners that precede the nouns in the writing. Notice when nouns are not preceded by determiners. How does this correspond to the rules you have just learned?

□   □   □

CHECKING YOUR OWN WORK

1. Read through each essay you wrote for this chapter. Look at the nouns in the essay. (It may be helpful to underline them lightly.) Notice the determiners that precede the nouns. Are they correct? Make sure that what you have done corresponds to the rules you have just learned.
2. Check other writing that you have done recently to make sure that you used determiners correctly.
3. As an added check, work with a classmate to make sure that you have used determiners correctly in your writing.

Learning from One Another

PREREADING ACTIVITIES

1. In a small group, describe an experience in which you felt embarrassed because you did not know how to behave due to language or cultural differences. Choose one of the experiences expressed in your group, and share it with your class.
2. What differences in behavior have you noticed in the way that people eat in your home culture and in your new culture?
3. How do people learn proper behavior in a new culture? What should someone do when a newcomer makes a mistake in acceptable behavior?

VOCABULARY DEVELOPMENT

Look at the italicized words in the following sentences, and try to decide the meaning of each word based on the context of the sentence. Then choose the definition that seems closest to the meaning of the word as it is used in the sentence.

1. The first time our family was invited out to dinner in America, we *disgraced* ourselves while eating celery. We had emigrated to this country from China, and during our early days here we had a hard time with American table manners.

   a. embarrassed   b. showed off   c. hurt

2. Most Chinese don't care for dairy products, and in those days I wasn't even ready to drink fresh milk. Sour cream sounded perfectly *revolting*.

   a. delightful   b. beautiful   c. disgusting

3. Our family shook our heads *in unison*.

   a. happily   b. sadly   c. at the same time

4. "Why don't we just order four complete dinners *at random*?" he suggested. "Isn't that risky?" asked Mother.

   a. carefully   b. without careful choice   c. from the menu

The All-American Slurp

Lensey Namioka

Although she now lives in Seattle, Washington, Lensey Chao Namioka was born in Beijing, China. Her husband was born in Himeji, Japan. She has written travel books, one on Japan and one on China. Namioka is also well known for her adventure books, which are set in feudal Japan and focus on two young samurai warriors, Zenta and Matsuzo. "The All-American Slurp" is about problems faced by the members of a Chinese family, the Lins, as they adjust to differences in culture and customs in the United States.

The first time our family was invited out to dinner in America, we 1 disgraced ourselves while eating celery. We had emigrated to this country from China, and during our early days here we had a hard time with American table manners.

In China we never ate celery raw, or any other kind of vegetable raw. 2 We always had to disinfect the vegetables in boiling water first. When we were presented with our first relish tray, the raw celery caught us unprepared.

We had been invited to dinner by our neighbors, the Gleasons. After 3 arriving at the house, we shook hands with our hosts and packed ourselves into a sofa. As our family of four sat stiffly° in a row, my younger brother and I stole glances at our parents for a clue° as to what to do next.

°not naturally

°helpful idea

Mrs. Gleason offered the relish tray to Mother. The tray looked pretty, 4 with its tiny red radishes, curly sticks of carrots, and long slender stalks of pale green celery. "Do try some of the celery, Mrs. Lin," she said. "It's from a local farmer, and it's sweet."

°pieces of celery

Mother picked up one of the green stalks,° and Father followed suit. 5 Then I picked up a stalk, and my brother did too. So there we sat, each with a stalk of celery in our right hand.

Mrs. Gleason kept smiling. "Would you like to try some of the dip, 6 Mrs. Lin? It's my own recipe: sour cream and onion flakes, with a dash of Tabasco sauce."

Most Chinese don't care for dairy products, and in those days I 7 wasn't even ready to drink fresh milk. Sour cream sounded perfectly revolting. Our family shook our heads in unison.

Mrs. Gleason went off with the relish tray to the other guests, and we 8 carefully watched to see what they did. Everyone seemed to eat the raw vegetables quite happily.

Mother took a bite of her celery. *Crunch.* "It's not bad!" she whis- 9 pered.

Father took a bite of his celery. *Crunch.* "Yes, it *is* good," he said, look- 10 ing surprised.

°exciting

I took a bite, and then my brother. *Crunch, crunch.* It was more than 11 good; it was delicious. Raw celery has a slight sparkle, a zingy° taste that you don't get in cooked celery. When Mrs. Gleason came around with the relish tray, we each took another stalk of celery, except my brother. He took two.

There was only one problem: long strings ran through the length of 12 the stalk, and they got caught in my teeth. When I help my mother in the kitchen, I always pull the strings out before slicing celery.

I pulled the strings out of my stalk. *Z-z-zip, z-z-zip.* My brother followed 13 suit. *Z-z-zip, z-z-zip, z-z-zip.* To my left, my parents were taking care of their own stalks. *Z-z-zip, z-z-zip, z-z-zip.*

Suddenly I realized that there was dead silence except for our zip- 14 ping. Looking up, I saw that the eyes of everyone in the room were on our family. Mr. and Mrs. Gleason, their daughter Meg, who was my friend, and their neighbors the Badels—they were all staring at us as we busily pulled the strings of our celery.

°abundantly

That wasn't the end of it. Mrs. Gleason announced that dinner was 15 served and invited us to the dining table. It was lavishly° covered with platters of food, but we couldn't see any chairs around the table. So we helpfully carried over some dining·chairs and sat down. All the other guests just stood there.

Mrs. Gleason bent down and whispered to us, "This is a buffet dinner. 16 You help yourselves to some food and eat it in the living room."

°rushed
°embarrassed
°ate slowly

Our family beat a retreat° back to the sofa as if chased by enemy sol- 17 diers. For the rest of the evening, too mortified° to go back to the din- ing table, I nursed° a bit of potato salad on my plate.

Next day Meg and I got on the school bus together. I wasn't sure how 18 she would feel about me after the spectacle our family made at the party. But she was just the same as usual, and the only reference she made to the party was, "Hope you and your folks got enough to eat last night. You certainly didn't take very much. Mom never tries to figure out how much food to prepare. She just puts everything on the table and hopes for the best."

I began to relax. The Gleasons' dinner party wasn't so different from 19 a Chinese meal after all. My mother also puts everything on the table and hopes for the best.

Meg was the first friend I had made after we came to America. I even- 20 tually got acquainted with a few other kids in school, but Meg was still the only real friend I had.

My brother didn't have any problems making friends. He spent all his 21 time with some boys who were teaching him baseball, and in no time he could speak English much faster than I could—not better, but faster.

I worried more about making mistakes, and I spoke carefully, making 22 sure I could say everything right before opening my mouth. At least I had a better accent than my parents, who never really got rid of their

Chinese accent, even years later. My parents had both studied English in school before coming to America, but what they had studied was mostly written English, not spoken.

Father's approach to English was a scientific one. Since Chinese verbs 23 have no tense, he was fascinated by the way English verbs changed form according to whether they were in the present, past imperfect, perfect, pluperfect, future, or future perfect tense. He was always making diagrams of verbs and their inflections, and he looked for opportunities to show off his mastery of the pluperfect and future perfect tenses, his two favorites. "I shall have finished my project by Monday," he would say smugly.

Mother's approach was to memorize lists of polite phrases that would 24 cover all possible social situations. She was constantly muttering things like "I'm fine, thank you. And you?" Once she accidentally stepped on someone's foot, and hurriedly blurted, "Oh, that's quite all right!" Embarrassed by her slip, she resolved to do better next time. So when someone stepped on *her* foot, she cried, "You're welcome!"

In our own different ways, we made progress in learning English. But 25 I had another worry, and that was my appearance. My brother didn't have to worry, since Mother bought him blue jeans for school, and he dressed like all the other boys. But she insisted that girls had to wear skirts. By the time she saw that Meg and the other girls were wearing jeans, it was too late. My school clothes were bought already, and we didn't have money left to buy new outfits for me. We had too many other things to buy first, like furniture, pots, and pans.

The first time I visited Meg's house, she took me upstairs to her room, 26 and I wound up trying on her clothes. We were pretty much the same size, since Meg was shorter and thinner than average. Maybe that's how we became friends in the first place. Wearing Meg's jeans and T-shirt, I looked at myself in the mirror. I could almost pass for an American— from the back, anyway. At least the kids in school wouldn't stop and stare at me in the hallways, which was what they did when they saw me in my white blouse and navy blue skirt that went a couple of inches below the knees.

When Meg came to my house, I invited her to try on my Chinese 27 dresses, the ones with a high collar and slits up the sides. Meg's eyes were bright as she looked at herself in the mirror. She struck several sultry° poses, and we nearly fell over laughing.

°sexy

The dinner party at the Gleasons' didn't stop my growing friendship 28 with Meg. Things were getting better for me in other ways too. Mother finally bought me some jeans at the end of the month, when Father got his paycheck. She wasn't in any hurry about buying them at first, until I worked on her. This is what I did. Since we didn't have a car in those days, I often ran down to the neighborhood store to pick up things for her. The groceries cost less at a big supermarket, but the closest one was many blocks away. One day, when she ran out of flour, I offered to borrow a bike from our neighbor's son and buy a ten-pound bag of flour at the big supermarket. I mounted the boy's bike and waved to Mother. "I'll be back in five minutes!"

Before I started pedaling, I heard her voice behind me. "You can't go 29 out in public like that! People can see all the way up to your thighs!"

"I'm sorry," I said innocently. "I thought you were in a hurry to get 30 the flour." For dinner we were going to have pot-stickers (fried Chinese dumplings), and we needed a lot of flour.

"Couldn't you borrow a girl's bicycle?" complained Mother. "That way 31 your skirt won't be pushed up."

"There aren't too many of those around," I said. "Almost all the girls 32 wear jeans while riding a bike, so they don't see any point buying a girl's bike."

We didn't eat pot-stickers that evening, and Mother was thoughtful. 33 Next day we took the bus downtown and she bought me a pair of jeans. In the same week, my brother made the baseball team of his junior high school, Father started taking driving lessons, and Mother discovered rummage° sales. We soon got all the furniture we needed, plus a dart board and a 1,000-piece jigsaw puzzle (fourteen hours later, we discovered that it was a 999-piece jigsaw puzzle). There was hope that the Lins might become a normal American family after all.

°secondhand

Then came our dinner at the Lakeview restaurant. 34

The Lakeview was an expensive restaurant, one of those places where 35 a headwaiter dressed in tails conducted you to your seat, and the only light came from candles and flaming desserts. In one corner of the room a lady harpist played tinkling melodies.

Father wanted to celebrate, because he had just been promoted. He 36 worked for an electronics company, and after his English started improving, his superiors decided to appoint him to a position more suited to his training. The promotion not only brought a higher salary but was also a tremendous boost to his pride.

Up to then we had eaten only in Chinese restaurants. Although my 37 brother and I were becoming fond of hamburgers, my parents didn't care much for western food, other than chow mein.

But this was a special occasion, and Father asked his coworkers to rec- 38 ommend a really elegant restaurant. So there we were at the Lakeview, stumbling after the headwaiter in the murky dining room.

At our table we were handed our menus, and they were so big that to 39 read mine I almost had to stand up again. But why bother? It was mostly in French, anyway.

Father, being an engineer, was always systematic. He took out a pocket 40 French dictionary. "They told me that most of the items would be in

French, so I came prepared." He even had a pocket flashlight, the size of a marking pen. While Mother held the flashlight over the menu, he looked up the items that were in French.

"*Pâté en croûte*," he muttered. "Let's see . . . *pâté* is paste . . . *croûte* is 41 crust . . . hmm . . . a paste in crust."

The waiter stood looking patient. I squirmed and died at least fifty 42 times.

At long last Father gave up. "Why don't we just order four complete 43 dinners at random?" he suggested.

"Isn't that risky?" asked Mother. "The French eat some rather pecu- 44 liar things, I've heard."

"A Chinese can eat anything a Frenchman can eat," Father declared. 45

The soup arrived in a plate. How do you get soup up from a plate? I 46 glanced at the other diners, but the ones at the nearby tables were not on their soup course, while the more distant ones were invisible in the darkness.

Fortunately my parents had studied books on western etiquette be- 47 fore they came to America. "Tilt your plate," whispered my mother. "It's easier to spoon the soup up that way."

She was right. Tilting the plate did the trick. But the etiquette book 48 didn't say anything about what you did after the soup reached your lips. As any respectable Chinese knows, the correct way to eat your soup is to slurp. This helps to cool the liquid and prevent you from burning your lips. It also shows your appreciation.

We showed our appreciation. *Shloop,* went my father. *Shloop,* went my 49 mother. *Shloop, shloop,* went my brother, who was the hungriest.

The lady harpist stopped playing to take a rest. And in the silence, our 50 family's consumption of soup suddenly seemed unnaturally loud. You know how it sounds on a rocky beach when the tide goes out and the wa- ter drains from all those little pools? They go *shloop, shloop, shloop.* That was the Lin family, eating soup.

At the next table a waiter was pouring wine. When a large *shloop* 51 reached him, he froze. The bottle continued to pour, and red wine flooded the tabletop and into the lap of a customer. Even the customer didn't notice anything at first, being also hypnotized by the *shloop, shloop, shloop.*

It was too much. "I need to go to the toilet," I mumbled, jumping to 52 my feet. A waiter, sensing my urgency, quickly directed me to the ladies' room.

I splashed cold water on my burning face, and as I dried myself with 53 a paper towel, I stared into the mirror. In this perfumed ladies' room, with its pink-and-silver wallpaper and marbled sinks, I looked completely out of place. What was I doing here? What was our family doing in the Lakeview restaurant? In America?

The door to the ladies' room opened. A woman came in and glanced 54 curiously at me. I retreated into one of the toilet cubicles and latched the door.

Time passed—maybe half an hour, maybe an hour. Then I heard the 55
door open again, and my mother's voice. "Are you in there? You're not
sick, are you?"

There was real concern in her voice. A girl can't leave her family just 56
because they slurp their soup. Besides, the toilet cubicle had a few draw-
backs as a permanent residence. "I'm all right," I said, undoing the
latch.

Mother didn't tell me how the rest of the dinner went, and I didn't 57
want to know. In the weeks following, I managed to push the whole thing
into the back of my mind, where it jumped out at me only a few times a
day. Even now, I turn hot all over when I think of the Lakeview restaurant.

But by the time we had been in this country for three months, our 58
family was definitely making progress toward becoming Americanized. I
remember my parents' first PTA meeting. Father wore a neat suit and
tie, and Mother put on her first pair of high heels. She stumbled only
once. They met my homeroom teacher and beamed as she told them
that I would make honor roll soon at the rate I was going. Of course
Chinese etiquette forced Father to say that I was a very stupid girl and
Mother to protest that the teacher was showing favoritism toward me.
But I could tell they were both very proud.

The day came when my parents announced that they wanted to give 59
a dinner party. We had invited Chinese friends to eat with us before, but
this dinner was going to be different. In addition to a Chinese-American
family, we were going to invite the Gleasons.

"Gee, I can hardly wait to have dinner at your house," Meg said to me. 60
"I just *love* Chinese food."

That was a relief. Mother was a good cook, but I wasn't sure if people 61
who ate sour cream would also eat chicken gizzards stewed in soy sauce.

Mother decided not to take a chance with chicken gizzards. Since we 62
had western guests, she set the table with large dinner plates, which we
never used in Chinese meals. In fact we didn't use individual plates at
all, but picked up food from the platters in the middle of the table and
brought it directly to our rice bowls. Following the practice of Chinese-
American restaurants, Mother also placed large serving spoons on the
platters.

The dinner started well. Mrs. Gleason exclaimed at the beautifully 63
arranged dishes of food: the colorful candied fruit in the sweet-and-sour
pork dish, the noodle-thin shreds of chicken meat stir-fried with tiny
peas, and the glistening pink prawns in a ginger sauce.

At first I was too busy enjoying my food to notice how the guests were 64
doing. But soon I remembered my duties. Sometimes guests were too
polite to help themselves and you had to serve them with more food.

I glanced at Meg, to see if she needed more food, and my eyes nearly 65
popped out at the sight of her plate. It was piled with food: the sweet-

and-sour meat pushed right against the chicken shreds, and the chicken sauce ran into the prawns. She had been taking food from a second dish before she finished eating her helping from the first!

Horrified, I turned to look at Mrs. Gleason. She was dumping rice out 66 of her bowl and putting it on her dinner plate. Then she ladled prawns and gravy on top of the rice and mixed everything together, the way you mix sand, gravel, and cement to make concrete.

I couldn't bear to look any longer, and I turned to Mr. Gleason. He 67 was chasing a pea around his plate. Several times he got it to the edge, but when he tried to pick it up with his chopsticks, it rolled back toward the center of the plate again. Finally he put down his chopsticks and picked up the pea with his fingers. He really did! A grown man!

All of us, our family and the Chinese guests, stopped eating to watch 68 the activities of the Gleasons. I wanted to giggle. Then I caught my mother's eyes on me. She frowned and shook her head slightly, and I understood the message: the Gleasons were not used to Chinese ways, and they were just coping the best they could. For some reason I thought of celery strings.

When the main courses were finished, Mother brought out a platter 69 of fruit. "I hope you weren't expecting a sweet dessert," she said. "Since the Chinese don't eat dessert, I didn't think to prepare any."

"Oh, I couldn't possibly eat dessert!" cried Mrs. Gleason. "I'm simply 70 stuffed!"

Meg had different ideas. When the table was cleared, she announced 71 that she and I were going for a walk. "I don't know about you, but I feel like dessert," she told me, when we were outside. "Come on, there's a Dairy Queen down the street. I could use a big chocolate milkshake!"

Although I didn't really want anything more to eat, I insisted on pay- 72 ing for the milkshakes. After all, I was still hostess.

Meg got her large chocolate milkshake and I had a small one. Even 73 so, she was finishing hers while I was only half done. Toward the end she pulled hard on her straws and went *shloop, shloop.*

"Do you always slurp when you eat a milkshake?" I asked, before I 74 could stop myself.

Meg grinned. "Sure. All Americans slurp." 75

Reading and Thinking Strategies

Discussion Activities

Analysis and Conclusions

1. What is the problem with the celery? With the dip?
2. What is a buffet? Where in the story does Namioka tell you what this

word means? Why was the Lins' behavior incorrect for eating a buffet dinner?

3. Why was the daughter embarrassed at the Lakeview restaurant? How are people expected to eat in an elegant restaurant?

4. What do the Americans do that show incorrect table manners at the Lin family dinner? How do the Lins expect the Gleasons to behave?

Writing and Point of View

1. Why does Namioka begin by showing the mistake that the Lin family made and end by showing the mistake that the Gleason family made? How do these two incidents connect with each other?

2. *Onomatopoeia* involves a word that imitates the natural sound associated with the action it refers to. What examples of onomatopoeia can you find in this story? What effect do they have on you as a reader?

3. What is the tone or mood of this story—sad, humorous, silly, serious, depressing? What specific incidents in the story support your answer?

4. How many examples does Namioka provide to illustrate American customs? How many examples illustrate Chinese customs? What details were the strongest for you as a reader? Why?

5. Namioka shifts time periods in this story. What words does she use to let her reader know to which time period she is referring? What different verb tenses are used in the story?

Personal Response and Evaluation

1. What is Namioka's main idea in this story? What evidence do you have in the story to support your answer?

2. Why does Mr. Lin tell the teacher that his daughter is a stupid girl when the teacher says that she is going to make the honor roll? Why does Mrs. Lin say that the teacher must be showing favoritism? What does this tell the reader about Chinese culture?

3. What is the significance of the last line in the story?

4. How do you compare the idea of becoming Americanized as presented in this story and in the Klein selection in Chapter One?

Role Playing

1. Act out the Namioka short story with one student playing the narrator and other students playing the characters. One more student can read the background information. You might want to record this and play it back for the class or for individual students who wish to review the story.

2. Act out the following situation in your class. One person is not sure how to behave in a new situation. Role-play this situation using members of the class to play the individuals who might be involved in the discussion.

Journal Writing

"Should I marry him?" I asked myself in English.
"Yes."
"Should I marry him?" I asked myself in Polish.
"No."

EVA HOFFMAN, *Lost in Translation*

"The All-American Slurp" is about cultural differences. Have you ever felt confused or conflicted in your new culture? Have you ever felt that you did not know the behavior that was expected of you? How did you handle the situation? Write your thoughts in your journal.

Writing Strategies

Essay Strategies

Narration: Telling a Story

Every day of our lives, all of us tell stories. For example, we come home from school and tell our families what happened in class. We might discuss a bus trip and describe one of the people on the bus. We fill our stories with details that will capture the imagination of the listener. We tell stories to give ourselves pleasure and to give our listeners pleasure. Writer Joan Didion said, "We tell ourselves stories in order to live." Stories are a way of making sense of the world.

When we tell stories, we are aware of beginnings and endings. We usually tell a story in the order in which it happened; when we listen to stories, we also like to hear them in the correct order. Have you ever been telling a child an old, familiar story and, in trying to rush through it, left out a part? The child will usually stop you and beg you to tell the story "right," with all its parts in the right order. The rules we follow when we tell stories to friends and family are similar to the rules we follow when we write stories that will be shared with teachers and classmates.

"The All-American Slurp" is an example of narration that uses *chronological order,* which means that events are told in the order in which they occurred. The Namioka story begins, "The first time our family was invited out to dinner in America . . ." Reread the story, noticing each time that Namioka uses expressions of time as transitions throughout the story. How do these help you follow the story?

In addition, Namioka includes many details that describe the members of the Lin family and their life. When you write a narration, you can make your writing more interesting and richer by adding details that help the reader feel and see the experience. Writers do this by adding sensory details, details that help a reader see, hear, smell, feel, and taste the experiences that are being described. Reread the Namioka story, noticing the specific details she provides. Decide whether the details help the reader see, hear, smell, feel, or taste each of the particular experiences she is describing.

When writing a narrative or a story of your own, always consider chronological order and the inclusion of sensory details to help your reader understand and enjoy your story.

□   □   □

EXERCISES

1. Compare the writing in Hemingway's story in Chapter Three with the writing in the story in this chapter. Which selection do you prefer and why?
2. What kinds of reading do you do just for your own enjoyment? Share with a classmate the best article, book, or story that you have read in the past few months. What makes a piece of writing appeal to you?

Essay Form

The Conclusion

Writers conclude their writing in different ways, depending on the type of writing they are doing and the purpose for which it is being written. In concluding a short story, the writer may want to make a specific point, to make a connection between the beginning of the story and the end, or to leave the readers with a particular feeling.

Namioka ends "The All-American Slurp" in the following way:

"Do you always slurp when you eat a milkshake?" I asked, before I could stop myself.

Meg grinned. "Sure. All Americans slurp."

What is the purpose of this conclusion?

Hemingway ends "A Day's Wait" in the following way:

But his gaze at the foot of the bed relaxed slowly. The hold over himself relaxed too, finally, and the next day it was very slack and he cried easily at little things that were of no importance.

What is the purpose of this conclusion?

In concluding an essay, an author may have similar goals as when concluding a short story: to make a specific point, to make a connection between the beginning of the story and the end, or to leave readers with a particular feeling. The conclusion can be humorous, and it can be short.

However, the most basic type of conclusion is a short restatement of the thesis or main idea of the essay. The concluding paragraph in this case is about three or four sentences long. For this type of conclusion, it may help to picture the essay as a clock with the introduction starting at 12 o'clock, the body of the essay moving through the hours of the day, and the conclusion arriving back at 12 o'clock to form a complete circle.

Let's look at some of the conclusions that have appeared in the essays in this book and examine their purposes and effects.

Grimes concluded his essay on fashion in the following way:

No wonder men tend to shy away from the fashion game. The risk of making a mistake, of looking silly, looms too large. They are happy, for once, to step back and take the passive role of spectator. But they do know enough to cheer when they see the game played well.

What is the purpose of this conclusion? What is the tone? Is it serious, humorous, sarcastic, angry? If you haven't read this article, what does it seem to be about?

Klein concluded his essay on a young immigrant from Haiti in the following way:

Such perverse propriety cannot last long. Immigrants become Americans very quickly. Some lose hope after years of menial labor; others lose discipline, inebriated by freedom. "There's an interesting phenomenon," says Philip Kasinitz of Williams College. "When immigrant kids criticize each other for getting lazy or loose, they say, 'You're becoming American.'" (Belizaire said she and the Russians would tease each other that way at Madison.) It's ironic, Kasinitz adds. "Those who work hardest to keep American culture at bay have the best chance of becoming American success stories." If so, we may be fixed on the wrong issue. The question shouldn't be whether immigrants are ruining America, but whether America is ruining the immigrants.

What is the purpose of this conclusion? What is the tone? Is it serious, humorous, sarcastic, angry? If you haven't read this article, what does it seem to be about?

◻ ◻ ◻

EXERCISES

1. Read conclusions from any of the selections in this book. What seems to be the purpose of each of the conclusions? Choose one that you think is particularly effective, and explain to the class why you chose that one.

2. You will find many excellent pieces of student writing throughout this book. Select two that you particularly like. Look at their conclusions. Try rewriting one of the conclusions. What effect does the new conclusion have on the essay?

3. Rewrite the conclusion to an essay you have written. Then read the original and the rewritten essay. (This is especially easy to do on the computer. You can save both versions and easily compare them.) Which do you prefer? Why? Discuss the question with a partner to find out if you agree.

Suggestions for Writing

You may want to look at your journal or try brainstorming or free-writing before you begin to write on these topics. Always spend some time thinking before you begin to write. (Try the suggestion in the next section, "Getting Started," if you need help in beginning your writing.)

The first two suggestions are narratives. When you write a narrative, keep in mind chronological order, sensory details, and the use of dialogue. Be sure to start a new paragraph each time a new person starts to speak, even if the words take up only one line.

1. Write a narrative about an experience in which people from two cultures meet, conflict, and resolve their differences.

2. Write a narrative in which you describe the learning of some type of behavior—table manners, ways of meeting and greeting new people, or school conduct, for example. Describe one or more incidents that illustrate the behavior and how a person learns what is expected.

3. Write an essay describing how to cook a particular dish from your culture. Reread pages 32–33 on how to write a process essay. Explain the steps involved, including gathering the supplies necessary, preparing the ingredients, cooking them, and serving them. Be specific and clear.

4. Write an essay describing a holiday in your country for which people wear special clothes, eat special foods, or engage in particular celebratory activities. Explain this holiday to an audience that is not familiar with the customs of your culture.

5. Namioka writes that when the teacher told the Lins that their daughter would make the honor roll, the father said that she was a stupid girl and the mother said that the teacher showed favoritism. Write an essay in which you explain a type of behavior that is traditional etiquette in your country but would seem unusual in the United States. Explain using a specific incident and dialogue.

Getting Started

Brainstorming

Whenever possible, you should write about something that interests you. You will then have ideas on the subject and will probably be able to come up with something to say. Even if you are writing about a topic that interests you, however, you may have problems writing an essay. As you have discovered when doing it with a classmate, brainstorming is a good technique to use to help you come up with ideas that will develop into your essay.

When you brainstorm on your own, you may want to write out some questions. The questions will vary with the topic. For example, the following sample questions were used to brainstorm for an essay about a conflict between two cultures.

Who has the conflict?
My two best friends. One is from Russia, and the other is from the Dominican Republic.

What makes it difficult to resolve?
They don't want to hurt each other's feelings, but they feel very angry because one student wouldn't let the other one speak in class.

Where did they meet?
In our English class.

When did you realize that the conflict was a problem?
They stopped talking to each other completely. I tried to talk to both of them, but it didn't work.

How do they treat each other?
They act as if they do not see each other. This makes me nervous and worried.

Why do you want to write about them?
I think that writing can help you understand a problem and find a solution. I hope it will this time.

The next step is reading through the questions and answers and deciding what to emphasize in the writing. As you read through what you have written, this may become obvious. Although brainstorming is a good technique for getting started, you can use it at any time during the writing process. If you are stuck in the middle and need more support or more details, brainstorming can be helpful. It is a useful tool to help a writer create a rich, fully developed essay.

□ □ □

EXERCISES
1. Brainstorm about one or more of the following: a conflict, cultural differences, problems in your school or classes. Write down your questions and answers. They will be helpful when you begin writing.
2. Brainstorm with a classmate. One of you will ask the questions; the other will write down the answers. Then repeat the activity with your roles reversed. At the end of the two sessions, you should have material for two essays.

Revising

After you have finished writing your first draft, give yourself some time to separate from your words and ideas so that you will be able to view your writing from a new perspective.

During this time, read the student essay that follows. Answer the following revision questions about this essay.

1. Does Castro's introduction make you want to read more? Is it clear what her essay will be about?
2. What connects the first paragraph to the second paragraph, the second to the third, and so forth?
3. Are there enough details and information to support the ideas?
4. What did you like best about this essay? Why?
5. Does the conclusion tie together the ideas of the essay?

After you use these questions to discuss the Castro essay, rewrite them to use as you revise your own essay. Share your revision with a classmate.

A Student Essay

Culture Shock

In general, anybody that comes from another country experiences "culture shock." Many foreigners in the United States have similar experiences with the different cultures. We are sometimes disappointed, embarrassed, insulted, and confused when we have problems. When I came from Colombia, I experienced a deep culture shock. I felt strange living in this country. I thought that life would be similar to life in Colombia, knowing people and being together with friends. But these expectations did not come true.

As much as my relatives living here tried to make me feel comfortable, they were too busy working to really help me. I was still very depressed because the rest of my relatives and friends were back in Colombia. My oldest sister would come to our house with her friends, but I didn't feel a part of them. I was usually in my bedroom every time they visited because I wanted to be alone with my memories of Colombia.

Another impression about American people was that they were like the weather of their country. One day they seemed to be warm and friendly, and the next day they were cool. I felt that every person I met was very different from me. I did not think it was going to be so difficult to communicate with native Americans and make friends and to know more information about living here, but I could not understand life here because I did not know what the people around me were talking about.

When I started studying in college, English was harder than I expected. I was very disappointed at the time because I had taken an English conversation course for a few months in Colombia before I came, but it wasn't enough for me. I realized that I had to "start from scratch." I was aware I would have to learn the proper structure of English sentences because translating them into my language made them sound backwards to me. I needed to think English, see English, feel English.

Another observation I made involved my professors. In my country, the professor helped students understand the lesson. If a student didn't understand it, the professor would help with the basics after class. Also, the teacher talked with the students' parents about how the student was doing in class. In this country, professors are very nice but tend to keep their distance.

Classroom environment was also very different from that in Colombia. The classrooms in Colombia were very clean and quiet. On the other hand, in United States classrooms, students chewed gum and ate. I never did these things in my school. In the United States, some students interrupt the professor while he is explaining the lesson. In addition, they never stop talking until the professor tells them to stop. In Colombia, students never talk except to answer questions after being called upon.

Living in the USA, I have learned about many different peoples' cultures and customs because I have tried to be patient in learning about them.

I realized that I needed to achieve my goal of speaking English as much as I could. But I was often disappointed and embarrassed during my six-year stay. If we learn to communicate across cultural barriers, we would learn what to say and how to say it better.

Now I understand and speak English better. I do not criticize the American coolness because I understand that this is part of their culture. Also, I like the American lifestyle. Nobody here looks into your affairs, but in Colombia it is very common for your neighbor to know your business.

Iris Castro, Colombia

Editing Strategies

Mechanics

Capital Letters

When editing for errors, many writers have difficulty with capital letters. Test your knowledge of capital letters by trying to find the 32 missing capital letters in the following paragraph.

Tatyana moved to illinois from russia. She attends the university of illinois in champaign-urbana and lives in a dorm with a roommate from missouri. In march, Tatyana began to work on wednesday, thursday, and friday afternoons in the college library. It is one of the biggest college libraries in the united states. She practices english with everyone who borrows books. One day a student borrowed *anna karenina* by leo tolstoy. She asked Tatyana about the book and soon invited her to a saturday night buffet dinner at st. joseph's church. She met some interesting people from the college at the dinner. They took her to a school game, where she learned "hail to the orange," the school song. Tatyana is starting to feel more at home in the midwest. She is teaching some of her new friends russian, and they are helping her with english. She bought an old chevrolet blazer from a student and plans to visit chicago and lake michigan in july.

Turn to page 357 to check your answers. If you made more than two mistakes, review the following rules.

Capital letters are used for the following terms:

1. The first word in a sentence, names of people, and the pronoun *I*:

    My friend thinks that I will be able to read Shakespeare soon.

2. Names of the months, days of the week, and holidays:

Miguel was born in November, on the fourth Thursday, Thanksgiving Day.

3. Names of particular places, languages, and nationalities:

The Brazilian girl in my class speaks French because she went to Le Havre High School in Montreal.

Note: Do not use capital letters if the specific names are not used:

He enjoys attending college and working in a store, but he likes to have time to visit museums and churches.

4. Titles of books, magazines, newspapers, stories, articles, films, television programs, songs, and poems:

When I saw Nina, she was carrying *The Silent Language, Omni,* and the *Washington Post.*
She was going to see the movie *Hamlet* with her class.

5. The first word in a direct quotation:

Tony said, "You can really do a lot if you try."

6. Brand names of products:

The man bought Pampers and Pepsi-Cola at the A&P.

7. Names of religious and political groups, companies, corporations, and clubs:

Françoise joined the Republican party when she was in college, but she became less active when she started to work for General Motors because she was very busy with her job, the Catholic Students' League, and Literacy Volunteers of America.

□   □   □

EXERCISE

The following paragraph has 35 missing capital letters. Can you find them all?

when mikhail and fatima volunteered to work one afternoon in the western college post office, they were in for a surprise. in one corner, there were many boxes piled high. they found three heavy cartons of french language tapes addressed to professor maude cousteau, now of the ford foundation. she had left the school back in february and had moved to new mexico. fatima accidentally opened a box filled with the microsoft windows programs needed for the college ibm computers. "mr. smith, this post office is a mess," mikhail told the postmaster. "i know it, son. we just have to get a little more organized. the u.s. mail has to go through, and we will do it soon." mikhail and fatima left there wondering if the college mail would ever get through.

The answers are on page 357.

Editing Practice

Editing Other People's Writing

All writers make errors in their first drafts. Sometimes it is difficult to find your own errors, but practice will help you improve your editing skills. Here we present a draft that contains errors involving subject-verb agreement, the use of *the,* plurals, and capital letters. Find and correct these errors. Answers are on page 357.

Marie learn languages very easily. She was born in haiti and has spoken the french and the creole all her lives. Now marie also know the english, spanish, and italian. She has a special technique that always work for her. At night she go to sleep by hypnotizing herself as she stare at a poster of the stained-glasses window of nôtre-dame cathedral in the paris. Her sony walkman tape deck is on her head, and she listen to a different language tapes each night.

Editing Your Own Writing

Reread an essay that you wrote for this chapter, asking yourself the following questions:

1. Did I format my paper correctly?
2. Did I start new paragraphs when necessary?
3. Did I use final sentence punctuation and apostrophes correctly?

4. Did I use the past tenses correctly?

5. Did I use the present tenses correctly? Do my subjects and verbs agree?

6. Did I use quotation marks correctly?

7. Did I use pronouns correctly? Do the pronouns agree with their antecedents?

8. Did I form plurals correctly?

9. Did I use *the* correctly?

10. Did I use capital letters where they are needed?

When you rewrite your essay, make any changes that will improve your writing.

Grammar Strategies

Sentence Variety

Writers use a variety of sentences to keep their writing interesting and lively. Too many short sentences can sound choppy and immature, just as too many long sentences can be dull and difficult to read. Writers maintain a balance of different lengths and types of sentences.

Sentences are made up of various types and numbers of clauses. A clause is any part of a sentence that contains a subject and a predicate.

An independent clause can stand alone as a sentence.

A dependent clause cannot stand alone. It needs an independent clause to make it a complete sentence.

When students do their homework, they should focus on their work.
     DEPENDENT CLAUSE   INDEPENDENT CLAUSE

Clauses determine four major sentence types:

1. A *simple sentence* has one independent clause:

   We always had to disinfect the vegetables in boiling water.
   Mrs. Gleason offered the relish tray to Mother.
   Our family shook our heads in unison.

2. A *compound sentence* has two or more independent clauses:

   We had emigrated to this country from China, and during our

early days here we had a hard time with American table manners.

It was lavishly covered with platters of food, but we couldn't see any chairs around the table.

Father wore a neat suit and tie, and Mother put on her first pair of high heels.

3. A *complex sentence* has one independent clause joined to one or more dependent clauses. A complex sentence contains either a subordinating word such as *although, when,* or *because* or a relative pronoun such as *that, who,* or *which:*

When we were presented with our first relish tray, the raw celery caught us unprepared.

Since we didn't have a car in those days, I often ran down to the neighborhood store to pick up things for her.

Before I started pedaling, I heard her voice behind me.

Although my brother and I were becoming fond of hamburgers, my parents didn't care much for western food, other than chow mein.

While Mother held the flashlight over the menu, he looked up the items that were in French.

4. A *compound-complex sentence* has two or more independent clauses and one or more dependent clauses:

My brother didn't have to worry, since Mother bought him blue jeans for school, and he dressed like all the other boys.

Several times he got it to the edge, but when he tried to pick it up with his chopsticks, it rolled back toward the center of the plate again.

The first time I visited Meg's house, she took me upstairs to her room, and I wound up trying on her clothes.

☐ ☐ ☐

EXERCISES

1. With a partner, write sentences about the Namioka story, practicing each of these sentence types.
2. Reread the Grimes essay in Chapter Four to find examples of the four sentence types.
3. Reread the Althen selection in Chapter Five to find examples of the four sentence types.
4. What differences did you find in the types of sentences used in these pieces of writing? What was the predominant type in each story? How does the use of a sentence type affect you as a reader? Is one type of sentence easier to read than another for you?

5. Working with a partner, read one essay that each of you has written to find examples of each of the four sentence types.

The Compound Sentence

To form compound sentences, join two related independent clauses with a semicolon (;), or use a coordinating word. Some commonly used coordinators are *and, but, or, yet, for, so,* and *nor.* Use a comma before the coordinator.

Each of the following sentences uses some type of coordination. Underline the comma and the coordinating word. Read the two independent clauses. Can each one stand alone?

1. The daughter was friendly with Meg, for they enjoyed many of the same things.

2. The family had recently arrived in the United States from China, and they had very little experience eating in an American home.

3. The daughter didn't want to sit at the table with her family, nor did she want to try eating strange food.

4. The celery looked tasty and fresh, but it had long strings that were hard to chew.

5. They could sit down at the table by themselves, or they could take their plates back to the living room with the other guests.

6. My parents seemed embarrassed, yet they stayed and tried to be cheerful.

7. The family wanted to meet new people, so they went to the buffet at the Gleason home.

Write two compound sentences of your own.

Complex Sentences

Commas with Subordinate Clauses

There are several types of sentences that we can use when we write. Most writers vary sentence types to make their writing more interesting to the reader. If you examine professional writing, you will usually find a combination of short sentences and long sentences.

Subordinators are special words that are used to make connections. Some commonly used subordinators are *after, as, because, before, if, since, until, when, where,* and *while.*

Each of the following sentences uses some type of subordination. Underline the word that indicates subordination.

1. Although I have lived in the United States for six years, I am still unable to think about my home country with detachment.

2. As I practiced more, my English began to improve.

3. I have to return to my home country one day because I want to know myself better.

4. When I try to review my life, I feel both happy and sad.

Write two complex sentences of your own. Then, on the basis of what you have observed in this exercise, complete the following sentences.

When two complete sentences are connected by a subordinator and

the subordinating word is the first word in the sentence, a comma

_____ needed. If the subordinating word occurs in the middle of the
(is/is not)

sentence, a comma _____ needed.
(is/is not)

Now write two complex sentences of your own describing your feelings about the Namioka story.

□   □   □

EXERCISES

1. Reread one of the nonfiction selections, essays, and textbook excerpts in this book that you have enjoyed. Notice the different types of sentences in the selection. Do you find more of one type of sentence than another?

2. Reread one of the stories in the book. Notice the different types of sentences in the story. Do you find more of one type of sentence than another? What differences, if any, do you find in the types of sentences that are used in essays and those that are used in stories?

□   □   □

CHECKING YOUR OWN WORK

1. Read through each essay you wrote for this chapter. Look at the sentences you used in the essay. Notice whether you used simple, compound, complex, or compound-complex sentences. Is there a

variety of sentence types? Do you think you need to change the balance of types of sentences?

2. Check other writing that you have done recently to make sure that you have used a variety of sentence types.

3. As an added check, work with a classmate to make sure that you have a variety of sentence types in your writing.

Considering Our Roles

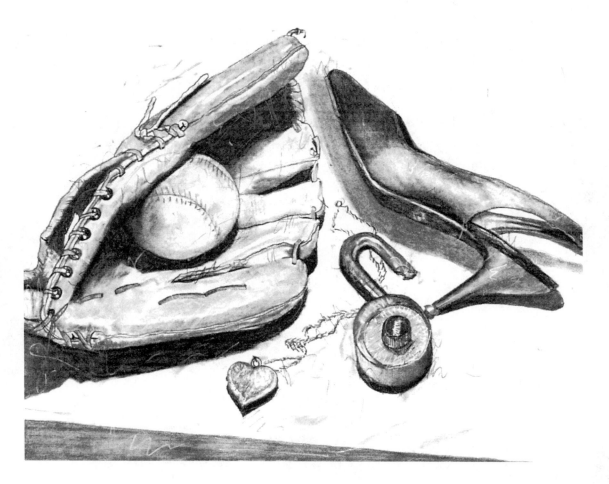

CHAPTER SEVEN

Dating Practices

PREREADING ACTIVITIES

1. In a group, discuss your observations about dating in the United States. Think about what you have seen on your college campus, on the streets, and at parties. What patterns have you observed in relation to who asks for the date, who pays, and how people act on dates?
2. In a group, discuss the way dating is portrayed on television, in books, and in the movies. What patterns have you observed in relation to who asks for the date, who pays, and how people act on dates?
3. Compare your personal observations with what is presented in the media. What differences do you find? How do you explain these differences?

VOCABULARY DEVELOPMENT

Ullman uses some idiomatic and slang expressions to express her ideas about dating. Look at the italicized expressions in the following excerpts from her article, and try to decide what each expression means. Then choose the definition that seems closest to the meaning of the expression as it is used in the sentence.

1. Students have fewer anxiety attacks when they ask somebody to play tennis than when they plan a formal dinner date. They enjoy last-minute "let's make dinner together" dates because they not only avoid *hassling* with attire and transportation but also don't have time to agonize.

   a. worrying about   b. preparing in advance   c. buying and selling

2. Casual dating also encourages people to form healthy friendships prior to starting relationships. My roommate and her boyfriend were friends for four months before their *chemistries clicked.*

   a. they took a chemistry class together   b. the relationship became more serious   c. their relationship ended

3. John whipped out his wallet on our first date before I could suggest we *go Dutch.* During our after-dinner stroll, he told me he was interested in dating me on a steady basis. After I explained I was more interested in a friendship, he told me he would have understood had I paid for my dinner.

   a. the man pays for the woman   b. the woman pays for the man   c. each person pays his or her own way

4. "I've practically stopped *treating* women on dates," he said defensively. "It's safer and more comfortable when we each pay for ourselves." John had assumed that because I graciously accepted his treat, I was in love.

   a. paying for someone else   b. paying for oneself   c. paying on credit

Will You Go Out with Me?

Laura Ullman

The following article from Newsweek *was written by Laura Ullman when she was a student. Today she is a freelance writer living in Los Angeles with her husband and two daughters. Ullman enjoyed writing this article about the dilemma of whether or not a woman should ask a man out on a date, and she continues to write articles about personal life experiences.*

E very day I anxiously wait for you to get to class. I can't wait for us to smile at each other and say good morning. Some days, when you arrive only seconds before the lecture begins, I'm incredibly impatient.° Instead of reading the *Daily Cal*, I anticipate your footsteps from behind and listen for your voice. Today is one of your late days. But I don't mind, because after a month of desperately desiring to ask you out, today I'm going to. Encourage me, because letting you know I like you seems as risky to me as skydiving° into the sea.

    I know that dating has changed dramatically in the past few years, and for many women, asking men out is not at all daring. But I was raised in a traditional European household where simply the thought of my asking you out spells "naughty." Growing up, I learned that men call, ask and pay for the date. During my three years at Berkeley, I have learned otherwise. Many Berkeley women have brightened their social lives by taking the initiative with men. My girlfriends insist that it's essential for women to participate more in the dating process. "I can't sit around and wait anymore," my former roommate once blurted out. "Hard as it is, I have to ask guys out—if I want to date at all!" Wonderful. More women are inviting men out, and men say they are delighted, often relieved, that dating no longer depends solely on their willingness and courage to take the first step. Then why am I digging my nails into my hand trying to muster° up courage?

    I keep telling myself to relax since dating is less stereotypical° and more casual today. A college date means anything from studying together to sex. Most of my peers prefer casual dating anyway because it's cheaper and more comfortable. Students have fewer anxiety attacks when they ask somebody to play tennis than when they plan a formal dinner date. They enjoy last-minute "let's make dinner together" dates

°not patient; wanting to do something right away

°parachuting from an airplane

°gather
°conventional or typical; characteristic

1

2

3

because they not only avoid hassling with attire and transportation but also don't have time to agonize.

Casual dating also encourages people to form healthy friendships 4 prior to starting relationships. My roommate and her boyfriend were friends for four months before their chemistries clicked. They went to movies and meals and often got together with mutual friends. They alternated paying the dinner check. "He was like a girlfriend," my roommate once laughed—blushing. Men and women relax and get to know each other more easily through such friendships. Another friend of mine believes that casual dating is improving people's social lives. When she wants to let a guy know she is interested, she'll say, "Hey, let's go get a yogurt."

Who pays for it? My past dates have taught me some things: you don't 5 know if I'll get the wrong idea if you treat me for dinner, and I don't know if I'll deny you pleasure or offend you by insisting on paying for myself. John whipped out his wallet on our first date before I could suggest we go Dutch. During our after-dinner stroll, he told me he was interested in dating me on a steady basis. After I explained I was more interested in a friendship, he told me he would have understood had I paid for my dinner. "I've practically stopped treating women on dates," he said defensively. "It's safer and more comfortable when we each pay ⁰politely for ourselves." John had assumed that because I graciously° accepted his treat, I was in love. He was mad at himself for treating me, and I regretted allowing him to.

Larry, on the other hand, blushed when I offered to pay for my meal 6 on our first date. I unzipped my purse and flung out my wallet, and he looked at me as if I had addressed him in a foreign language. Hesitant, I asked politely, "How much do I owe you?" Larry muttered, "Uh, uh, you really don't owe me anything, but if you insist . . ." Insist? I thought, I only offered. To Larry, my gesture was a suggestion of rejection.

Men and women alike are confused about who should ask whom out 7 and who should pay. While I treasure my femininity, adore gentlemen and delight in a traditional formal date, I also believe in equality. I am grateful for casual dating because it has improved my social life immensely by making me an active participant in the process. Now I can not only receive roses but also give them. Casual dating is a worthwhile adventure because it works. No magic formula guarantees "he" will say yes. I just have to relax, be Laura and ask him out in an unthreatening manner. If my friends are right, he'll be flattered.

Sliding into his desk, he taps my shoulder and says, "Hi, Laura, what's 8 up?"

"Good morning," I answer with nervous chills. "Hey, how would you 9 like to have lunch after class on Friday?"

"You mean after the midterm?" he says encouragingly. "I'd love to go 10 to lunch with you."

"We have a date," I smile. 11

Reading and Thinking Strategies

Discussion Activities

Analysis and Conclusions

1. Why does Ullman think that men are pleased that women are asking them out?

2. At the end of paragraph 5, why was John "mad at himself for treating" Ullman to dinner? In paragraph 6, why was Larry upset? Explain Larry's attitude about paying for a date.

3. According to Ullman, how has casual dating changed the dating situation in her college? How has it changed her social life?

4. What does Ullman mean when she writes, "Casual dating is a worthwhile adventure because it works"? What works?

Writing and Point of View

1. To whom is the first paragraph of the article addressed? Who is "you"?

2. The final paragraph is only one sentence long. Is this an effective conclusion to the article? Would you change it in any way?

3. What is Ullman's main idea? Did she convince you? What examples did she use to support her ideas?

Personal Response and Evaluation

1. Do you think it is easier for a woman to ask a man for a casual date or a formal date? Explain, using your observations or experiences.

2. Should women ask men out on dates? Explain, using your observations or experiences.

3. Who should pay for a date? Why? Would you ever "go Dutch" on a date?

4. What problems could develop from young people dating in the way Ullman describes? What advantages are there to this kind of dating?

Small Group Discussion

In a small group, discuss the best way to deal with one or more of the following situations:

1. Someone asks you on a date and you do not want to go, but you want to be polite to the other person.

2. Someone asks you on a date and your parents do not allow you to date yet.

3. Many of your college friends are dating, and one of them wants to set up a date for you. However, in your culture, people do not date casually.

4. You ask someone on a date. The person refuses and tells you that you two should just be friends.

As a class, discuss the results of your discussions. Some groups may role-play some of these situations for the entire class.

Journal Writing

It is well to understand as early as possible in one's writing life that there is just one contribution which every one of us can make: we can give into the common pool of experience some comprehension of the world as it looks to each of us.

DOROTHEA BRANDE, *Becoming a Writer*

What do you think about Ullman's essay? Should she have asked her classmate out? Is it ever wrong for women to ask men on dates?

What do you think about dating customs in the United States? In what ways are they similar to or different from those in your culture? Write about these ideas in your journal.

Writing Strategies

Essay Strategies

Use of the Anecdote

Reread the first paragraph and paragraphs 8 through 11 of Ullman's article. Her essay begins and ends with an anecdote, a short, amusing story taken from her own experience. Many writers use anecdotes from their experience to enrich and personalize their writing. Using anecdotes is also an effective way to engage the reader, that is, to get the reader interested in reading what you have written. Audience engagement is an important aspect of successful writing. If the reader is interested in your writing, communication is going on between writer and reader. This is the real purpose of writing.

Any anecdote you use should relate to the topic of your essay. Be sure you make a smooth transition from the anecdote to the body of your essay.

□   □   □

EXERCISES

1. Reread the Althen article in Chapter Five. What anecdotes does he include about students' perceptions of higher education in the United States? How do these anecdotes connect to the main idea of the selection?

2. Reread the Grimes article in Chapter Four. What anecdotes or short stories does he tell that relate to his main idea? What was the tone of the anecdotes—humorous, serious, critical, angry?

3. Reread the Wenden selection in Chapter Two. How does Wenden interweave her students' stories into the selection? In what ways do they connect to the main idea of her selection?

4. Reread the Lay essay in Chapter Two. What anecdotes does Lay tell to help her reader understand the importance of her father's store in her experience of learning English?

5. Reread the Klein article in Chapter One. The writer tells a short story about Berenice Belizaire's life. In what tense is it written? Why? What is the purpose of including these anecdotes about Belizaire? How do they support Klein's main idea?

6. Which of these authors uses anecdotes most effectively, in your opinion? Support your opinion with examples from the writer's work.

7. Choose one of the student essays that have appeared so far in this book. Read it with a partner. Does the writer use anecdotes? If so, what is the purpose of the anecdotes? If not, what kinds of anecdotes would you suggest that the writer add to make the piece more effective?

8. Reread your own essays. How can you improve the way you use anecdotes in your writing?

Essay Form

Writing an Explanation

In Ullman's article, the author is explaining the dating patterns on her campus so that you will understand why she is going to ask out a male student. When you explain something in writing, you are making it clearer to a reader. Steps that are useful in helping a writer explain or teach something to a reader include these:

1. *Look around you* as you did in the "Prereading Activities" for this chapter. Observe patterns in the way people act and think in relation to the subject you are going to explain. Or carefully observe the process you are going to explain in your writing. What in Ullman's article tells you that she looked around her before she began writing?

2. *Define* your subject. Some writers use the dictionary or another source book to help them define the process or pattern about which they are writing. What does Ullman define?

3. *Describe* in detail the steps that are needed to understand the process or pattern. Readers see the picture through your words, so make them clear and direct. What specific descriptions did you find in the Ullman article? How do they add to its overall effectiveness?

4. *Compare* your subject to others. What two types of dating does Ullman compare in this essay? Why does she make this comparison?

5. *Analyze* the parts or steps of the pattern or process you are explaining. Then tell how these steps work together. Tell the reader about the history and the future of your subject. What does Ullman include about her personal history in relation to dating? What does she tell the reader about the history of dating on her campus? What predictions does she make about the future of dating?

6. *Evaluate* the reasons why the pattern or process you are explaining is important for the reader to think about and know. What does Ullman write to convince you that the issue she is explaining is important to you as a reader?

You will not need to use all six of these steps in every essay that you write, but keeping them in mind can help you write clear and effective essays. Reread other essays in this book to evaluate which of these steps the writers used and how effectively they used them.

Suggestions for Writing

Choose one of the following topics to write about. Before you start writing, you may want to try the paired clustering activity in the next section, "Getting Started."

1. Describe a first date, real or imagined. Use lots of detail to make the experience come alive for the readers. What made this date unique? Why did you choose to write about this particular date?

2. "There is no such thing as love at first sight. For love to be real, people must know each other for a long time and have many shared experiences." Do you agree or disagree? Support your point of view with your own experiences or observations.

3. Compare a casual date with a formal date. Consider such things as where people go, what they wear, and who pays for the date.

4. On the basis of your own observations, do you think that dating patterns have really changed in recent years? If you are a woman, would

you ask a man out? If you are a man, would you go out with a woman who invited you? Would you go on a Dutch date? Should the man always treat?

5. "When a man wants to show a woman that he cares and respects her, he pays for their date." Do you agree or disagree with this statement? Support your point of view with your own experiences and observations.

6. Many people believe that men and women cannot really be friends. They feel that there is always an attraction between people of the opposite sex. Write an essay analyzing your feelings on this subject. Give examples from your experiences and observations.

Getting Started

Paired Clustering

In Chapter Three, you used clustering to help you think of ideas and get started writing. In this chapter, you will use a similar technique, except that you will work with a partner. One of you should write the word *dating* on a blank piece of paper. Draw a circle around the word, and say all the words that come to your mind about dating. Each of you writes down words on the page as quickly as they occur to you. After about five minutes, stop and look at the cluster you have created.

Next each of you should choose as many of the words and ideas from the big cluster as you need to form your own personal cluster, which you will use when you begin to write.

A Student Essay

In recent years, dating patterns have changed: girls pay for guys, ask 1 guys out, and are much less shy than they used to be.

In my family, my mom doesn't agree with girls paying for guys. 2 However, it doesn't always go the old way anymore. When I go out with my girlfriend, she sometimes pays for the date. She doesn't believe that guys should pay all the time. She said that by letting guys pay, they tend to get the wrong ideas. By paying for the date, the guy would not have any wrong ideas.

When I was growing up, girls were not supposed to ask guys out. They 3 would have to wait until guys asked them out. But now that has changed. My friend, Peter, was asked by a girl to go out on a date. He told me he was surprised to hear a girl ask him out, but he liked the idea of girls asking guys out.

Today's girls are not shy anymore. They see guys who are good- 4
looking and they ask them out. In the old days, it was shameful to see
girls asking guys out. Today it's not shameful; it's courageous.

I feel it is a good change for the girls because it gives them the right 5
to choose anyone they want to go out with. There are many ways that dating has changed, some bad and some good, but I think girls asking out
guys is good.

Koan Ung, Cambodia

Revising

With a partner, answer the following questions, looking at Koan
Ung's essay on dating.

1. What in this essay tells you that the writer looked around and observed the way people act and think?
2. Did the writer define any terms or ideas?
3. What specific descriptions do you find in this essay? How do they add
   to the overall effectiveness of the essay?
4. What specific comparisons can you find in this essay?
5. Does the writer tell you about the history and the future of the subject of the essay? If not, would this add to your understanding of the
   subject?
6. Where in the essay does the writer evaluate the reasons why the subject is important for you to know about?

Next, with your partner, answer the same questions, looking at the
draft of the essay that you have just written. Do the same with your partner's essay. Revise your draft, keeping in mind what you have discussed.
Then share your revision with your partner.

Editing Strategies

Mechanics

The Comma

All the commas have been left out of the following letter. Fill in
the commas where you think they belong. Then check your answers on
pages 357–58.

5516 Buena Vista Avenue
Miami FL 33158
March 14 1996

Dear Aunt Millie

Because I am so excited I had to write to you today. I have some special news so I wanted you to be one of the first people to know about it. I just got engaged to Jorge your best friend Luisa's oldest son. Just like that you have a wedding to attend. After we made our plans we talked for hours about everything. When he told me about his memories of you and Luisa I knew I had to write to you right away. He remembers you of course from when he was a little boy. He said you always treated him like he was worth $1000000. You do remember him don't you? If you do write soon. Millie send me any pictures or tell me any stories you recall. By the way my parents are doing very well and we just opened a new store. Even though you have not seen our first store yet I am sure you will be impressed with this one. The new store is big elegant and beautifully decorated. Working so hard together we all feel very proud. Everyone says "Hi!" Please write soon.

Love always
Blanca

Commas are used in a great many ways.

1. Commas are used with dates:

   March 14, 1996

2. Commas are used with openings and closings of personal letters:

   Dear Aunt Millie,
   Love always,

3. Commas are used with addresses:

   5516 Buena Vista Avenue, Miami, FL 33158

4. Commas are used with numbers:

   10,000
   1,000,000

5. Commas are used between complete thoughts that are connected by coordinating words such as *for, or, and, yet, nor, so,* and *but:*

I have some special news, so I wanted you to be one of the first people to know about it.

Send me any pictures, or tell me any stories you recall.

Note: If the complete thoughts are very short, no comma is necessary:

I arrived and he met me.

6. Commas are used to separate introductory material from the rest of the sentence:

Just like that, you have a wedding to attend.

By the way, my parents are doing very well, and we just opened a new store.

7. Commas are used after introductory clauses beginning with *after, although, as, as if, because, before, even, even though, if, since, so that, though, unless, until, when, whenever, where, wherever, whichever, while,* and *whoever:*

Because I am so excited, I had to write to you today.

Even though you have not seen our first store yet, I am sure you will be impressed with this one.

If you do, write soon.

Note: If these introductory clauses are short, the comma may occasionally be omitted.

8. Commas are used after introductory *-ing* phrases:

Working so hard together, we all feel proud.

9. Commas are used to set off words that identify or repeat something in a sentence or words that could be omitted without changing the meaning of the sentence:

Millie, send me any pictures or tell me any stories you recall.

He remembers you, of course, from when he was a little boy.

10. Commas are used to set off quotations:

Everyone says, "Hi!"

11. Commas are used between items in a series:

The new store is big, elegant, and beautifully decorated.

12. Commas are used before tag questions (short questions added to a statement to seek confirmation):

You do remember him, don't you?

☐ ☐ ☐

EXERCISE

Insert commas where they are necessary in the following paragraph.

Traveling to a different country whether it is returning home or going to a new destination is exciting. When the airplane arrives in the airport safely even people who travel often are glad. Suddenly they are in a new exciting world. Feeling tired they get off the plane and they head for their destination. They convert their money wait in line for taxis and spend too much money on foolish things. On the way home they feel mixed emotions but overall most of them are glad they took the chance and traveled.

Check your answers on page 358.

Editing Practice

Editing Other People's Writing

The letter on page 154 is all one paragraph. Decide where there should be paragraph breaks. Rewrite the letter, inserting the paragraph indentations and all necessary commas.

Editing Your Own Writing

Reread an essay that you wrote for this chapter, asking yourself the following questions:

1. Did I format my paper correctly?
2. Did I start new paragraphs when necessary?
3. Did I use final sentence punctuation and apostrophes correctly?
4. Did I use the past tenses correctly?
5. Did I use the present tenses correctly? Do my subjects and verbs agree?
6. Did I use quotation marks correctly?

7. Did I use pronouns correctly? Do the pronouns agree?
8. Did I form plurals correctly?
9. Did I use *the* correctly?
10. Did I use capital letters where they were needed?
11. Did I use commas correctly?

When you rewrite your essay, make any changes that will improve your writing.

Grammar Strategies

Modal Auxiliaries

Modal auxiliaries are verbs that are used before other verbs to change the meaning of the verb they precede. Some modal auxiliaries are *can, could, may, might, must, shall, should, will, would,* and *ought to.*

1. Modal auxiliaries *never* have verb endings (*-s, -ed, -ing*).
2. They are followed by the simple form of the verb:

He *can* swim.
She *ought to* go to school.

3. They are made negative by adding *not* after the modal and before the verb:

I *will not* swim.
They *should not* eat that apple.

4. They form questions by placing the modal auxiliary before the subject:

May I have some coffee?
Will you register for the writing class?

5. They have a continuous form with *be* and a verb with the *-ing* ending:

He *should be sailing* by the end of summer.
They *will be speaking* English by the end of this course.

(This form of the modal predicts a future outcome.)

6. They have a perfect form with *have* and a past participle:

   He *should have learned* to swim when he was a boy. (It is understood that he did not.)
   They *would have studied* English in their country, but they had to leave too quickly. (It is understood that they did not.)

7. Modals are not indicators of time and tense, although most users of English agree that "I can swim" has a different time meaning from "I could swim."

Some Expressions with Meanings Similar to Modals

Expression	Meaning or use	Example
be able to	ability	He is able to swim.
be allowed to	permission	She is allowed to stay out after midnight.
be obliged to	necessity	Teachers are obliged to help their students.
be permitted to	permission	They are permitted to drive alone.
be supposed to; be expected to	obligation	You are supposed to work hard.
have to	strong necessity	We all have to pay taxes.
not have to	lack of necessity	You don't have to do anything.
have got to	strong necessity	You have got to work hard if you want to succeed.
know how to	ability	I know how to drive now.

These expressions do change for tense and person; for example:

I am supposed to work hard in all my classes.
He is supposed to work hard in all his classes.
You were supposed to work hard in all your classes.
We will be expected to work hard in all our classes next year.

Uses and Meanings of Modals

Modal	Meaning or use	Example
can	ability	She can dance well.
	potential	They can learn English.
	request	Can you help me?
	advice	You can try doing it that way.

could	ability (past)	I could swim when I was a boy.
	request	Could you help me?
	possibility	It could be Marie at the door.
	possibility (future)	You could do better next time.
	advice	You could try it that way.
had better	necessity	They had better work harder.
may	possibility	It may be Marie at the door.
	possibility (future)	It may rain later.
	request	May I borrow your book?
might	advice	You might like this kind of pie.
	advice (future)	You might try it this way next time.
	possibility (future)	It might rain later.
	possibility (past)	I was afraid that I might be sick.
must	necessity	You must do all your homework if you want to pass the class.
	necessity (future)	You must try harder next time.
ought to	advice	She ought to talk to her teacher.
should	obligation	I should send my application now.
	advice (future)	You should try it my way.
will	future	They will begin working harder.
won't	negative of *will*	She won't do it your way.
shall*	future (first person)	I shall do that next week.
would	action (future)	Irina said she would do her work over the weekend.
would like	polite offer	Would you like some tea?
	wish or desire	I would like to visit Brazil. She would like to be a doctor
would rather	preference	I would rather have tea than coffee.

Shall is rarely used in American English but is current in British English.

□ □ □

EXERCISE   Fill in the blanks with the modal that seems most appropriate. Then, with a classmate, answer the questions that you have created.

1. What _____ you do if you want to do well in your courses in

   college?

2. _____ you stop to help someone who has been hurt?

3. _____ you go to school or get a job next summer?

4. What _____ you do when you were in your country that you

   _____ not do now?

5. What _____ you do now that you _____ not do when

   you were younger?

6. _____ you _____ to study in the morning or in the

   evening?

7. What city in the United States _____ you _____ to

   visit?

8. _____ you _____ to visit an art museum or a science

   museum?

9. Do you think parents _____ help their children with home-

   work?

Using Modals to Express the Future Aspect

will

When we write about the future, we often use *will*. As with all modals, the verb directly following *will* is in the simple form.

   I will be in school tomorrow.
   You will be in school tomorrow.
   He will be in school tomorrow.
   She will be in school tomorrow.

It will rain tomorrow.
We will be in school tomorrow.
You will be in school tomorrow.
They will be here tomorrow.

be going to

The second method for indicating future is by using the phrase *be going to*. When this is spoken, *going to* often sounds like "gonna," but when it is written, it should be written in its entirety.

I am going to be in school tomorrow.
You are going to be in school tomorrow.
He is going to be in school tomorrow.
She is going to be in school tomorrow.
It is going to rain tomorrow.
We are going to be in school tomorrow.
You are going to be in school tomorrow.
They are going to be in school tomorrow.

To form a question, invert (reverse) the *be* verb and the subject of the sentence. For example, "they are going" becomes "are they going." To form a negative, insert *not* after the *be* verb. For example, "he is going" becomes "he is not going."

□   □   □

EXERCISE

Fill in the blanks to make the questions refer to the future. Then, with a classmate, answer the questions.

1. What classes _____ you register for next semester?

2. Whom _____ you study with for the next test?

3. When _____ you meet with your writing teacher?

4. What papers _____ to go over with your teacher?

5. What essays _____ you include in your portfolio or folder?

Modals in the Perfect Aspect

Modals have a special meaning when they are used in the perfect aspect: describing an unreal past. The formula is modal (*not*) + *have* + past participle.

Expression	Meaning or use	Example
could have	past possibility (action never took place)	She could have gotten married in her twenties.
could not have	past impossibility	We could not have learned as much on our own as we did in class.
might have	past possibility (action never took place)	They might have learned to drive before, but they didn't.
should have	past advisability (action never took place)	You should have bought the camera when it was on sale.
should not have	past inadvisability	They should not have left all their money in their hotel room.
would have	past possibility (action never took place)	If he had known about the election, he would have voted.
would not have	past choice	Even if she had known about the election, she would not have voted.
would rather have	preference	I would rather have won the election, but I must accept the results.

☐ ☐ ☐

EXERCISE

Fill in the blanks in the following questions with a modal used in the perfect aspect. Then discuss the answers with a classmate.

1. If you _____ changed one historical event, what would it be and why?

2. If you _____ born at a different moment in time, what would it be and why?

3. If you _____ voted in the last election in this country, whom _____ you _____ voted for and why?

4. In the past year, what _____ the president _____ done for the United States that he did not do? Why?

5. What changes _____ made in television that have not been made? Why?

6. What other laws _____ passed in the United States that have not been passed? Why?

□   □   □

EXERCISES

1. Answer the following questions, using some of the modals you have read about.

   a. What does an adult who wants to learn how to swim do?

   _____

   b. What does it mean if it looks very cloudy and overcast outside?

   _____

   c. What advice helps students do well in their English classes?

   _____

   d. How does a person get a driver's license?

   _____

   e. How does a person find out about admission to your college?

   _____

   f. What is the best way to meet new people in your school?

   _____

   g. Where is the best place for people to go to practice their English?

   _____

h. What do people do to find out which movies are playing in your area?

2. Read the following paragraph about the Ullman article, and underline the following modal auxiliaries: *can, can't, has/have to, had better, may, might, must, ought to, should, will, won't,* and *would rather.*

Ullman writes that at the University of California in Berkeley, women may ask men out on dates. They can feel comfortable because it is done all the time. Men ought to feel flattered, not threatened, when they are asked out by a woman. Some women would rather have men ask them out, but like Ullman, occasionally they will ask men out on a casual date. The only problem is that women had better get ready to be rejected once in a while, too. Ullman thinks that dating in college should be casual and relaxed. Casual dating may help men and women feel at ease with each other, and, in the long run, that will help them when they have to make future partner choices.

Examine the use of the modal auxiliaries in the paragraph; then answer the following questions.

a. Is there any ending on the verb that follows the modal auxiliary?
b. In a group, reread each of the sentences and decide the meaning of each modal auxiliary as it is used.
c. In a group, rewrite this paragraph in the past tense. What changes would you have to make in the sentences and in the modal auxiliaries? Why would you make those changes?

Writing Practice

Using Modals in Your Writing

Write an essay on one of the following topics:

1. Write an essay in which you give advice to someone going on a first date. Use words like *should, must, ought to, had better,* and *might.*
2. Write an essay in which you give advice to someone about passing a course in your college. Use some of the modals you have studied in this chapter.

3. Write an essay in which you describe your life five years from now. What will you be doing then? Use some of the modals you have studied in this chapter.

4. Describe something you wish you had done. Why would it have been better if you had done it that way? Use the modals you studied in this chapter.

5. Write an essay in which you describe something you wish you had not done. Why would it have been better if you hadn't done this? Use the modals you studied in this chapter.

6. Reread the situations described in "Small Group Discussion" on pages 148–49. Write an essay using modals in which you describe how you would handle the situation.

Share your essays with your class. Discuss the modals you chose and how they helped you in your writing.

☐ ☐ ☐

EXERCISE

Reread one of the selections in this book that you have enjoyed. Notice the way that modals are used in the selection.

☐ ☐ ☐

CHECKING YOUR OWN WORK

1. Read through each essay you wrote for this chapter. Look at the modals used in the essay. (It may be helpful to underline them lightly.) Does each modal make sense? If you are not sure, check the meaning for the modal in the "Grammar Strategies" section. Is there an ending on the verb that follows the modal?

2. Repeat check 1 for other writing that you have done recently.

3. With a classmate, check to make sure that you have used modals correctly in your writing.

CHAPTER EIGHT

Comparing the Sexes

PREREADING ACTIVITIES

1. The title of the textbook excerpt you are about to read is "Gender-Role Identity." What does the word *gender* mean? What expectations are associated with your gender? What does the word *role* mean? What roles do you play in your life?
2. In a small group, discuss whether you feel that males and females are treated differently in your home, in school, in your neighborhood, and in society in general. Each group should present its ideas to the class as a whole.
3. In a small group, discuss the advantages and disadvantages of being a male or being a female. Each group should present its ideas to the class as a whole.

VOCABULARY DEVELOPMENT

One way to learn new words is to study the vocabulary of a particular new discipline. Learning one word or root often helps you learn many more words. For example, let's take the word *genetics*. Craig uses the words *genetics, genetically,* and *genetic programming* in her article.

She writes: "Gender is genetically determined, and some [observers] suggest that men and women are inherently and dramatically different in intellect, personality, adult adjustment, and style—primarily because of genetic programming."

Look up the word *gene* in the dictionary. You will find that it refers to any of the units that occur at particular points on a chromosome. Hereditary characteristics are determined by and transmitted through genes. Once you know this, you can determine what people study when they study genetics. What does "genetically determined" mean? Does such determination occur before or after birth? What is genetic programming? Can people do this sort of programming to you after you are born?

According to what you know about genetics, what do you think *inherently* means in Craig's statement? Does it mean "educationally," "usually," or "naturally"? How did you decide?

Gender-Role Identity

Grace J. Craig

Grace J. Craig teaches psychology at the University of Massachusetts. The following is an excerpt from her popular textbook, Human Development. *The selection describes and then questions some of the "well-established" differences between males and females.*

Gender is genetically determined, and some [observers] suggest   1
that men and women are inherently and dramatically different in
intellect, personality, adult adjustment, and style—primarily because of
genetic programming. The opposite point of view contends that men
and women are different because of the way they are treated by their
parents, their teachers, their friends, and their culture throughout life.
When we argue about whether genetics or culture is more important in
determining gender-role identity, we are probably addressing the wrong
issue. Genetics and culture may set the outer limits of gender-role identity, but they interact like two strands of a rope in forming personality or
psychosexual identity. We need to look more closely at this interplay
throughout the life span.

Although gender-role identity is established in early childhood, it re-   2
mains a developmental issue well into adulthood. Gender-role identity is
perhaps our most fundamental self-concept, but it is not a permanent,
rigid personality trait. Before we consider how gender-role identity can
change as a result of life situations, let us examine some of the clear differences between the genders and how these genetic "givens" may determine some aspects of behavior.

Male-Female Differences

Studies have shown that male babies, on average, are born slightly   3
longer and heavier than are female babies. Newborn girls have slightly
more mature skeletons, and they seem to be a bit more responsive to
touch. As toddlers, boys are a bit more aggressive, and girls have a slight
edge in verbal abilities. By age 8 or 10, boys are beginning to outperform
°referring to space   girls in spatial° skills and in mathematics. By age 12, the average girl
°sudden burst   is well into the adolescent growth spurt° and maturation, while the
average boy is still considered a preadolescent, physically. By mid-
adolescence, the girl's superiority in verbal skills increases, and the boy's
edge in spatial skills and mathematics increases. By age 18, the average
female has roughly 50% less muscular strength than the average male.
In adulthood, the male body carries more muscle and bone. The average female body carries more fat as insulation. There are built-in health
°flexible, movable   advantages for women, including more pliable° blood vessels and the
ability to process fat more efficiently. By middle age, males are suc-
°falling victim to   cumbing° much faster to health hazards, such as emphysema, arte-
riosclerosis, heart attacks, liver disease, homicide, suicide, or drug ad-
diction. By age 65, there are only 68 men alive for every 100 women; at
age 85, women outnumber men almost two to one. At the age of 100,
there are five times as many women as there are men (McLoughlin et
al., 1988).

Many of these differences between males and females appear to be   4
genetically caused. For example, Maccoby and Jacklin (1980) suggest
°before birth   that the greater aggressiveness in males may be due to their prenatal° ex-

posure to higher levels of some sex hormones. Tieger (1980) disagrees and states that there is no biological predisposition toward aggressiveness in males; rather, the difference in aggressiveness between males and females is due to sex-role socialization. A more recent review (Hyde, 1984) suggests that even these "well-established" differences between males and females in aggression—as well as in mathematical skills and verbal abilities—should be looked at with caution. After examining hundreds of studies, Hyde concluded that the differences noted between the average male and the average female were not found consistently.

Equally important are the findings in areas where males and females 5 do *not* differ. Ruble (1988) reviewed many studies on sex-role differences and noted areas in which differences were not established. There appeared to be no consistent differences due to gender, for example, in sociability, self-esteem, motivation to achieve, or even in rote° learning and certain types of analytical skills.

°mechanical

Furthermore, the differences that actually exist between males and 6 females are small, often less than 5% of the full range. In many studies conducted in the mid-1980s, these tendencies were not as strong as previously believed (Halpern, 1986; Ruble, 1988). Men average only slightly higher in activity level, aggression, or mathematical reasoning, and women score only slightly higher in empathy.° What is more, many of the personality differences that do exist are modifiable° with training, with the situation, or with changes in cultural expectations.

°feeling for others
°changeable

References

Halpern, D. F. (1986). *Sex differences in cognitive abilities.* Hillsdale, NJ: Erlbaum.

Hyde, J. S. (1984). How large are gender differences in aggression? A developmental metanalysis. *Developmental Psychology, 20,* 722–736.

Maccoby, E. E., and Jacklin, C. N. (1980). Sex differences in aggression: A rejoinder and reprise. *Child Development, 51,* 964–998.

McLoughlin, M., Shryer, T. L., Goode, E. E., and McAuliffe, K. (August 8, 1988). Men vs. women. *U.S. News & World Report.*

Ruble, D. (1988). Sex-role development. In M. Bornstein and M. E. Lamb (Eds.), *Developmental psychology: An advanced textbook* (2nd ed., pp. 411–460). Hillsdale, NJ: Erlbaum.

Tieger, T. (1980). On the biological basis of sex differences in aggression. *Child Development, 51,* 943–963.

Reading and Thinking Strategies

Discussion Activities

Analysis and Conclusions

1. Some writers refer to the argument described in paragraph 1 as the difference between genetics and culture; others refer to it as nature

or nurture; others refer to inborn versus learned behaviors. What is the argument, and what is Craig's position regarding it?

2. Why is it difficult to answer whether differences between males and females are inborn or learned?

3. What differences does Craig point out between males and females? Which of these appear at birth? During childhood? At adolescence? In old age?

4. Why does Craig think that even "well-established" differences between males and females should be looked at with caution?

Writing and Point of View

1. To what do the names and dates in parentheses refer? How do these provide support for Craig's arguments?

2. Does Craig quote from other researchers? How does she present their findings?

3. What statistics does Craig include? How do these support her arguments?

Personal Response and Evaluation

1. Later in the chapter, Craig writes: "Because the term *sex* has many meanings, there is some preference for the use of the word *gender* when we talk about maleness or femaleness. Some major authors, though, continue to use the terms *sex* and *gender* interchangeably (Ruble, 1988)." What is the difference in meaning between *gender* and *sex?*

Debate

While working on this chapter, it might be interesting to have several class debates. Divide the class into men and women, or use any other division that seems to work. Each group is given a point of view on a topic. Together the group members create an argument based on facts and observations. Then the actual debate can begin. It might be useful to tape-record or videotape the debate for later class discussions.

The following are some points of view that might be considered for debate.

Team A	*Team B*
Women are the weaker sex.	Men are really the weaker sex.
Children should be brought up as equals; there should be no differences in treatment.	Boys and girls should be brought up differently. This is necessary for their future roles in life.

Women are not psychologically equipped to hold positions of power.	Women can deal with positions of power at least as well as men can.
There can never be true equality between men and women.	Men and women must develop true equality for there to be peace in the world.

Note Taking

Practice taking notes during the class debates. Take notes as if you were planning to study or write an essay from them. Then meet in a small group to compare your notes. Discuss how you decided what to write down. What do you think are the most important ideas? Justify your choices.

Journal Writing

The claim that men and women grow up in different worlds may at first seem patently absurd. Brothers and sisters grow up in the same families, children to parents of both genders. Where, then, do women and men learn different ways of speaking and hearing?

DEBORAH TANNEN, *You Just Don't Understand*

When you write in your journal, think about what it means to be male or female in our society today. Have your views about relationships between men and women changed since you came to America? Have your views changed since you started college? Write about what it means to be a man or a woman in today's society and about the ways in which your ideas have changed about male and female relationships.

Extra Reading

The Story of an Hour

Kate Chopin

Kate Chopin (1851–1904) was born and raised in St. Louis. After her husband's death in 1883, she began writing to support herself and her six children. "The Story of an Hour," one of Chopin's most famous short stories, deals with the complexities of love and loss.

Knowing that Mrs. Mallard was afflicted with a heart trouble, great care was   1
taken to break to her as gently as possible the news of her husband's death.

It was her sister Josephine who told her, in broken sentences; 2
veiled hints that revealed in half concealing. Her husband's friend
Richards was there, too, near her. It was he who had been in the newspaper office when intelligence° of the railroad disaster was received,
with Brently Mallard's name leading the list of "killed." He had only
taken the time to assure himself of its truth by a second telegram, and
had hastened to forestall° any less careful, less tender friend in bearing
the sad message.

She did not hear the story as many women have heard the same, with 3
a paralyzed inability to accept its significance. She <u>wept</u> at once, with
sudden, wild abandonment,° in her sister's arms. When the storm of
grief had spent itself she went away to her room alone. She would have
no one follow her.

There stood, facing the open window, a comfortable, roomy arm- 4
chair. Into this she sank, pressed down by a physical exhaustion that
haunted her body and seemed to reach into her soul.

She could see in the open square before her house the tops of trees 5
that were all aquiver° with the new spring life. The delicious breath of
rain was in the air. In the street below a peddler was crying his wares.
The notes of a distant song which some one was singing reached her
faintly, and countless sparrows° were <u>twittering</u>° in the eaves.°

There were patches of the blue sky showing here and there through 6
the clouds that had met and piled one above the other in the west facing her window.

She sat with her head thrown back upon the cushion of the chair, 7
quite motionless, except when a sob came up into her throat and
shook her, as a child who has cried itself to sleep continues to sob in its
dreams.

She was young, with a fair, calm face, whose lines bespoke° repression 8
and even a certain strength. But now there was a dull stare in her eyes,
whose gaze was fixed away off <u>yonder</u> on one of those patches of blue
sky. It was not a glance of reflection, but rather indicated a suspension
of intelligent thought.

There was something coming to her and she was waiting for it, fear- 9
fully. What was it? She did not know; it was too subtle and elusive to
name. But she felt it, creeping out of the sky, reaching toward her
through the sounds, the scents, the color that filled the air.

Now her bosom rose and fell tumultuously.° She was beginning to 10
recognize this thing that was approaching to possess her, and she was
striving to beat it back with her will—as powerless as her two white slender hands would have been.

When she abandoned herself a little whispered word escaped 11
her slightly parted lips. She said it over and over under her breath: "free,
free, free!" The vacant stare and the look of terror that had followed
it went from her eyes. They stayed keen and bright. Her pulses beat

---

°information

°prevent

°surrender to feelings

°shaking; trembling

°small brown birds
°making light, chirping
  sounds
°under the edges of the
  roof

°gave evidence of;
  showed

°violently

°racing

fast, and the coursing° blood warmed and relaxed every inch of her body.

She did not stop to ask if it were or were not a monstrous joy that held 12 her. A clear and exalted perception enabled her to dismiss the suggestion as trivial.

°except; but

She knew that she would weep again when she saw the kind, 13 tender hands folded in death; the face that had never looked save° with love upon her, fixed and gray and dead. But she saw beyond that bitter moment a long procession of years to come that would belong to her absolutely. And she opened and spread her arms out to them in welcome.

There would be no one to live for her during those coming years; she 14 would live for herself. There would be no powerful will bending hers in that blind persistence with which men and women believe they have a right to impose a private will upon a fellow-creature. A kind intention or a cruel intention made the act seem no less a crime as she looked upon it in that brief moment of illumination.

And yet she had loved him—sometimes. Often she had not. What did 15 it matter? What could love, the unsolved mystery, count for in face of this possession of self-assertion which she suddenly recognized as the strongest impulse of her being!

"Free! Body and soul free!" she kept whispering.   16

Josephine was kneeling before the closed door with her lips to the 17 keyhole, imploring for admission. "Louise, open the door! I beg; open the door—you will make yourself ill. What are you doing, Louise? For heaven's sake open the door."

°medicine said to prolong
  life

"Go away. I am not making myself ill." No; she was drinking in a very 18 elixir° of life through that open window.

Her fancy was running riot along those days ahead of her. Spring 19 days, and summer days, and all sorts of days that would be her own. She breathed a quick prayer that life might be long. It was only yesterday she had thought with a shudder that life might be long.

°repeated demands
°unknowingly

She arose at length and opened the door to her sister's importuni- 20 ties.° There was a feverish triumph in her eyes, and she carried herself unwittingly° like a goddess of Victory. She clasped her sister's waist, and together they descended the stairs. Richards stood waiting for them at the bottom.

°calmly
°suitcase

Some one was opening the front door with a latchkey. It was Brently 21 Mallard who entered, a little travel-stained, composedly° carrying his gripsack° and umbrella. He had been far from the scene of the accident, and did not even know there had been one. He stood amazed at Josephine's piercing cry; at Richards' quick motion to screen him from the view of his wife.

But Richards was too late.   22

When the doctors came they said she had died of heart disease—of 23 joy that kills.

Discussion Activities

1. What is the theme of "The Story of an Hour"?

2. "Storm of grief" is a very poetic expression of Mrs. Mallard's feelings. What does this expression mean? How do you picture a "storm of grief"?

3. Describe the characters. What insights do you get from their experiences?

4. What makes this story appropriate for a chapter on gender relationships?

5. The final paragraph is only one sentence long: "When the doctors came they said she had died of heart disease—of joy that kills." What do you think killed Louise Mallard?

Writing Strategies

Essay Strategies

Using Definitions in Your Writing

In writing technical and scientific material or textbooks, writers often define unusual or difficult words or concepts to help their readers understand the material. Whether a writer is creating an explanation, a comparison, an analysis, or a persuasive piece of writing, a definition can add substance or comprehensibility. In "Gender-Role Identity," Craig did not define her terms. As a reader, you had to do some work to understand the selection.

When you are using difficult terms in your writing or when you just want to make sure that your reader understands the way you define a term, you may include a definition in your essay. Some writers do this in the introduction. They may begin their essay by asking, "What is a _____ ?" After stating what is to be defined, the writer explains the special characteristics of the term or concept. The writer makes sure to let readers know why they should be interested in knowing more about the term or concept.

If you are not sure which terms need to be defined, ask a classmate to read your essay. Find out if that person was unsure of the meaning of any word or concept in the essay. If you were using a word in a particular way, make sure your reader understood your definition.

□   □   □

EXERCISE   With a classmate, decide which terms you would define if you were to rewrite the Craig selection to make it easier for readers to understand. Together, rewrite part of the article, defining some of the terms you have chosen.

Essay Form

Comparison and Contrast

In "Gender-Role Identity," Craig compared and contrasted males and females. When a writer compares two things, the writer looks for the similarities. When a writer contrasts two things, the writer looks for the differences. We compare and contrast things every day. We may compare how quickly the bus came this morning with how quickly it came yesterday. We may contrast the experience of walking to school with the experience of taking the bus. It is a human activity to compare and contrast. We do it in our minds, and we do it aloud with our friends. For many writers, however, the comparison-and-contrast essay can create problems.

Comparison-and-contrast essays may follow two basic patterns of organization. Both may contain the same information, but it is presented in a different manner. In the first method, the writer follows this basic pattern:

Introduction

Body paragraph(s) A—presenting all the information about A

Body paragraph(s) B—presenting all the information about B

Conclusion—sums up and makes final comparisons and contrasts

The second method involves alternating within each paragraph. It is organized as follows:

Introduction

Body paragraph—about one aspect of the comparison

   Point A

   Point B

   Point A

   Point B

Body paragraph—about another aspect of the comparison

   Point A

   Point B

   Point A

   Point B

Conclusion

Many writers find the first method, the block approach, easier to organize. In this method, all the information about one side of an issue or problem is presented, and then all the information about the other side is given. Using this method, it is also possible to present all the similarities and then all the differences. In the second method, the alternating method, a point from one side is given, then a point from the other side. This is a good method to use for longer pieces of writing because it is easy to follow. For this reason, readers may prefer this method.

The following paragraph is from an essay that uses the block form; it presents the information about women's physical superiority. We can assume that the writer will next give us all the information about the areas of male superiority.

Women, on the average, have a better sense of smell than men. Women hear better at the upper range. Women have more physical endurance than men. They generally live longer and do not usually suffer from hypertension and heart disease.

Using the alternating method, the writer of an essay about male and female differences makes the comparison within the paragraph itself. The paragraph that follows uses the alternating method to compare the health problems of men and women.

Women, on the average, have a better sense of smell than men. Men, however, have keener eyesight. Women hear better at the upper range, whereas men often have more acute hearing at the lower range. The estimated life span for men is 74 years; for women it is 78 years.

The comparison-and-contrast essay is a popular form of writing. The following student paragraph is written in the comparison-and-contrast mode. Does it follow the block pattern or the alternating pattern?

There are differences between men and women. Men usually live a shorter time than women. Women have a higher range of hearing. Men have a lower range of hearing, but they can see better for a long distance. Women have long-term strength. At night they take care of the baby and then go to work the next day. Men have short-term strength. They go to work during the day and then when they get home, they complain that they are very tired. Most men spend their time outside the house. Women stay home and do the chores. Men are usually taller and women are shorter. More crimes are done by men, but women commit crimes, too. Both women and men have vices like gambling and smoking. Both genders often marry more than once.

Marina Ibea, The Philippines

In comparison-and-contrast writing, we use special transition words:

To compare	*To contrast*
also	but
as . . . as	not as . . . as
as well as	however
likewise	nevertheless
similarly	conversely
too	in contrast

Reread the Craig selection, and decide which method she uses. What words and phrases does she use to compare and contrast her ideas?

□   □   □

EXERCISES

1. Write a paragraph comparing and contrasting the behavior of males and females in college.
2. Write a paragraph contrasting living in your native country with living in the United States.
3. Write a paragraph comparing and contrasting a book with the movie made from that book.
4. Write a paragraph comparing and contrasting the teaching methods of two teachers you have had.

Suggestions for Writing

Before you start to write your essay, try making quadrants, as shown in the "Getting Started" section, to help you develop ideas for writing.

1. Write an essay comparing and contrasting the way girls are raised with the way boys are raised. Use your own observations and experiences as evidence.
2. Write an essay comparing and contrasting the teaching methods in your native country with those in the United States.
3. What are some of the differences between men and women? Include information from the Craig article, as well as your own observations and experiences.
4. The characteristics that a person looks for in a friend may be very different from the ones that are important in a future husband or wife. Compare and contrast these characteristics.
5. Each language is unique, although there may be some similarities between certain languages. Compare and contrast your first language with English. Consider such characteristics as the ways in which questions are constructed, where adjectives are placed, the use of articles,

how nouns are made plural, and whether or not the language is pho-
netic.

Getting Started

Making Quadrants

Before you begin to write, spend some time thinking of ideas that relate to the process or pattern you are writing about. To help you come
up with ideas, fold a piece of paper into four sections.

In one section, write the word *describe*. In that section, write the following four questions:

What do you see?

What do you hear?

What do you feel?

What do you taste?

In another section, write the words *compare* and *contrast*. Then write the
following questions:

What is it similar to?

What is it different from?

In the next section, write the word *analyze*. Then write the following
questions:

What parts does it have?

How do they work together or not work together?

In the remaining section, write the word *argue*. Then write the following
questions:

Why is it a good idea?

Why would people think it is a bad idea?

In each of the sections, think about the process or pattern you are going to write about; then write answers to the questions. Reread these answers when preparing to write your essay.

A Student Essay

In my native country, the Dominican Republic, from the day girls or
boys are born, they learn their place in society. Men are taught to be   1

strong; as boys they are given guns to play with. The boys go with their fathers from time to time to help them on the farm, if they have one. The women are taught to do housework. As girls, they are given dolls and kitchen sets to play with. The girls help their mothers while they cook by passing the foods to be prepared. Afterward, they either help cleaning or doing the dishes.

In the Dominican Republic, men are the leaders of the house. They 2 are the ones to go out to work and bring the bread home. When they are not able to, they sometimes feel less than a man because of their ego. Women stay home doing the housework and taking care of the children. That, I believe, is because that is what they are trained to do and also because they do not get a wider education.

In the United States, more men are sharing the housework and are 3 helping out with the care of the children. Men are more liberal; they have a different perspective of their role as a man. They believe in equality and sharing decisions. Women's roles are different. They go out to work outside of the house, and they bring money home. This makes it easier on the man by having fewer financial problems. Sometimes the man would have a career that does not require him to go outside to work while his wife might have. In this case, he would probably be the one to have to cook more often. This, I believe, is good because there are lots of men who cook better than women.

Although I am Dominican, I do not share the belief that the woman's 4 place is at home and that the men should be the leaders of the family. I share and believe the role of the United States. I feel that women should have the same rights as men. They should have equality. Women should go out and work too. In this way, their family would have more money to manage and have a better future.

Nowadays things are changing in my native country—slowly, but they 5 are. Women are getting themselves more educated, and they, too, are going outside to work. This pleases me very much because I believe that society should not tell you your place as a human being or what role you should follow but that each individual must have the right to choose for herself or himself.

Rosmenia Vásquez, Dominican Republic

Revising

With a partner or in a small group, reread the student essay; then answer the following questions about it.

1. What is the main idea of this essay? How did you know?

2. Which method of comparison did the writer use in this essay?

3. What do you like about this essay? Why?

4. What would you like to add to this essay? Why?

5. What would you like to delete from this essay? Why?

6. Try to move one sentence in the essay. Which sentence did you move? Why? How does it change the rest of the essay?

7. What is the best sentence in the essay?

8. What audience do you think the writer had in mind? What in the essay told you this?

Working with a partner or in a small group, use these same questions to discuss your own draft and to help you prepare to revise it. After you have revised your writing, share it with the same classmate or group again.

Editing Strategies

Mechanics

Subject-Verb Agreement

In English, a verb must agree with its subject. In the simple present tense, it is important that third person singular subjects (*he, she, it, one, an apple,* and so on) be followed by a verb ending in *s.* Plural subjects are followed by the simple form of the verb in the simple present tense.

Singular	*Plural*
She *lives* in a big city.	They *live* in a big city.
A tree *grows* tall.	Trees *grow* tall.

Rules for Deciding Whether to Add the *s* Ending

1. The following indefinite pronouns are singular and require singular verbs in writing.

   anybody, anyone, anything
   each, each other
   either, neither
   everybody, everyone, everything
   nobody, no one, nothing
   somebody, someone, something

EXAMPLES

Anything is possible if you work hard enough.
Each of the people in the world is unique.*
Either of those apartments is acceptable to me.*
Everybody deserves to pass the course.
Nobody wants to go to jail.
Somebody answers the phone each time I call.

In the following sentences, decide which is the correct verb form.

a. No one _____ what to do about violence in our society.
(know/knows)

b. Each of the triplets _____ hungry right now.
(is/are)

c. Everybody who works in the company's offices _____ to work
(has/have)

overtime until the crisis is over.

2. Collective nouns such as *audience, class, committee, couple, family, government, group,* and *troop* are treated as singular in the United States. (In Britain, they are treated as plural.)

The government makes decisions for its citizens.
The committee meets every Thursday.

In the following sentences, decide which is the correct verb form.

a. The couple _____ to the movies every Saturday night.
(go/goes)

b. The audience _____ when the conductor appears.
(clap/claps)

c. The group _____ who will be the next leader.
(decide/decides)

3. Words such as *athletics, economics, politics, physics, statistics, measles, mumps, news,* and *United States* are singular, even though they end in *s.*

No news is good news.
Economics is my favorite subject.

In the following sentences, decide which is the correct verb form.

a. Mumps _____ a serious illness for adults.
(is/are)

b. Physics _____ a required course in my college.
(is/are)

*Notice that the verbs agree with the singular subject *each* and *either.* They are not affected by the prepositional phrases "of the people" or "of those apartments."

4. Prepositional phrases have no effect on the verb form.

   The researchers from Harvard are in our school right now.

   The prepositional phrase "from Harvard" has no effect on the verb, which agrees with the subject, *researchers*.

   The puppies in the window need a home.

   The prepositional phrase _____ has no effect

   on the verb *need,* which agrees with the subject, _____ .

   The chapter on the use of articles _____ important.
   _(is/are)

5. When *or* or *nor* is used between subjects, the verb agrees with the closer subject.

   Neither a computer nor books make a person a good writer.
   Neither books nor a computer makes a person a good writer.
   Either the cat or the kittens follow me around the house.
   Either the kittens or the cat follows me around the house.

   In the following sentences, decide which is the correct verb form.

   a. Neither the soloist nor all the singers _____ every day.
   _(rehearse/rehearses)

   b. Neither all the singers nor the soloist _____ every day.
   _(rehearse/rehearses)

6. The verb agrees with the subject that follows it when the sentence begins with *there.*

   There are two problems to be discussed tonight.
   There is a student waiting at my door.

   In the following sentences, decide which is the correct verb form.

   a. There _____ many good television programs on tonight.
   _(is/are)

   b. There _____ no need to get upset right now.
   _(is/are)

   c. There _____ some papers on the floor.
   _(is/are)

7. When *any, each,* or *every* is used as an adjective, its subject needs a singular verb.

Any child learns her own language.
Each teacher and student needs to come to the meeting.
Every male and female baby starts out with enormous potential.

In the following sentences, decide which is the correct verb form.

a. Every baby _____ special and unique.
   (is/are)

b. Each man and woman _____ to find happiness in life.
   (want/wants)

c. Every bird and bee _____ how to fly.
   (know/knows)

8. When *one of the* is the subject of the sentence, it requires a singular verb.

One of the cars has a flat tire.
One of the windows is broken.

□ □ □

EXERCISES

1. Many people have problems with the subject-verb agreement involved in the simple present tense. Decide whether to use the final *s* on the verbs in the following sentences:

   a. Many ambitious parents _____ their children to succeed in
      (want/wants)

      school.

   b. One of the smartest children in our class _____ as she
      (yawn/yawns)

      _____ that she _____ till after midnight every night.
      (explain/explains)   (study/studies)

   c. Her classmates _____ her that she _____ too much and
      (tell/tells)   (study/studies)

      _____ too little.
      (sleep/sleeps)

   d. This student _____ that she _____ to do as well in school as
      (feel/feels)   (need/needs)

      her twin brother, who always _____ straight A's in his classes.
      (receive/receives)

   e. The problem faced by this student _____ to be related to
      (seem/seems)

      family expectations.

   f. The group of students _____ angry at the tuition increase.
      (is/are)

  g. There _____ so many people standing in line tonight.
     (is/are)

  h. The children in the stories _____ not very realistic.
          (is/are)

  i. One of my friends _____ your school.
        (attend/attends)

  j. Either the table or the chairs _____ on sale tomorrow.
          (go/goes)

2. Review the sentences in Exercise 1, and decide which of the uses of the simple present tense they illustrate.

3. On your own or with a partner, reread the essay that you have written for this chapter or any other essay that you have written this semester, focusing on the simple present tense. Notice when and why you use the simple present tense in your writing, and make sure that you have used the correct verb endings.

Editing Practice

Editing Other People's Writing

  The following is a draft that has not been corrected for errors. Correct all the errors you can find. (If you have any difficulty with the comparatives, see pages 184–185.) Answers are on page 358.

  Anyone who have a baby care more that the baby is healthy then if it is a boy or a girl. But each mother and father have expectations. Some people think a boy baby should be strongest than a girl baby. He is supposed to be biggest, fastest, and smartest. People needs to know that girl and boy babies all over the world is more similar than different. Some girls babys are bigger, faster, and smartest, but it doesn't matter. When one of the babys are your baby than all that matters are that the baby is alive and healthy.

Editing Your Own Writing

  Reread an essay that you wrote for this chapter, asking yourself the following questions:

1. Did I format my paper correctly?
2. Did I start new paragraphs when necessary?
3. Did I use final sentence punctuation and apostrophes correctly?

4. Did I use the past tenses correctly?

5. Did I use the present tenses correctly? Do my subjects and verbs agree?

6. Did I use quotation marks correctly?

7. Did I use pronouns correctly? Do the pronouns agree with their antecedents?

8. Did I form plurals correctly?

9. Did I use *the* correctly?

10. Did I use capital letters where they were needed?

11. Did I use commas correctly?

12. Did I use modals correctly?

When you rewrite your essay, make any changes that will improve your writing.

Grammar Strategies

Comparatives and Superlatives

One of the most basic uses of language is to express similarities and differences, to compare and contrast. Comparisons can be expressed using adjectives, adverbs, nouns, and verbs. Comparatives are used to compare two things; superlatives are used when comparing three or more.

1. Comparisons using adjectives:

    COMPARATIVE: Rose is *smarter than* Marie (is).
    SUPERLATIVE: Rose is *the smartest* student in the room.
    COMPARATIVE: Harry is *less competitive than* Roland (is).
    SUPERLATIVE: Harry is *the least competitive* one in his family.

2. Comparisons using adverbs:

    COMPARATIVE: Han walks *slower than* Thuy (walks, does).
    SUPERLATIVE: Han walks *the slowest of* all the students in the class.
    COMPARATIVE: Mimi talks *less frequently than* Jenny (talks, does).
    SUPERLATIVE: Mimi talks *the least frequently of* all the girls.

3. Comparisons using nouns:

    COMPARATIVE: Li has *more* books *than* Ping (has, does).
    SUPERLATIVE: Li has *the most* books *of* all the students.

COMPARATIVE: Sam has *fewer* books *than* Howard (has, does). (*Books* is a countable noun.)

SUPERLATIVE: Sam has *the fewest* books *of* all the brothers.

COMPARATIVE: Sam has *less* money *than* Howard (has, does). (*Money* is an uncountable noun.)

SUPERLATIVE: Sam has *the least* money *of* all the brothers.

4. Comparisons using verbs:

COMPARATIVE: Hong weighs *more than* Pedro (weighs, does).

SUPERLATIVE: Hong weighs *the most of* all the fighters.

COMPARATIVE: My school costs *more than* your school (costs, does).

SUPERLATIVE: My school costs *the most of* all the schools in this state.

The rules for using *-er* or *more* and for using *the . . . -est* and *the most* are as follows:

1. Use *-er* or *the . . . -est* with one-syllable adjectives and adverbs and with two-syllable adjectives that end in *y* (which changes to *i*), *ple, ble,* and sometimes *tle* and *dle.*

big, bigger, the biggest; little, littler, the littlest

2. Use *-er* or *more* or *the . . . -est* or *the most* with two-syllable adjectives that end in *ly, ow, er,* and *some.*

early, earlier, the earliest

3. Use *more* or *the most* with other adjectives and with adverbs of two or more syllables.

intelligent, more intelligent, the most intelligent

Irregular Comparative and Superlative Forms

Base Form	*Comparative Form*	*Superlative Form*
much	more	the most
many	more	the most
little	less	the least
good	better	the best
bad	worse	the worst
far	farther (literal)	the farthest
	further (figurative)	the furthest

□ □ □

EXERCISES   1. Fill in the blanks, using the examples as your guide.

Base form	Comparative form	Superlative form
cute	cuter	the cutest
nice	_____	_____
pretty	prettier	the prettiest
happy	_____	_____
ample	ampler	the amplest
simple	_____	_____
lovely	lovelier	the loveliest
manly	_____	_____
friendly	_____	_____
hollow	hollower	the hollowest
mellow	_____	_____
handsome	handsomer *or* more handsome	_____
beautiful	more beautiful	_____
brilliant	_____	the most brilliant
extraordinary	_____	_____

2. Fill in the blanks with the words needed to make the sentences comparative.

a. The male's lack of a second X chromosome makes him in many

respects the _____ sex.
        (weak)

b. The death rate for men is _____ than it is for women.
                    (high)

c. Both sexes have "male" as well as "female" hormones, but the proportion of male hormones is _____ in men and that of
(great)

female hormones is _____ in women.
(great)

d. Men tend to be _____ and to have _____ mathemat-
(aggressive) (great)

ical ability women tend to be _____ and _____.
(nurturant) (emotional)

e. Male babies are _____ than females; female babies smile
(active)

_____ and are _____ to warmth and touch than
(readily) (sensitive)

males.

Commonly Confused Words

than/then

Helene called Thomas when she saw that the movie star he liked better than any other was starring in a new movie in their neighborhood. Then they went to see it together. When it ended, they talked in front of the movie theater more than usual. They thought the movie was better than the star's last one. Then they went to get something to drink and then they continued talking. Then it was almost midnight and they both had to rush home.

Examining the use of *than* and *then* in this paragraph should help you complete the following definitions.

_____ means "at that time."

_____ is used to show comparisons.

Fill in the blanks in the following sentences with *than* and *then*.

She lived in Ecuador until she was 5; _____ she moved to the United States. _____ she started school, where she found it was easier for her to understand English _____ to speak it. Her teachers thought she knew less _____ she really did because they did not know how to communicate with her

_____ .

☐ ☐ ☐

EXERCISE

Reread one of the selections in this book that you have enjoyed.

Notice the way that comparatives and superlatives are used in the selection.

□   □   □

CHECKING YOUR OWN WORK

1. Read through each essay you wrote for this chapter. Look at the way you used comparatives and superlatives in the essay. (It may be helpful to underline them lightly.) Did you use them appropriately and correctly? If you are not sure, check the descriptions of comparatives and superlatives in the previous section. Did you use the word *the* with superlatives? Did you use the word *than* and not *then* when making comparisons?
2. Repeat check 1 with other writing that you have done recently.
3. As an added check, work with a classmate to make sure that you have used comparatives and superlatives correctly in your writing.

CHAPTER NINE

Aging and Living

PREREADING ACTIVITIES

1. The following excerpt is from an autobiography written by a 93-year-old man. Before you read it, what do you expect him to write about in this piece, titled "Age and Youth"?
2. Pablo Casals, the writer of "Age and Youth," was a famous musician who traveled all over the world. Discuss your ideas about the life of a professional musician. Do you think professional musicians should retire when they reach a particular age?
3. Pablo Casals lived his last years in Puerto Rico. Where is Puerto Rico? What do you know about its land and climate?

VOCABULARY DEVELOPMENT

One way to learn new vocabulary is to learn groups of words that relate to a particular discipline or subject. Casals, being a musician, refers to musical terms in this selection. Before you begin to read, discuss with your class what the following words mean:

conduct	Maestro	orchestra
piano	rehearse	concerts
Bach	preludes	fugues

Age and Youth
Pablo Casals

"Age and Youth" is an excerpt from Joys and Sorrows, *the autobiography of the great musician Pablo Casals. An autobiography is a nonfiction account of a person's life. This excerpt reveals Casals's feelings about his life at the age of 93.*

On my last birthday I was ninety-three years old. That is not young, of course. In fact, it is older than ninety. But age is a relative matter. If you continue to work and to absorb the beauty in the world about you, you find that age does not necessarily mean getting old. At least, not in the ordinary sense. I feel many things more intensely than ever before, and for me life grows more fascinating.

Not long ago my friend Sasha Schneider brought me a letter addressed to me by a group of musicians in the Caucasus Mountains in the Soviet Union. This was the text of the letter:

°distinguished conductor, composer, or performer of music

Dear Honorable Maestro,°

I have the pleasure on behalf of the Georgian Caucasian Orchestra to invite you to conduct one of our concerts. You will be the first musician of your age who receives the distinction of conducting our orchestra.

Never in the history of our orchestra have we permitted a man under one hundred years to conduct. All of the members of our orchestra are over one hundred years old. But we have heard of your talents as a conductor, and we feel that, despite your youthfulness, an exception should be made in your case.

We expect a favorable response as soon as possible.

We pay travel expenses and of course shall provide living accommodations during your stay with us.

Respectfully,
Astan Shlarba
President, 123 years old

°unbelievable

Sasha is a man with a sense of humor; he likes to play a joke. That letter was one of his jokes; he had written it himself. But I must admit I took it seriously at first. And why? Because it did not seem to me implausible° that there should be an orchestra composed of musicians older than a hundred. And, indeed, I was right! That portion of the letter was not a joke. There is such an orchestra in the Caucasus. Sasha had read about it in the *London Sunday Times.* He showed me the article, with photographs of the orchestra. All of its members were more than a hundred years old. There were about thirty of them—they rehearse regularly and give periodic concerts. Most of them are farmers who continue to work in the fields. The oldest of the group, Astan Shlarba, is a tobacco grower who also trains horses. They are splendid-looking men, obviously full of vitality. I should like to hear them play sometime—and, in fact, to conduct them, if the opportunity arose. Of course I am not sure they would permit this, in view of my inadequate age.

°enthusiasm

There is something to be learned from jokes, and it was so in this case. In spite of their age, those musicians have not lost their zest° for life. How does one explain this? I do not think the answer lies simply in their physical constitutions or in something unique about the climate in which they live. It has to do with their attitude toward life; and I believe that their ability to work is due in no small measure to the fact that they do work. Work helps prevent one from getting old. I, for one, cannot dream of retiring. Not now or ever. Retire? The word is alien and the idea inconceivable to me. I don't believe in retirement for anyone in my type of work, not while the spirit remains. My work is my life. I cannot think of one without the other. To "retire" means to me to begin to die. The man who works and is never bored is never old. Work and interest in worthwhile things are the best remedy for age. Each day I am reborn. Each day I must begin again.

For the past eighty years I have started each day in the same manner. 5 It is not a mechanical routine but something essential to my daily life. I go to the piano, and I play two preludes° and fugues° of Bach°. I cannot think of doing otherwise. It is a sort of benediction° on the house. But that is not its only meaning for me. It is a rediscovery of the world of which I have the job of being a part. It fills me with awareness of the wonder of life, with a feeling of the incredible marvel of being a human being. The music is never the same for me, never. Each day it is something new, fantastic and unbelievable. That is Bach, like nature, a miracle!

I do not think a day passes in my life in which I fail to look with fresh 6 amazement at the miracle of nature. It is there on every side. It can be simply a shadow on a mountainside, or a spider's web gleaming with dew, or sunlight on the leaves of a tree. I have always especially loved the sea. Whenever possible, I have lived by the sea, as for these past twelve years here in Puerto Rico. It has long been a custom of mine to walk along the beach each morning before I start work. True, my walks are shorter than they used to be, but that does not lessen the wonder of the sea. How mysterious and beautiful is the sea! how infinitely variable! It is never the same, never, not from one moment to the next, always in the process of change, always becoming something different and new.

°opening section of fugue
°musical compositions with two interacting themes or melodies
°Johann Sebastian Bach (1685–1750), a great German composer
°blessing

Reading and Thinking Strategies

Discussion Activities

Analysis and Conclusions

1. What attitude does Casals have toward life? Give examples from the text to support your point of view.
2. What does retirement mean to Casals? Support your answer with examples from the text.
3. Why does Casals live by the sea? What effect does the sea have on him?

Writing and Point of View

1. Why do you think Casals included the letter in this essay instead of just telling the reader about it? What effect did reading the letter have on you?

2. The excerpt is from an autobiography. What is the difference between an autobiography and a biography? If you could interview any famous person to write that person's biography, who would you most want to interview? Explain why.

3. In the first seven lines of paragraph 3, the pronoun *it* is used four times. What does each *it* refer to?

4. If this had been a biography, would it be written in the first person or the third person? Why? What biographies or autobiographies have you read that you would recommend to your classmates?

Personal Response and Evaluation

1. Have you ever known any older person with an especially positive attitude toward life? Describe that person.

2. Casals discusses his love of music. How has music influenced your life? Do you like classical music, jazz, rock 'n' roll, or country music? What other kinds of music do you like?

3. Some people believe that Americans do not respect older people enough and do not treat them with enough care and kindness. In your experience, does this seem to be true? Explain.

Interviewing

Ask a classmate the following questions and any others about this topic that you think would be interesting. Take notes about what your partner tells you.

1. Who is one older person that influenced your life?
2. How old was the person?
3. What memory about this person stands out in your mind?
4. What did you learn from knowing this person?
5. How would you describe this person so that I can see him or her through your eyes?

Then reverse the process, with the classmate asking you questions and taking notes. After you have finished your interviews, write a report of what you learned from your partner. Share your report with the class.

Journal Writing

The journal is an excellent tool with which the writer may begin to see his or her experience as unique in the world. Although we may focus on the same aspect of life in our journals, each of our views of the world will be personal and distinctive.

Your representation of the world differs from mine, and this is not only insofar as the world has used us differently—that is to say we have had differing experiences of it. It is also because your way of representing is not the same as mine. We are neither of us cameras. . . . I look at the world in the light of what I have learned to expect from past experiences of the world.

JAMES BRITTON, *Language and Learning*

Let us examine age and the aging process in our journals. Although we are not necessarily old, we are all constantly aging. Casals tells us that age is relative. "If you continue to work and to absorb the beauty in the world about you, you find that age does not necessarily mean getting old." He encourages us to question what it means to be old and what it means to be young. Imagine yourself as an old person. Imagine yourself as a young child. How does this make you feel? Think about this when you write in your journal.

Writing Strategies

Essay Strategies

Finding a Controlling Idea

One technique that can help focus your writing is to concentrate on a few words or a theme that illustrates the main idea of your essay. In your writing, you may not actually state this theme, but you will think about it in deciding on appropriate supporting details. For example, Pablo Casals never writes that "life is a great gift," but every example he provides about the orchestra, his music, and the beach are illustrations of this controlling idea or theme. Sometimes these controlling ideas are clichés or overused expressions, so you should not include them in your essay. However, keeping them in mind as you write can help you focus and decide on appropriate supporting details. Here are some examples of controlling ideas:

You learn from adversity.

Persistence is rewarded.

Wealth isn't always measured in terms of money.

☐   ☐   ☐

EXERCISES

1. Choose one of the themes just listed, or write a theme of your own that will assist you in describing a person. Make a list of supporting

details that illustrate the theme and also create a picture of the person you want to describe.

2. Write a description of the person, keeping the theme in mind but never stating it. Share your writing with a classmate, and ask the classmate to tell you what your theme was.

Essay Form

Description: Writing about an Event

When Casals writes about receiving the letter, his daily routine, or walking on the beach, he is writing about important events that define who he is as a person. When you write about an event, you can focus on the *person,* the *place,* or the *feelings* associated with the event. First, you must decide what to concentrate on to describe the event from your own perspective. Once you have decided on your focus, in your first draft, practice using the four processes listed here as you write your essay. When you write your final draft, you may find that you do not need all the steps, and you may delete some or add others that work better for you.

1. *Observe.* Look closely at the event in your memory, in pictures, or in real life. Notice the specific or unusual details, the moments that stand out, so that your readers will be able to see and feel the event through your words.

2. *Describe.* Ask yourself *who, what, where, when, why,* and *how* questions about the event. Write out your answers, and include in your essay as many as seem necessary to re-create the event for your reader.

3. *Compare and contrast.* Tell the reader what event yours is similar to or different from and why. Tell your reader why this is important to understanding the event.

4. *Evaluate.* Tell your readers why this event is important to you or to others.

□   □   □

EXERCISES

1. Reread the Casals excerpt to determine which of the listed steps he used in his writing.
2. Reread another selection in the book to determine which steps the author used.
3. Reread one of your own essays describing an event to determine which steps you used. Rewrite one of your own essays, adding information using one of the steps you did not use in your earlier version. Reread both versions. Which version of your essay do you prefer? Why?

Suggestions for Writing

Choose one of the following topics that interests you. Before you begin to write, try the suggestion in the next section, "Getting Started."

1. Describe an older person who has had an important influence on your life. Include a lot of detail so that the reader can picture the person. Tell a story about the person so that the reader can understand why this person means so much to you.

2. "Work helps prevent one from getting old," Casals writes. Do you agree or disagree? Support your point of view with your experience or observations.

3. Should people be forced to retire at a certain age to give opportunities to young people? Support your point of view with your experience or observations.

4. Casals says that no day passes in his life in which he fails to look with amazement at the miracle of nature. Analyze his statement, and explain whether you have ever felt inspired by the "miracle of nature." Give examples from your own life.

5. "Young people in this country have been accused of not caring for their parents in the way they would have in the old country, in Puerto Rico, in the Old South, or in Italy. And this is true, but it is also true that old people in this country have been influenced by an American ideal of independence and autonomy. The most important thing in the world is to be independent. So we live alone, perhaps on the verge of starvation, in time without friends, but we are independent." Margaret Mead, a famous anthropologist, wrote this statement in an essay on grandparents. Respond to the statement on the basis of your observations and experiences.

6. There are now more people in the United States over the age of 65 than there have ever been before. What types of problems can this create? What advantages can this offer? What are some ways of dealing with these situations?

Getting Started

Directed Freewriting

Before you begin to write your essay, take a blank piece of paper. Write the title or the main idea of your essay at the top of the paper. Close your eyes for about a minute, concentrating on those words at the top of the page. Open your eyes, and begin to write anything at all that comes into your mind. Write for at least ten minutes without putting down the pen, even if what you are writing seems unrelated to the topic. Just keep writing until you have filled a page or two with ideas. Then stop writing and read what you have written, underlining any idea that relates to your topic. When you begin to write your essay, read your freewriting again. You may find other connections with your topic, or you may decide to change your essay topic to one you find more interesting.

A Student Essay

MEMORIES OF PAPA VICTOR

When I was growing up in my country of origin, Ecuador, I remember 1
spending my summer vacation at my grandfather's farm. The farm was about eight hours away from our home at the capital city, Quito. For some reason during this summer, I waited for my vacation very impatiently. I had a feeling inside of me that made me react in a different way.

My grandfather, Papa Victor, always waited for me at the main house, 2
seated on a very comfortable chair, smoking a wooden homemade pipe and homeground tobacco. This tobacco has been highly valued by the Spanish colonies for centuries. My grandfather had come to this farm around twenty-five years ago. He was a man with the body shape of a black bear and the heart of a nun. He was welcomed and respected wherever he went. He was also known for his generosity toward the less fortunate.

On the first night of my arrival, the old man had ordered several em- 3
ployees to the kitchen to prepare my favorite meal—grilled codfish, baked potato, chicken soup, and homemade wine. After a delicious dinner with my grandfather, we sat down outside the dining room, where we chatted for several hours, trying to catch up on the news and the rumors about the government. We headed to our respective rooms after midnight. He had advised me that the next day's trip would be a special one. The old man used to take me on fishing trips that were filled with fun and adventure. Most of the trips were far away from the farm. On this occasion, two of the biggest horses at the farm were ready for the next day's adventure.

Before the sun came up in the morning, about twenty employees who 4
worked at the farm were serving breakfast. Included in the group were men and women from different ethnic groups of the region. The horses were panting and ready to go. My grandfather was lighting his pipe, leaving behind a smell of respect and tradition. We had to ride through valleys and mountains for about five hours until we reached the peak of the biggest mountain, where we found a hidden lake of crystal clear waters. Here the fish could not hide from our eyes. All the fatigue was erased from my body and mind when we saw so much surrounding us. The

sense of peace and harmony was unmeasurable. The fresh air and the gliding fish in the clear water made a heavenly panorama. My grandfather and I spent the night next to the lake talking about our life experiences and sharing his pipe.

On the way back to the farm, I looked around the mountains with the evergreens that lined up along the horizon. The rest of my vacation I spent helping around the farm, doing the chores like any other employee. This job filled me with pride and also enlarged my ego. 5

Soon after I left the farm, we received the bad news that the man was one more victim of time. The death of my beloved Papa Victor caused part of my heart to succumb, too. He died from natural causes, and he was buried on the land that we loved so much. 6

The following summer I went back to the farm to work. This time was different. I did not have anybody waiting for me at the house. I felt an emptiness in my heart. I asked one of the employees to take me to where I went the last time with my grandfather, but something rare happened. None of them could find the place where my grandfather and I had shared the secrets of life. Many times I have tried to find this place without any luck. Now I do not look for it anymore because I know that he is watching me from heaven. He is also there waiting for me as he used to do at the farm each summer. 7

Victor Ortiz, Ecuador

Revising

Ask yourself the following questions about Victor Ortiz's essay.

1. What is the purpose of Ortiz's essay? What was the writer trying to say?
2. Which words or phrases best describe Papa Victor? Explain your choices.
3. How does Ortiz connect the first and last paragraphs in this essay?
4. What references to time are used in the essay? How do these connect with the essay's main idea?
5. How did this essay make you feel? What specifically in the essay contributed to that feeling?
6. What do you like best about this essay? Why?

After you have thought about Ortiz's work, rewrite the questions so that you can use them with an essay you wrote for this chapter. Read your essay with a classmate, and discuss your writing. Decide what changes you would like to make. Revise your essay, and share it with the same classmate.

Editing Strategies

Mechanics

Finding and Correcting Run-ons

A run-on occurs when two or more complete sentences are joined with no punctuation or connecting word between them. Another type of run-on is the comma splice, in which two complete sentences are joined only by a comma. Run-ons present editing problems for many writers. Every sentence in the following paragraph is a run-on. Circle the place in each run-on where a correction should be made.

Jeanne Calment is the oldest woman in the world, her age has been officially documented. She lives in Arles, France, she was born on February 21, 1875. She met the painter Vincent Van Gogh in 1888 or 1889, she was not impressed. She thought he was ungracious, and impolite, consequently she did not want to spend time with him. Calment's mother lived to be 86 her father lived to be 93. Unfortunately, her husband died in 1942 her daughter died even earlier, in 1934. Calment gave up smoking when she was 117 she stopped riding a bicycle at the age of 100. Reporters asked her about herself, she said that she had to wait until she turned 110 to become famous. In 1953, there were 200 centenarians (people who are 100 years of age or over) in France, by 2050 it is predicted that there will be as many as 150,000.

ADAPTED FROM THE *NEW YORK TIMES*, FEBRUARY 22, 1995

You can use the accompanying chart to check whether a sentence is a run-on. If you had any difficulty correcting the run-ons in the paragraph, read the following explanations.

There are five basic methods for correcting run-ons:

1. Use a period to end the first sentence and a capital letter to begin the next.

   Jeanne Calment is the oldest woman in the world. Her age has been officially documented.

2. Use a subordinating word such as *when, because, if, although, as,* or *since* or a relative pronoun such as *who, which, that,* or *whose.*

   <u>When</u> reporters asked her about herself, she said that she had to wait until she turned 110 to become famous.

3. Use a comma and a coordinating word: *for, or, and, yet, nor, so,* or *but.*

   She met the painter Vincent Van Gogh in 1888 or 1889<u>, but</u> she was not impressed.

4. Use a semicolon to connect the two sentences when the second sentence begins with a transition word such as *however, consequently, therefore,* or *furthermore.* The transition word should be set off with a comma.

   She thought he was impolite and ungracious<u>; consequently,</u> she did not want to spend time with him.

5. Use a semicolon or a colon to connect the two sentences when the idea in the second sentence is a continuation of the idea in the first sentence.

   Calment's mother lived to be 86<u>;</u> her father lived to be 93.

Run-on Checklist

	Subject	*Verb*	*Complete Thought*
Jeanne Calment is the oldest woman in the world,	√	√	√
her age has been officially documented.	√	√	√
(This is a run-on because two complete sentences are connected only by a comma.)			
Calment's mother lived to be 86	√	√	√
her father lived to be 93.	√	√	√
(This is a run-on because two complete sentences are linked with no break between them.)			
She thought he was impolite and ungracious,	√	√	√
consequently she did not want to spend time with him.	√	√	√
(This is a run-on because two complete sentences are connected with a transition word that is punctuated incorrectly.)			

□ □ □

EXERCISES

1. Correct the remaining run-ons in the paragraph about Jeanne Calment, using the chart and a variety of the techniques just presented.

2. Correct the following run-ons, using any of the illustrated techniques. Try several approaches, as this adds variety to your writing.

a. He always loved music Pablo Casals learned to play the cello.

b. His friend Sasha Schneider played a joke on him Schneider sent Casals a letter inviting him to conduct an orchestra.

c. Casals liked to live near the sea he enjoyed early-morning walks on the beach.

d. Looking at nature makes Casals very happy he feels connected to life in that way.

e. Some elderly people continue to work and absorb beauty around them they feel that aging does not mean getting old.

f. Casals had a routine he started every day by walking on the beach and playing the piano.

g. He went to the piano he played two preludes and fugues by Bach.

h. Casals believes there is something to be learned in jokes this was true of Schneider's joke as well.

i. All the members of the orchestra are healthy they are all over 100 years old.

j. The oldest of the group is Astan Shlarba he is a tobacco grower and a horse trainer.

Editing Practice

Editing Other People's Writing

The following is an unedited draft. It contains many errors, including many run-on sentences. Correct as many errors as you can. (If you have difficulty correcting the preposition problems, read pages 201–205.) Answers are on page 358.

Jacqueline Kennedy Onassis died on May 1994 at the age of 64, she was loved by much Americans because of her grace, beauty, and style. Jackie, as people called her, was the first lady for a shortest time then almost any other first lady, yet she made a huge impact in people all over the world. Her first husband President John Kennedy was assassinated on 1963 so Jackie became a widow in the age of 34. She was raising her two children Caroline and John alone later she married one of the richest man on the world, Aristotle Onassis. After he died Jackie never remarried. She had worked as an editor and she enjoyed her friends, children and grandchildren until the end. Everyone will miss Jackie she was a great women.

Editing Your Own Writing

Reread an essay that you wrote for this chapter, asking yourself the following questions:

1. Did I format my paper correctly?
2. Did I start new paragraphs when necessary?
3. Did I use final sentence punctuation and apostrophes correctly?
4. Did I use the past tenses correctly?
5. Did I use the present tenses correctly? Do my subjects and verbs agree?
6. Did I use quotation marks correctly?
7. Did I use pronouns correctly? Do the pronouns agree with their antecedents?
8. Did I form plurals correctly?
9. Did I use *the* correctly?
10. Did I use capital letters where they were needed?
11. Did I use commas correctly?
12. Did I use modals correctly?
13. Did I use comparatives correctly?
14. Are all the sentences complete, with no run-ons?

When you rewrite your essay, make any changes that will improve your writing.

Grammar Strategies

Prepositions

Prepositions are a group of words that indicate relationships such as time, place, position, direction, comparison, contrast, reason, manner, and possession. They do not change form and have no special endings for tense or number. Their use is very idiomatic.

Prepositions often appear in *prepositional phrases,* expressions that contain a preposition and a noun phrase, such as *in the office* or *on the desk.*

Verb-preposition combinations, often called two-word verbs, alter the meaning of the verbs and are very common in English.

The babysitter *looked after* the child every evening.
She *looked at* the page for a long time.
The retiring teacher *looked back* on her favorite classes.
He *looked down* on anyone he thought was poorer than he was.
I *looked for* you all over school.
The students *looked forward to* their vacation.
The police *looked into* the robbery.
They *looked out* the window at the snow.
We *looked through* the catalog and decided to order a few things.
The employees *looked up* to their boss.

□   □   □

EXERCISES

1. Discuss the meanings of the different uses of *look* just illustrated. What other two-word verbs can you cite that use the verb *look*?
2. With your classmates, make a list of other two-word verbs you know and use frequently.
3. Consult a dictionary to find other two-word verbs you know and might use. Make a class list, and add to it as you think of other two-word verbs.

Prepositions of Time and Place

in/on/at/by (**time**)

Although preposition use is very idiomatic, certain rules apply with *in, on, at,* and *by* as they are used for time.

In is usually used for a block of time:

in a million years	in the fall
in my lifetime	in the winter
in 1997	in June
in the spring	in a week
in the summer	in a little while

On is more specific:

on December 27	on the Fourth of July
on the eighteenth of the month	on Thanksgiving
on weekends	on Tuesday
on my birthday	on the day

At is the most specific of all; it is used to pinpoint an exact time:

at midnight   at 6 P.M.

at dawn   at 10:15

at noon   at 2 o'clock

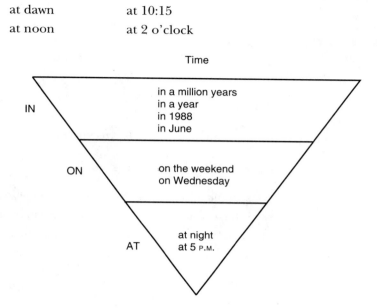

A birthday would be expressed in one of the following ways:

I was born in 1970, in May, on the tenth of the month at 9:15 P.M.
I was born on May 10 in 1970 at 9:15 P.M.

By has a special meaning with time. "I will be there by 6 o'clock" means that I will be there before or just at 6 o'clock but no later than that. "I will graduate by 2001" means that I will graduate before or at 2001 but not after that date.

in/on/at (place)

In is usually used for large land areas:

space	in the universe, in the world
continent	in Africa
country	in France
state	in Oregon
county	in Essex County
city	in Miami
town	in New Paltz, in that community

But there are exceptions:

on a planet, *on* Earth, *on* Venus, *on* the moon

On is usually slightly more specific:

part of town	on the East Side
street	on Bay Street, on the next block
floor	on the tenth floor

Exceptions:

> *in* an apartment, *in* Apartment 10G

At is the most specific of all:

specific address	at 700 Lincoln Boulevard
intersection	at the corner of Morrison Street and Broadway
specific place	at the museum, at the zoo, at the movies, at the office

Exceptions:

> I work *in* a museum, *in* an office, *in* a school, *in* a hospital.

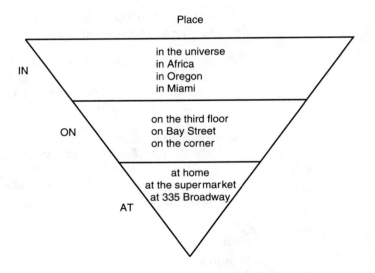

Place

IN — in the universe / in Africa / in Oregon / in Miami

ON — on the third floor / on Bay Street / on the corner

AT — at home / at the supermarket / at 335 Broadway

Many other prepositions have particular uses:

To express time:

> about, after, around, before, by, during, for, from . . . to, since, until

To express place, position, or direction:

> above, against, along, among, around, behind, below, beside, between, by, close to, down, far from, from . . . to, in back of, in front of, inside, into, near, next to, off, out, out of, outside, over, under, up, upon, within

To express comparison:

> as many as, as much as, the same as, different from, less than, more than, similar to, better than

To express contrast:

> despite, in spite of

To give a reason:

> because of, due to

To express manner:

> as, as well as, by, like, such as, through, with, without

To show possession:

> of

□   □   □

EXERCISES

1. Fill in each of the following blanks with *in, on,* or *at.*

a. Pablo Casals was born _____ 1876, _____ Vendrell, Spain, _____ December 29.

b. He lived _____ Puerto Rico for many years of his life.

c. _____ a typical day _____ his life, he got up _____ dawn.

d. He made his debut _____ the age of 22 _____ Paris _____ 1898.

    e. Casals founded the Barcelona Orchestra _____ 1919.

    f. _____ 1950, he organized and played _____ the first of the chamber music festivals _____ Prades, France.

    g. He also founded the Casals Festival _____ Puerto Rico _____ the 1950s.

2. Fill in each of the following blanks with *as many as, as much as, the same as, different from, less than, more than, better than,* or *similar to.*

    a. My brother is __*the same*__ age _____*as*_____ I am. We are twins.

    b. She drinks _____ coffee _____ she can every day.

    c. They play _____ tennis _____ possible, even though they both have very demanding jobs.

    d. My friends want an apartment with _____ rooms _____ possible because they have a big family.

    e. Speaking English is _____ writing English, and I prefer writing because I can revise what I have written.

    f. Her diet worked. She now weighs ten pounds _____ she did last month.

    g. My grade on the math exam was 99. I did _____ I expected to do on it.

    h. Living in a dormitory is _____ living at home when you go to college.

3. Fill in the blanks with *despite, in spite of, because of,* or *due to.*

    a. _____ the rain, I went to the concert in the park.

b. _____ Casals's age, he remained active and creative.

c. _____ the demand for writing classes, I had to wait a se-

mester to get into the class I wanted.

4. Write a short essay describing your life in the school you are attending right now. Try to use many prepositions in your essay. Share it
   with a classmate, and together discuss your use of prepositions.

Idiomatic Use of Prepositions with Verbs

Certain verbs are almost always followed by particular prepositions.
Here is a list of some of the most common ones.

Verbs followed by at

frown	laugh	stare
glance	marvel	wink
hint	point	

Verbs followed by for

care	pray	wait
cry	qualify	watch
hope	shop	wish
long		

Verbs followed by from

abstain	escape	retire
differ	recover	shrink
emerge	result	

Verbs followed by in

believe	engage	result
confide	excel	succeed
end	participate	

Verbs followed by of

approve	consist	dispose
beware	disapprove	smell

Verbs followed by **on**

act	feed	plan
count	insist	reflect
decide	knock	rely
depend	live	shine

Verbs followed by **to**

consent	object	respond
like	point	subscribe
listen	reply	

Verbs followed by **with**

associate	deal	join
cooperate	interfere	unite

☐   ☐   ☐

EXERCISES

1. Write the correct preposition in each blank.

   a. She likes to listen _____ the radio when she does her

      homework.

   b. The mother laughed _____ the child as he tried to wink

      _____ her.

   c. They wished _____ a new car and counted _____

      winning the lottery to buy it.

   d. Casals reflected _____ his long life and hoped

      _____ a healthy, productive future.

   e. Shoppers have to beware _____ high prices when they

      shop _____ bargains.

2. Reread one of the selections in this book that you have enjoyed.
   Notice the way that prepositions are used in the selection. Copy out
   any prepositional phrases (combinations of prepositions and other
   words) that you find interesting or would like to use yourself.

□　□　□

CHECKING YOUR OWN WORK

1. Read through each essay you wrote for this chapter. Look at the way you used prepositions. (It may be helpful to underline them lightly.) Did you use them appropriately and correctly? If you are not sure, check the list of prepositions in the previous section.
2. Repeat check 1 with other writing that you have done recently.
3. As an added check, work with a classmate to make sure that you have used prepositions correctly in your writing.

Concentrating on Work

Chapter Ten: Looking at the Economy

> Naisbitt and Aburdene describe the changes occurring as we move from an industrial to an information economy.

Chapter Eleven: Enjoying Your Work

> Psychologist Robbins examines the factors that contribute to job satisfaction.

Chapter Twelve: Getting a Job

> Suyin tells the story of a young woman in Beijing trying to get her first job.

Looking at the Economy

PREREADING ACTIVITIES

1. What is a global economy? In what ways does the economy today seem more global than in the past? Why might this be so?
2. What abilities and skills do immigrants and international students have that are needed in a global economy?
3. What types of professions are well suited to a global economy?
4. What kinds of problems may develop in a global economy that would not develop in an economy tied to local issues?

VOCABULARY DEVELOPMENT

Use the context in which they occur to help you decide what the italicized words mean.

1. The United States is constantly *replenishing* and enhancing this rich mix of talent. In 1988 it admitted 643,000 legal immigrants, more than all other countries put together.

   a. resupplying   b. rejecting   c. revisiting

2. That year was a *benchmark* year—just before the OPEC oil crisis and the subsequent rise in inflation, just before the emergence of Japan as the leading industrial power.

   a. sports-filled   b. unusual   c. establishing a standard of reference

3. After that year, male incomes *declined* precipitously. But by 1985 those incomes had regained the 1973 level. . . . Women's wages did not suffer the same dip as men. Women have moved steadily upward.

   a. went down   b. went up   c. stayed the same

4. After that year, male incomes declined *precipitously.* But by 1985 those incomes had regained the 1973 level. . . . Women's wages did not suffer the same dip as men. Women have moved steadily upward.

   a. predictably   b. steeply   c. on average

Megatrends 2000

John Naisbitt and Patricia Aburdene

In their 1990 best-selling book Megatrends 2000: Ten New Directions for the 1990's, *the authors present their optimistic view that as we enter the new millennium, our world will enjoy an economic boom. Technological changes have made our world safer, more efficient, and more ecologically aware. As our interactions become more global, we will learn to relate to one another and to depend on one another in new and exciting ways. Naisbitt and Aburdene recognize problems, but they are optimistic that, working together, we will be able to solve them.*

The United States . . . has the richest mix . . . of ethnic groups, racial groups, and global experience that the world has ever known, and it is the *richness* of this mix that yields America's incredible creativity and innovation. . . . [1]

°refilling

The United States is constantly replenishing° and enhancing this rich mix of talent. In 1988 it admitted 643,000 legal immigrants, more than all other countries put together. Indeed, since 1970 the United States has allowed more legal immigration than the rest of the world combined. [2]

°willing to start a business

Who are these immigrants? Currently, most are Asian and Hispanic. More important, they are the most aggressive, most entrepreneurial,° most assertive people, who fight fiercely to get to the United States. [3]

It is the habit of Americans to brag about previous immigrants and to complain about the current ones. [4]

These immigrants are adding immeasurably to America's talent pool and at a time when birthrates in the United States are down. Contrast this with immigration policies in European countries whose birthrates are even lower. Germany is the oldest country in the world (average age), followed by the Netherlands and then the Scandinavian countries. These aging countries with their low birthrates have some of the toughest immigration laws in the world. They won't let anybody in. Japan, also growing older faster, won't let anybody in either. [5]

In the 1990's the United States will have a younger population than either of its major competitors—Europe and Japan. [6]

°period of 1,000 years

America's great import is people. Yet Americans have not even begun to experience the real potential of their fantastic human resource mix, which will be their competitive edge in the global economy as we move toward the next millennium.° . . . [7]

A study of wages during the past fifteen years tracks the shift from an industrial to an information economy. In 1973 the median income for males aged thirty-five to forty-four was $26,026. Those between forty-five and fifty-four earned $25,718. [8]

°last great moment

°momentous, decisive

That year was a benchmark year—just before the OPEC oil crisis and 9 the subsequent rise in inflation, just before the emergence of Japan as the leading industrial power. In effect, 1973 was the last hurrah° of the industrial period, when union bargaining power arguably reached its height.

After that fateful° year, male incomes declined precipitously. But by 10 1985 those incomes had regained the 1973 level. Males between thirty-five and forty-four earned $25,886, just under the 1973 figure, and those between forty-five and fifty-four earned $26,702, about $1,000 above it. Wages have increased ever since.

When we compare the incomes of men and women, an interesting 11 trend emerges. Women's wages did not suffer the same dip as men. Women have moved steadily upward. In 1973 women from thirty-five to forty-four earned $13,673. By 1985 their earnings had increased to $16,114. Still a lot lower than male wages but moving steadily upward. That is because women were never a big part of the union-based high-wage phase of the industrial economy. And women have taken two thirds of all the new jobs of the information economy. . . .

°graduates

There is no doubt about it: Wages are down for unskilled, unedu- 12 cated male workers. In 1987 college grads° averaged $31,371; high school grads, $20,314. In the benchmark year of 1973 the unemployment rate for uneducated males was three times that of college graduates. Before the information economy really took off, well-educated baby boomers° were left out in the cold and the stories about college grads driving cabs were legend.

°the 76 million people born in the United States between 1945 and 1964

In today's information society, however, it is the unskilled who are 13 standing in the unemployment line. The unemployment rate for college graduates (one in four U.S. workers) is 1.7 percent; for people with one to three years of college, it is 3.7 percent. High school graduates have unemployment rates of 5.4 percent, and among high school dropouts unemployment is 9.4 percent—nearly six times that of college grads. Today half of all adults get at least some college, compared with one fourth in the 1950's.

Among those households earning $75,000 or more per year, two 14 thirds of the heads of households are college graduates.

Did the unskilled, uneducated white male have it made in the indus- 15 trial America? You bet. Those days are gone forever. . . .

If the industrial society was "a man's world," the information society 16 is wide open to the well educated and technically trained, be they male or female. The system also favors ambitious, intelligent immigrants and other go-getters° who can start off in "service" jobs that pay not $7,000 a year but $7 an hour. With experience—$10 an hour. How much better off are they than the last wave of immigrants who sweated it out in the factory jobs of industrial America?

°aggressive, ambitious people

The issue is not poor-quality jobs or low wages. It is not "death of the middle class" but the real potential for everyone to do well. The problem is how to educate and train people to qualify for an abundance of good jobs. 17

There are not nearly enough people with college degrees or advanced vocational and technical training to fill the more than 2 million new managerial, administrative, and technical jobs coming on-line annually. Without mass immigration from Western Europe (unlikely since it is entering its own boom years) or mass liberalization of immigration laws, there is no way the United States will have the optimum° work force needed for the information economy. 18

°most efficient

Finally, the 120 million people in the U.S. work force today must constantly upgrade their skills over the course of the 1990's. It will require a tremendous human resource effort to transform corporate America into the decentralized, customer-oriented model of the information society. Yet that is what is needed for the United States to participate fully in the booming global economy. With new markets, with a single-market Europe, and with new competitors from Asian countries, corporations need people who can think critically, plan strategically, and adapt to change. 19

That is the challenge of the information age. Let us address it and recognize once and for all that the information economy is a high-wage economy. 20

Reading and Thinking Strategies

Discussion Activities

Analysis and Conclusions

1. Why do Naisbitt and Aburdene think the United States is positioned well to succeed in a global economy?

2. What personal characteristics do the authors suggest are important for success in a global economy? Why would these be important? Why does the information society favor immigrants? Does it favor one type of immigrant over another?

3. What has happened to women in the information economy? What facts do the authors provide to support their claim? How might these changes affect the family positively? Negatively?

4. Which group has the highest unemployment rate in the United States? Why? What jobs used to be open to unskilled, uneducated individuals that are not open anymore?

5. What percentage of workers in the United States have a college degree?

Writing and Point of View

1. Find five facts in this selection. What ideas are these facts used to support?
2. Find five opinions in this selection. What facts are used to support these opinions?
3. The final paragraph begins "That is the challenge of the information age." To what does *that* refer?
4. The authors refer to numbers throughout the selection. What is the main point? How do the numbers support it? When do the authors spell out the numbers? When do they use figures? What rules do they seem to be following?

Personal Response and Evaluation

1. What problems exist today in the United States that might affect the success of a global economy? What worldwide problems might affect the success of a global economy?
2. What differences are there between the industrial society and the information age, according to Naisbitt and Aburdene? What does this mean to you as a college student?
3. Who do you think will benefit the most from the information age? Who will suffer the most? What do you think should be done about this?
4. Naisbitt and Aburdene suggest in paragraph 16 that there are no more sweatshops in America. Is this true? Do sweatshops exist in other parts of the world? In what ways have conditions in such factories changed? Who works in them today?
5. Look at the table below, which presents data for 1992. What information does the table provide? In what ways does the information support the claims made by Naisbitt and Aburdene?

THE LOW END GOES LOWER

Real wages for the least skilled workers have declined since 1979, making it harder than ever to work one's way out of poverty. Wages for [people] with more education and skills, in contrast, have risen, creating a widening gap in incomes. [Figures for full-time year-round workers aged 25 to 64 years, corrected for inflation]

(continued)

(continued from page 217)

Annual Wages in 1992

	Men		Women	
	Wages in 1992 ($)	Change from 1979 (%)	Wages in 1992 ($)	Change from 1979 (%)
High school dropout	21,620	−23.3	14,944	− 7.4
High school graduate	29,993	−17.0	20,372	+ 0.9
Some college	34,794	− 7.3	24,695	+ 7.6
4+ years of college	50,331	+ 5.2	34,429	+ 19.1

Source: New York Times, April 16, 1995. Data from U.S. Bureau of Labor Statistics.

Journal Writing

Reading about jobs makes us think about our own future. What will we do with our lives? Is it important to make a lot of money? Is it important to help people? Is it possible to do both? How do we decide on a job for the future?

This journal entry should focus on jobs, decision making, and finding your way in the world. What jobs have you considered for yourself? Why are these jobs attractive or meaningful to you? Did any one person influence you in your ideas about a future occupation? Did any experience in your life influence you in your ideas about a future occupation?

Class Presentation

1. Select an occupation that interests you, and do research on it in the library. Write a page or two describing the education needed, the kind of work, the starting salary, and any other information that you think would be useful to someone interested in that job. Present your findings to the class in a short oral report.

2. Interview someone who works in a job that interests you. Ask questions to find out about both the positive and the negative aspects of the job. Present your findings to the class in a short oral report.

Writing Strategies

Essay Strategies

Distinguishing Facts from Opinions

Writers use facts and opinions to support their main ideas or points. A factual statement is based on evidence that can be verified or proved. Writers may include the source of their factual information if it is derived from a written source or from an observation or experiment. Some facts are common knowledge, such as the fact that the sun rises in the east and sets in the west. There is no need to acknowledge the source for common information.

Opinions are based on feelings, ideas, or attitudes. Some opinions are also commonly accepted knowledge, such as the opinions that mothers love their babies and that babies need love to survive and grow.

1. What main idea or point of view do Naisbitt and Aburdene present in their selection? Is it stated directly in the selection? If so, where? If not, how did you recognize it?

2. Look at your answer to question 1 at the top of page 217. How effective are these facts in supporting the authors' point of view? What other facts would you have liked them to include? Why?

3. Look at your answer to question 2 at the top of page 217. How effective are these opinions in supporting the authors' view?

4. Who do you think the audience is for *Megatrends 2000*?

5. What facts does Craig include in "Gender-Role Identity" in Chapter Eight? How does she acknowledge the source of these facts? Who do you think the audience is for Craig's textbook, *Human Development*? How does audience affect the sources that writers use to support their point of view?

Essay Form

Persuasion

Persuasive writing involves trying to convince your readers of the strength of your ideas. You are trying to get readers to consider your point of view and perhaps change their minds. This type of writing calls for clear organization of your ideas.

Before you begin to write your essay, you need to organize your thoughts. First, think about the issue and determine a clear position that you can support with examples, facts, and ideas. Make notes to help you organize your ideas. In your notes, write your main idea or belief in a strong, clear sentence. You may decide not to use this sentence in your essay, but it will help you organize your thinking.

List the reasons why you believe as you do. Think about an event or incident that influenced your feelings about this subject. List any other specific examples or reasons that you will use to support your main point. Make sure you have enough examples or reasons to convince your readers.

When you begin to write, identify the problem in the first paragraph. You may decide to experiment with different models for writing an introduction (see pages 103–104 for ideas). Some writers state their position in the first paragraph, and some provide examples that begin to persuade the readers. Try various methods to see which is most effective for you.

Keep in mind the audience who will be reading your writing, and appeal to its needs and interests. You may want to discuss your reasons with a classmate before you begin to write. Choose your words carefully to make your point. Make your conclusion powerful and to the point (see pages 129–130 for ideas about writing a conclusion).

Let's examine paragraph by paragraph the following essay written by Fei Yu, a student from China, looking to see how he developed his ideas in this persuasive essay.

We are moving toward a more global economy where people work for companies based in different parts of the world, and this can create problems for employees and for companies. The United States is a democratic country, and people have more rights in America than in other countries. However, people's rights sometimes can be limited by the companies for which they work, especially companies based in different countries. I think the company has the right to tell its employees what they can or cannot do in the company. But the company should not interfere with its employees' personal lives and spare time.

What problem has Fei Yu identified? What is his position on this problem?

Every employee belongs to his or her company, and every individual is part of his or her company. Employees' dress, behavior, and words all reflect their company's form and quality directly. Therefore, if a company wants to show its customers good form, the company should have some discipline and tell its employees what they should or should not do during working hours. For instance, a company can tell its employees to wear the same uniforms and that they cannot eat during working time. Too many positive things may become negative sometimes. When a company makes discipline for its employees, it should limit its employees only when their behavior may affect the company's form.

What is the main idea of this second paragraph? How does Fei Yu support this main idea?

On the other hand, if the company makes too many limitations, it may infringe upon its employees' legal rights and go against the laws. I don't think any companies should interfere in their employees' spare time and personal life. During their own time, employees don't have any connection with their companies, and their behavior represents their own personalities. If a company wants to control its employees' personal lives, its action oversteps the power of office and also infringes on people's private rights. The employee can sue his or her company. I think no companies want to create "the stone" to squash their own feet.

What is the main idea of paragraph 3? How does Fei Yu support this main idea?

Sometimes it is difficult to distinguish between right or wrong. If employers and employees can have a better understanding of each other's situation, the company would have peace between employer and employee. This peace would make the global economy idea work more smoothly.

How does Fei Yu connect the conclusion to the introduction?

□ □ □

EXERCISES

1. As a class, reread the Naisbitt and Aburdene selection. Determine the main idea of the selection, and together, looking at the same questions asked about Fei Yu's essay, analyze the way the selection is structured. What is the main point of each paragraph? What examples, ideas, or facts are used to support the main point of each paragraph?

2. Read any persuasive essay you have written this semester. Use the same questions to analyze the essay. Then revise your essay to make it even more persuasive. Share your revised essay with a classmate.

Suggestions for Writing

1. In an essay, explain what particular characteristics give an immigrant or an international student an advantage in a global economy. Why would these characteristics be helpful?

2. Naisbitt and Aburdene suggest that financial success means success in today's world. Do you agree? Write an essay in which you explain what success means to you and why you feel this way.

3. "The problem is to educate and train people to qualify for an abundance of good jobs." Write an essay in which you describe specific steps that education, government, or whatever social institution you choose needs to take to make sure that enough people are qualified for the new jobs of the information age. Explain why these steps must be taken to ensure success in the future.

4. In an essay, describe one problem that the authors did not consider in the move toward a global economy. Explain why the problem you mention needs to be considered. What changes must be made to deal with the problem you describe?

5. What should high schools be doing to convince students of the importance of a college education today? Write an essay in which you describe two or three activities that high schools could undertake to inform their students of the benefits of higher education. Explain why high schools should include these activities in their plans.

Getting Started

Creating a Dialogue with Yourself

Before you write an essay, write a dialogue with yourself in which you ask yourself questions about your topic. Write down your answers, and then challenge those answers with more difficult questions. Keep challenging yourself until you think you have asked and answered the difficult questions about your subject. When you have answered the difficult challenges, you will have thought about your topic, and you will be prepared to write a thoughtful and credible essay.

Revising

A Student Essay

After you have finished writing your first draft, give yourself some time to separate from your words and ideas so that you will be able to view your writing from a new perspective.

During this time, read the following student essay. Then think about the questions that follow it.

OPPORTUNITIES FOR SUCCESS

I tend to believe that opportunities for achievement attract a great number of people from around the world to the United States. Educational opportunities, jobs, freedom of mobility, and an economic infrastructure allow its citizens to accumulate personal wealth. This differentiates the United States from many other countries.

Despite the well-known negative opinion among Americans, I am confident that higher education remains affordable for the majority of the American population. In addition to the fair costs of education, there are many different financial aid programs and grants available for qualified individuals. On the contrary, education in my native country, the former Soviet Union, is free of charge. However, nationalistic politics of the Russian government encouraged and supported quotas for national minorities of the former Soviet Republic. These quotas determined who would be allowed to enter college.

Higher education in the United States opens doors and qualifies one 3 for a high-paying professional job. In Russia, very often, an engineer or a superior earns less money than an unskilled laborer who takes orders from his underpaid superior.

Regardless of the widespread opinion about high unemployment 4 rates in the United States, I am convinced that an educated professional and a persistent person will always be able to find a job. The first thing I have learned about a job search in the United States is the fact that it is easier to look for a job while you are working than when you are out of work. Every Sunday, my wife and I spent some time looking through the employment advertisement section of the newspaper. Next we typed cover letters and sent out résumés. This job search is a great opportunity for the professional to achieve financial growth. I do not think many Americans take advantage of this.

Another opportunity that I probably enjoy the most is the freedom to 5 travel. That is a pleasure that many generations of my former country-men were denied. In the United States, you can go whenever and wher-ever you please. You can take a vacation and travel abroad. You can move from one part of the country to another. In the former Soviet Union, the situation was quite different until recently. For example, my grand-mother was denied permission to travel to the United States to visit her nephew. Her application was refused because her nephew was not con-sidered a close relative.

Every person in the Soviet Union possesses a passport. This docu- 6 ment represents one as a citizen and assigns a place of residence for the individual. Thus if a person chooses to move from one part of the coun-try to another, he or she would not be hired by any employer because, officially, that person does not live there.

Another advantage of the American lifestyle is the flexible financial 7 infrastructure. The existence of the middle class separates the American society from many countries. Usually, a family with two working parents belongs to the middle class and makes a decent living. A house in the suburbs and a new car are affordable items for the middle-class American family. Also, many different ways to save and invest are avail-able in the United States. IRA accounts, stocks, bonds, and different types of bank accounts allow American people to earn interest on their hard-earned money. This permits them to plan for their future and re-tirement. On the contrary, in Russia, only two types of investment are known to the general public: long- and short-term savings. The financial options of the American economy and the stability of American cur-rency give people extra insurance and confidence.

The opinions expressed in this essay may be considered by many peo- 8 ple as conservative and politically incorrect. However, the most success-ful people among immigrants that I know are conservatives. They just had a clear view of the opportunities for achievements that their new homeland offered them, and they did not hesitate to take advantage of them. America offers many opportunities for success for educated and persistent people.

Edward Geller, Ukraine

1. What is Edward Geller's main idea? Where is it stated?
2. To what "well-known negative opinion" is Geller referring in paragraph 2? How did you know this? Should he have made this clearer?
3. To what "widespread opinion" is Geller referring in paragraph 4? How did you know this? Should he have made this clearer?
4. In which paragraphs does Geller compare the United States and the former Soviet Union? What examples does he provide to support his ideas in these comparisons?
5. What is the strongest part of this essay? Explain your choice by referring to specific words and phrases in the essay.
6. Does the conclusion tie the ideas of the essay together? What makes this essay persuasive? Did Geller convince you of his opinion? Explain your answer.

After thinking about Geller's essay, rewrite these questions to fit your essay. Reread your draft, asking yourself these questions. Note down ideas to improve your essay. Then rewrite your essay and share the revised essay with a classmate.

Editing Strategies

Mechanics

Making Connections Using Transitional Words

One method that writers use to connect their ideas from sentence to sentence and from paragraph to paragraph is to use transitional words and phrases, such as *furthermore, therefore, nevertheless,* and *then.*

By far the most common idea and sentence connectors are *and, but, for,* and *so.* Commas usually precede these words when they connect independent clauses or sentences. (See pages 154–55 for more information about this.) Many other words are used to indicate types of relationships between ideas, sentences, and paragraphs.

1. One type of connection is to show *comparison.* This involves such expressions as *in the same manner, in the same way, likewise,* and *similarly.*
2. *Contrast* words include *although, but, even though, however, in contrast*

with, instead of, on the contrary, on the other hand, otherwise, rather than, still, and *yet.*

3. *Illustration* words include *as an example, as an illustration, for example, for instance, specifically, to illustrate,* and *to show what I mean.*

4. *Addition* words include *also, besides, besides that, furthermore, in addition,* and *moreover.*

5. *Emphasis* words include *actually, as a matter of fact, frankly, honestly, indeed, in fact, of course, really, to tell the truth,* and *truly.*

6. *Time* or *chronological-order words* are *after all, afterward, at last, at the end, at the same time, first, first of all, in conclusion, in the end, in the meantime, lately, later, meanwhile, next, recently, second, subsequently,* and *then.*

7. *Explanation* words are *in fact, in other words, namely, that is,* and *what I mean is.*

8. *Result* words include *as a result, because of that, consequently, due to that, for this reason, hence, therefore,* and *thus.*

□   □   □

EXERCISES

1. Fill in the blanks using the words showing comparison or contrast that best fit the meaning of the following paragraph.

_____ with an industrial economy, an information economy

favors people with better educations. _____ people who enjoy

working with technology and computers will do better than those

who prefer doing physical labor with their hands. _____ the

facts provided by Naisbitt and Aburdene do not take into account the

low-paying, menial jobs that provide employment for a large segment

of newcomers, even those with better educations, when they first en-

ter this country.

2. Fill in the blanks with the words used for illustration or addition that best fit the meaning of the following paragraph.

_____, students in my class often find jobs working at fast-

food restaurants, cleaning apartments, or taking care of young chil-

dren. _____ their parents sometimes have to do the same

kind of work even though they had professional jobs in their home countries. _____ I would like to tell about my friend Karl and his family.

3. Fill in the blanks with the words used for emphasis or chronological order that best fit the meaning of the following paragraph.

_____ Karl comes from a well-educated family. _____ I am not sure what his mother and father did when they lived in Russia. I _____ think his father was an engineer and his mother a doctor. I know they tried to get jobs in their fields, but _____ they took what they could get. _____ it doesn't matter because now they work at a fast-food restaurant.

4. Fill in the blanks with the words used for explanation or result that best fit the meaning of the following paragraph.

_____ it is hard to get a good job when you first arrive in a new country even if you have a good education. You need to learn the language, go to school and learn new skills, and learn the ways of the new country too. _____ I advise my friends to make it easier for themselves and try to learn the language as best they can before they come here. _____ I tell them to prepare themselves for hard work and big changes.

5. Reread the essay you have written in exercises 1–4 using transitional words. It now contains too many connecting words, and that makes the essay too predictable. Decide which connectors to eliminate and which ones to keep to make the essay more interesting to read.
6. Reread the essay you wrote for this chapter. Look at the ways you connected your ideas. Did you use any of the connecting words

listed in this section? Discuss with a classmate whether you used them appropriately and effectively.

7. In paragraph 2 of the Naisbitt and Aburdene article, the authors use the word *indeed*. What does it mean in the sentence? To what does it refer in the paragraph? Try using another transitional word or phrase with a similar meaning in its place. Does it change the meaning for you? Which do you prefer?

Editing Practice

Editing Other People's Writing

The following is an unedited draft. Too many connecting words are used in the essay. Underline them; then decide which ones to delete, which to change, and which to leave as they are. Answers will vary.

The Home Revolution

For example, more people are starting to work at home. In fact, thousands more people are choosing to work at home to be closer to their children and other family members. As a matter of fact, these people are trading in their cars for home computer systems. As a case in point, I'll describe a family that lives in my apartment building. To illustrate, they have two computers, connected to all the branches their office has. In fact, these people can be in touch with Tokyo, San Francisco, New York, Paris, Rome, Calcutta, and Ankara by computer in minutes. Instead of waiting for letters to be delivered all over the world, they just send them by modem to all their branch offices. Indeed, they get responses to their work right away, too. On the other hand, they now have more work than they can handle. As a result, they have convinced me to start thinking about buying a computer myself. To tell the truth, they tell me they could use my help, and I like the idea of getting on-line. Besides, I look forward to being in touch with the world from my bedroom. To be frank, I am tired of taking the bus to and from work each day.

Editing Your Own Writing

Reread an essay that you wrote for this chapter, asking yourself the following questions:

1. Did I format my paper correctly?
2. Did I start new paragraphs when necessary?
3. Did I use final sentence punctuation and apostrophes correctly?
4. Did I use the past tenses correctly?
5. Did I use the present tenses correctly? Do my subjects and verbs agree?
6. Did I use quotation marks correctly?
7. Did I use pronouns correctly? Do the pronouns agree with their antecedents?
8. Did I form plurals correctly?
9. Did I use *the* correctly?
10. Did I use capital letters where they were needed?
11. Did I use commas correctly?
12. Did I use modals correctly?
13. Did I use comparatives correctly?
14. Are all the sentences complete, with no run-ons?
15. Did I use connecting words appropriately?

When you rewrite your essay, make any changes that will improve your writing.

Grammar Strategies

Gerunds and Infinitives

Gerunds

A gerund consists of a verb + *-ing*. For example, *playing* and *talking* are gerunds. Gerunds can be used in three ways:

1. As the subject of a sentence:

   Dancing can be relaxing and fun.

2. As the object of a sentence:

   People enjoy talking.

3. As the object of a preposition:

The idea of dancing with my father made me very happy.
I am fond of eating out late at night.

Gerunds form negatives with the word *not:*

Would you consider not smoking here?

They can follow the preposition *to* with the expressions *admit to, be/get accustomed to, be/get used to,*[*] *confess to,* and *look forward to:*

She *admitted to stealing* the car.
It is easy to *get accustomed to driving* a new car.
I *am used to listening* to that radio program every morning.
They *confessed to making* the phone calls.
They *look forward to taking* a long vacation this summer.

The following is a list of some of the verbs that should be followed by a (gerund):

alternate	deny	include	regret[†]
appreciate	dislike	miss	report
avoid	discuss	mind	resent
consider	enjoy	postpone	resume
continue	escape	practice	stop[‡]
delay	finish	quit	suggest

The verb form that should follow most prepositions (*on, in, off, up, by, about, from, of*) is the *-ing* (gerund) form. Several examples of this from the Ullman article in Chapter Seven are reproduced here. Underline the preposition and the verb that follows it. The first one has been done for you.

1. Instead <u>of reading</u> the *Daily Cal,* I anticipate your footsteps from behind.

---

[*]Notice that the meaning of *be used to* and *get used to* is different from *used to*. *Be used to* and *get used to* mean "to become accustomed to." *Used to* refers to something done in the past that is no longer done, as in "I used to live with my grandmother when I was a child."

[†]In a formal letter, *regret* is followed by the infinitive form of the verb (*to* plus the simple form of the verb): "I regret to tell you . . ."

[‡]*Stop* can be followed by either the *-ing* form or the *to* form, but the meaning changes:

I *stopped talking* to my best friend. (We no longer talk.)
I *stopped to talk* to my best friend. (We spent some time talking.)

2. Many Berkeley women have brightened their social lives by taking the initiative with men.

3. A college date means anything from studying together to sex.

4. I don't know if I'll deny you pleasure or offend you by insisting on paying for myself. (There are two examples in this sentence.)

5. During our after-dinner stroll, he told me he was interested in dating me on a steady basis.

6. He was mad at himself for treating me, and I regretted allowing him to.

□   □   □

EXERCISE

In the following sentences, fill in each blank with a verb that makes sense to you as a reader.

1. The teacher finished _____ and then asked for questions about the examination that Thursday.

2. The students appreciated _____ about what would be on the test.

3. One of the students asked the teacher to postpone _____ the test until Monday.

4. The teacher told the students that they had to get used to _____ tests every week.

5. A few students considered _____ after class to study together in small groups.

Infinitives

An infinitive consists of *to* + the base form of a verb. For example, *to play* and *to talk* are infinitives. Infinitives can be used in four ways:

1. As the subject of a sentence:

   To learn English is critical to my success.
   To travel abroad is my goal.

   Often, however, such sentences begin with *it:*

   It is important to learn English.
   It is my goal to travel abroad.

2. As the object of a verb:

   I want to do my homework.
   The students tried to do well on their research paper.

3. As an adjective:

   There were only a few fresh vegetables to buy. (modifies *vegetables*)

4. As an adverb:

   The students were ready to take the test. (modifies *ready*)

Infinitives may occur after adjectives such as *afraid, determined, difficult, easy, fortunate, happy, lucky, necessary, nice, possible, ready,* and *sad:*

   I am afraid to walk home alone.
   She is determined to graduate from school.
   It is difficult to get an A in every course.
   We found it easy to learn to use the computer.

These are the most commonly used verbs that are followed by an infinitive:

agree	expect	manage	require
appear	fail	need	seem
ask	forget	plan	try
attempt	have	prepare	urge
cause	hope	pretend	wait
choose	know	promise	want
decide	learn	refuse	would like
deserve			

Employees *have to learn to deal* with irate customers. When they *decide to work* in a job in which they are on the "front line," they *choose to deal* with people and problems every day. Some employees *need to learn* how to expend emotional labor on their jobs. They *want to find out* the best way to listen to a resentful customer, negotiate the difficulty, and solve the problem without *forgetting to appear* courteous.

Some verbs can be followed by either an infinitive or a gerund:

begin	hate	prefer
can't stand	like	start
continue	love	

□   □   □

EXERCISES

1. Read the following sentences, underlining each verb and the infinitive that follows it. The first one has been done for you.

   a. He <u>agreed to work</u> as a secretary during the summer, but he <u>forgot to tell</u> his boss that he was majoring in accounting.
   b. There appear to be many job openings in the fast-food industry.
   c. The recent college graduate asked to meet the president of the company.
   d. He chose to work in a big city because he wanted to meet lots of new people.
   e. The advertisement attempted to make the job sound challenging and interesting.
   f. The new driver managed to get a job as a taxi driver.
   g. The waiter deserved to get a big tip, but his customers refused to give him anything.
   h. She planned to go back to school in September even though she expected to keep her job.

2. In the following sentences, fill in each blank with a verb in the infinitive form. There are many possibilities; decide what sounds good to you. The first one has been done for you.

   a. The man decided _to ask_ for an application.

   b. He knew he needed _____ a high school diploma, and he was prepared _____ the interviewer about his other job qualifications.

c. His friend promised _____ a copy of the records from his country.

d. He had _____ his birth certificate, his green card, and his passport for the interview.

e. Even though he knew how _____ many machines, he hoped _____ some training on the job.

f. In his country he had learned _____ a computer, and that knowledge seemed _____ important to the company.

g. As he waited _____ called for the interview, he tried _____ his nervousness.

h. The first thing he said to the interviewer was, "Good afternoon. I would like _____ for your company."

3. Fill in each of the following blanks with an appropriate verb. Choose either the infinitive or the gerund form of the verb.

a. The woman learned _____ the phone right away.

b. She enjoyed _____ to new people every day.

c. Still she missed _____ her own language.

d. She needed _____ with old friends at night.

e. She tried _____ together with them, but some nights she had _____ the date.

4. Reread one of the selections in the book that you have enjoyed. Notice the way gerunds and infinitives are used in the selection. Copy out any gerunds and infinitives that are unfamiliar to you or that you would like to use yourself.

□ □ □

CHECKING YOUR OWN WORK

1. Read through each essay you wrote for this chapter. Look at the way you used gerunds and infinitives. (It may be helpful to underline them lightly.) Did you use them appropriately and correctly? If you are not sure, check the lists of gerunds and infinitives in the previous section.
2. Repeat check 1 with other writing that you have done recently.
3. As an added check, work with a classmate to make sure that you have used gerunds and infinitives correctly in your writing.

CHAPTER ELEVEN

Enjoying Your Work

PREREADING ACTIVITIES

1. In a group, make a list of the qualities you would like to find in a job while you are a college student.
2. In a group, make a list of the qualities you would like to find in a job (or career) after you have completed college. What differences are there in the two lists? How do you account for the differences?
3. What do you think are the most important general qualities that make employees satisfied with their jobs?

VOCABULARY DEVELOPMENT

Learning one form of a word can lead you to discover new forms of the word and to increase your vocabulary. Find out the meaning of the word in each row of the following table, and fill in the blanks with the corresponding forms (if no word exists, no blank appears in the column). The first row has been done for you.

Noun	Verb	Adjective	Adverb
organization	organize	organizational	organizationally
activity	_____	_____	_____
_____	_____	satisfied	_____
employee	_____	_____	
performance	_____	_____	
_____	require	_____	

Using the dictionary, choose five other words from the selection that you would like to add to your vocabulary, and list all the word forms.

Job Satisfaction

Stephen P. Robbins

The following excerpt is from the fourth edition of a popular textbook called *Organizational Behavior: Concepts, Controversies, and Applications* (1989). Robbins states that he has tried to write in a logical way, to use a lively style, and to include examples whenever possible. He believes that although textbooks should be serious and intellectually demanding, they should also be interesting and clearly written. This selection is about the factors that influence job satisfaction.

Job satisfaction [refers to] an individual's general attitude toward 1
his or her job. This definition is clearly a very broad one. Yet this
is inherent° in the concept. Remember, a person's job is more than just
the obvious activities of shuffling papers, waiting on customers, or driving a truck. Jobs require interaction with co-workers and bosses, following organizational rules and policies, meeting performance standards, living with working conditions that are often less than ideal, and the like.° This means that an employee's assessment of how satisfied or dissatisfied he or she is with his or her job is a complex summation° of a number of discrete° job elements. . . .

What work-related variables° determine job satisfaction? An extensive 2
review of the literature° indicates that the more important factors conducive° to job satisfaction include mentally challenging work, equitable rewards, supportive working conditions, and supportive colleagues (Locke, 1976).

°essential

°similar things
°adding up, total
°separate
°items that may change
°articles on the subject
°leading

Mentally Challenging Work

Employees tend to prefer jobs that give them opportunities to use 3
their skills and abilities and offer a variety of tasks, freedom, and feedback on how well they are doing. These characteristics make work mentally challenging. Jobs that have too little challenge create boredom. But too much challenge creates frustration and feelings of failure. Under conditions of moderate challenge, most employees will experience pleasure and satisfaction.

Equitable° Rewards

°fair, reasonable

Employees want pay systems and promotion policies that they per- 4
ceive as being just,° unambiguous,° and in line with their expectations. When pay is seen as fair based on job demands, individual skill level, and community pay standards, satisfaction is likely to result. Of course, not everyone seeks money. Many people willingly accept less money to work in a preferred location or in a less demanding job or to have greater dis-

°fair
°clear

cretion in the work they do and the hours they work. But the key in linking pay to satisfaction is not the absolute amount one is paid; rather, it is the perception of fairness. Similarly, employees seek fair promotion policies and practices. Promotions provide opportunities for personal growth, more responsibilities, and increased social status. Individuals who perceive that promotion decisions are made in a fair and just manner, therefore, are likely to experience satisfaction from their job.

Supportive Working Conditions

⁰making easier

Employees are concerned with their work environment for both personal comfort and facilitating⁰ doing a good job. Studies demonstrate that employees prefer physical surroundings that are not dangerous or uncomfortable. Temperature, light, noise, and other environmental factors should not be at either extreme—for example, having too much heat or too little light. Additionally, most employees prefer working relatively close to home, in clean and relatively modern facilities, and with adequate tools and equipment.

Supportive Colleagues⁰

⁰co-workers

⁰real, physical

People get more out of work than merely money or tangible⁰ achievements. For most employees, work also fills the need for social interaction. Not surprisingly, therefore, having friendly and supportive co-workers leads to increased job satisfaction. The behavior of one's boss also is a major determinant of satisfaction. Studies generally find that employee satisfaction is increased when the immediate supervisor is understanding and friendly, offers praise for good performance, listens to the employee's opinions, and shows a personal interest in his or her employees.

Don't Forget the Personality–Job Fit!

⁰agreeing, matching
⁰careers, jobs

⁰reproduce, repeat

[John Holland's personality–job fit theory (see accompanying box) led him to conclude] that high agreement between an employee's personality and occupation results in a more satisfied individual. His logic was essentially this: People with personality types congruent⁰ with their chosen vocations⁰ should find that they have the right talents and abilities to meet the demands of their jobs; are thus more likely to be successful on those jobs; and, because of this success, have a greater probability of achieving high satisfaction from their work. Studies to replicate⁰ Holland's conclusions have been almost universally supportive (see Feldman and Arnold, 1985). It's important, therefore, to add this to our list of factors that determine job satisfaction.

5

6

7

MATCHING PERSONALITY AND JOBS

°idea

°tendency

°transformation through
willpower

John Holland's personality–job fit theory (1985) . . . is based on the no-tion° of fit between a person's interests (taken to be an expression of per-sonality) and his or her occupational environment. Holland presents six personality types and proposes that satisfaction and the propensity° to leave a job depends on the degree to which individuals successfully match their personalities with a congruent occupational environment.

Each one of the six personality types has a matching occupational en-vironment. Listed next is a description of the six types and examples of congruent occupations:

Type	*Occupations*
1. *Realistic*—involves aggressive behavior, physical activities requiring skill, strength, and coordination	Forestry, farming
2. *Investigative*—involves activities requiring thinking, organizing, and understanding rather than feeling or emotion	Biology, mathematics, news reporting
3. *Social*—involves interpersonal rather than intellectual or physical activities	Foreign service, social work, clinical psychology
4. *Conventional*—involves rule-regulated activities and sublimation°of personal needs to an organization or person of power and status	Accounting, finance, corporate manage-ment
5. *Enterprising*—involves verbal activities to influence others, to attain power and status	Law, public relations, small-business management
6. *Artistic*—involves self-expression, artistic creation, or emotional activities	Art, music, writing

References

Feldman, D. C., & H. J. Arnold (1985, June). Personality types and career pat-terns: Some empirical evidence on Holland's models. *Canadian Journal of Administrative Science,* pp. 192–210.

Holland, J. L. (1985). *Making vocational choices: A theory of vocational personalities and work environments,* 2nd ed. Englewood Cliffs, N.J.: Prentice Hall.

Locke, E. A. (1976). The nature and causes of job satisfaction. In M. D. Dunnette, ed. *Handbook of industrial and organizational psychology.* Skokie, Ill.: Rand McNally, pp. 1319–1328.

Reading and Thinking Strategies

Discussion Activities

Analysis and Conclusions

1. Why is mental challenge on the job an important factor in work satisfaction? Can there ever be too much mental challenge? Explain your answer.

2. Robbins lists "equitable rewards" as the second category. Look up the word *reward* in your dictionary. Do you agree with Robbins that pay systems and promotion policies are rewards? What other words could he have used to describe this category?

3. What characteristics make pay systems and promotion policies just, unambiguous, and in line with expectations? What could cause employees to be dissatisfied with the pay or promotion system?

4. What other occupations can you think of that would match with the personality types described in the Holland study?

Writing and Point of View

1. In the first sentence, Robbins uses the possessive pronouns *his* and *her.* Why does he include both? What other changes could he have made in this sentence to include both men and women? Where else in the selection does he make sure to include men and women?

2. In the fourth sentence, Robbins uses three commas. Explain why he uses each of the commas. If you have difficulty with this, review the comma rules on pages 154–56. Read through the selection to find other sentences in which he uses more than two commas, and discuss the reasons for each comma.

3. What words in paragraph 2 tell the reader what to expect in the four paragraphs that follow? Why do you think Robbins separates "Don't Forget the Personality–Job Fit?" from the other headings?

Personal Response and Evaluation

1. Of all the factors that the author mentions as contributing to job satisfaction, which is the most important to you? Explain your answer.

2. Many people find their jobs mentally challenging in the beginning and boring after they have been at the job for a while. What specific techniques can help a new employee learn a mentally challenging job? In what ways are these similar to what a student can do with a

mentally challenging new course? What techniques help eliminate boredom on the job? In the classroom?

3. Which characteristics in the Holland personality–job fit theory best correspond to your personality? What type describes you best?

4. What is the most satisfying job you have ever had? Discuss why this job was so satisfying. Do your reasons for liking the job correspond to the excerpt's analysis of job satisfaction?

5. Have you ever had a job that you did not like? If you have, describe the job to the class or to your group, and explain in detail why this job was not satisfactory to you.

Questionnaire

Most of us have had jobs or know people who have jobs. If we were to develop our own questionnaire dealing with job satisfaction, some of us might give responses similar to those given by the employees surveyed for this selection. Some of us, however, might have different expectations. Working is a very individual experience.

As a group, make a list of questions that you would ask to determine what factors people think are important for job satisfaction. (See pages 20–21 and 41–43 for information on writing questions.) Then make enough copies of the questionnaire to distribute at least five copies to everyone in the class.

To indicate which respondents are members of the class, each student should put a *C* in the top right-hand corner of his or her questionnaire. Each student should then fill out the questionnaire and ask four other people outside of class to answer the questionnaire.

As a class, add up the responses and compare the results of your survey with the findings in the excerpt. Did you find that most people thought mental challenge was the most important factor in job satisfaction? Did most people favor straight salaries? Were the responses from the class members, the *C* group, different from the other responses to the questionnaire? If so, what might explain this?

You will learn many things from doing this activity. You will learn how to create a questionnaire. You will learn how research is conducted, and you will be able to compare your results with the results of other researchers. You may then realize how interesting and often unpredictable research is.

Journal Writing

A student once wrote that the worst job she had ever had was stuffing feathers into pillows in an un-air-conditioned factory in the summertime. The feathers got stuck in her mouth and her lungs, and she coughed all the time. The workers couldn't turn on a fan because the feathers would blow all over the factory. The student couldn't quit the job because she spoke very little English and needed the money. So she stayed and coughed.

The story is unforgettable. Every detail of it—the feathers, the pillows, the heat, and the coughing—remain in the mind of the reader. In your journal entry, think about the best or worst job experience you have ever had. (If you have never worked, write about an experience of a friend or family member.) Recall as many details as you can—the smells, tastes, colors, voices. When you can see a picture of the job clearly in your mind, start to write. Write everything down, and concentrate on making the experience vivid and alive.

Writing Strategies

Essay Strategies

Making Connections Using Keywords and Phrases

Writers can connect their ideas throughout a piece of writing by using keywords (important words and phrases), synonyms (words that have the same meaning), and related words such as pronouns or words in the same category.

using keywords

Robbins uses several keywords in this essay to help his readers follow his ideas from paragraph to paragraph. Some of the keywords are *job, satisfaction,* and *employee.* Identify five other words that Robbins uses many times throughout his selection.

using synonyms and other related words

Robbins uses the words *pay* and *money* synonymously. He uses *boss* and *supervisor.* What other examples of synonyms can you find in the selection?

He also uses related words such as *physical surroundings, environmental factors, temperature, noise,* and *light.* What other words can you find that relate to the word *job?* The word *employee?* The word *rewards?*

using adjectives such as *this, that, these,* and *those*

In the first paragraph, Robbins uses the word *this* three times. To what does *this* refer each time it is used?

In paragraph 3, Robbins writes "these characteristics." To which characteristics is he referring? How did you know?

using special expressions or connecting words

In paragraph 1, Robbins uses the word *yet*. How does *yet* connect the ideas in the two sentences? (See pages 224–25 for more information about these kinds of words and phrases.)

In paragraph 4, Robbins uses the expression *of course*. What does this expression mean in this sentence? (See pages 224–25 for more information about these kinds of words and phrases.)

In paragraph 4, Robbins uses the word *similarly*. What is similar to what? Why is it followed by a comma?

In paragraph 4, he uses the word *therefore*. What is the result of what? Why does he use a comma and not a semicolon here? Where else in the selection does Robbins use *therefore*? In each case, what is its purpose?

In paragraph 5, Robbins writes "for example." What examples does he include? For what are they examples?

In paragraph 5, he uses the word *additionally*. What is being added to what?

Essay Form

Summary Writing

A summary condenses a piece of writing into its essential points. A summary can be used to include another writer's ideas in your own writing. A summary can be used to take notes from library material when doing research for term papers. The techniques for summary writing can be helpful when you take notes in class, by training you to listen for the essential points in a lecture.

What are the techniques for writing a summary? First, use your own words. Occasionally you may want to copy a few words or phrases from the original piece of writing, but in general, the most effective summary is written in your own words. Look for the main ideas in the writing, and include them in your summary. Then look for the important supporting or explanatory details.

Second, you do not have to follow the exact organizational pattern of the original author. The summary is yours, and it should reflect your way of thinking and writing.

Third, even though the summary is organized by you and is written in your own words, it should not contain your ideas. You are summarizing another writer's ideas for your own use.

Finally, use your own style of writing. Do not copy the original author's writing style.

Reread the Robbins selection at the beginning of this chapter; then read the following summaries. Although their styles are quite different, each is a good summary. Summary writing is individual.

Robbins lists four basic reasons for job satisfaction: mentally challenging work, equitable rewards, supportive working conditions, and supportive colleagues. In addition, he describes the 1985 John Holland personality–job fit theory. Holland listed six personality types: realistic, investigative, social, conventional, enterprising, and artistic. He also explained the kinds of jobs appropriate for each one.

What makes people like their jobs? Robbins explains the four most important reasons. They are: the work should be mentally challenging, but not too much; people should be paid fairly; people should work in a decent, comfortable work environment; and people like to work with others who are friendly and treat them honestly, especially bosses. He also describes Holland's list of personality types and the kinds of jobs that match up with those types.

Which summary do you prefer? One is more informal and uses fewer of the author's original words. Which would you find it easier to study from? Just as in any other form of writing, you should begin to develop your own style of writing summaries.

☐   ☐   ☐

EXERCISES

1. Write a summary of the text selection in Chapter Two, Chapter Five, or Chapter Eight.
2. In a small group, read your summary, or make a copy for each member of the group. Compare your summary with those of your classmates. Discuss what makes a good summary. Which summary in your group do you like best? Why?
3. Choose another selection in the book that you have read and write a summary of its contents.

Suggestions for Writing

Before you begin to write on the topic of your choosing, try writing an outline as described in the next section, "Getting Started." Many writers create outlines before doing any formal writing.

1. In essay form, write about your experiences creating the questionnaire, and discuss the results you obtained from it. How did your results compare with the findings in the article? What were the differences? How do you explain these differences?

2. Choose three factors that are most important to you in determining job satisfaction, and write an essay explaining your choices. Support your choices with details from your own experiences and observations.

3. Describe in detail the worst job you have ever had. Close your eyes, and try to recall how it felt to work in that place. When you begin to write, concentrate on trying to make your reader really feel what it

was like to work there. Use descriptive words and dialogue, if appropriate.

4. Following the same procedure as in suggestion 3, write about the best job you have ever had.

5. Use your imagination to write an essay describing your dream job. Begin your essay with the sentence "If I could have any job in the world, I would work as a _____ ." Fill your writing with details.

6. "People should be forced to change jobs every ten years. If they work at the same place for any longer than that, they begin to fall into dull routines, and their work is no longer as good as it was when the job was new and exciting." Do you agree or disagree? Write an essay, supporting your point of view with your own experiences or your observations of others.

Getting Started

Outlining

Many writers find outlining helpful in their prewriting organization, and some books teach very formal outlining techniques. However, writers can spend so much time outlining that they don't have enough time to write. The outlining technique presented here is simple and effective; it will help you think your essay through before you actually begin to write.

The outline is a guide that you will refer to as you are writing. It can be changed as you go along. Its purpose is to help you organize and to give you confidence that you will have something to say throughout your essay.

An outline does not have to be written in complete sentences. It is a list of ideas that you will develop more fully. The basic shape of an outline is as follows:

I. Main idea or topic sentence

   A. First supporting detail

      1. Development 1

      2. Development 2

   B. Second supporting detail etc.

To see how the outline works in the Robbins selection, examine the fourth paragraph more closely. Fill in the rest of the outline.

I. Employees want pay systems and promotion policies that they perceive as fair.

   A.

      1.

      2.

      3.

   B.

      1.

      2.

Your outline may be very different from the author's actual outline. You have the option of making your outline more detailed or very brief, with just a few keywords to help you remember what you wanted to write about. Keep in mind that all writers are different. Some writers find outlines essential to orderly writing; others say they do all their outlining in their head. In the following exercises, you will have the opportunity to try outlining to see if it works for you.

□   □   □

EXERCISES

1. Prepare an outline for one of the other paragraphs in the article.
2. Make a brief outline for the entire article.
3. Before you write your next essay, prepare a brief outline using the techniques you have just learned. See if the outline helps you organize your essay.

Revising

After you have finished writing your first draft, give yourself some time to separate from your words and ideas so that you will be able to view your writing from a new perspective.

During this time, read the student essay that follows.

A Student Essay

THE QUEEN OF QUEENS

"Could you come earlier tomorrow to finish all the cleaning before others come?" a woman asked sharply. "Yes," a hoarse man's voice replied.   1

I had heard that commanding voice on the phone interview yester-   2
day. When I arrived on the second floor of this two-story old building, the young Chinese man had just turned on the vacuum cleaner, which made a loud "vee vee" sound. I knocked at the door hard, and a Chinese woman in her late fifties, I guessed, noticed me.

"Good morning. I have an interview with Mary this morning. Is she ₃ around?" I said. "You must be Ivy. I am Mary. Please come here," Mary replied. She led me to a tiny room that had two desks and some chairs.

It was in September 1992, an excellent morning with warm sunshine ₄ and a refreshing breeze. Since it was the second week I had stayed in New York City, I still had to check bus and subway maps for transportation. Knowing how to go throughout the city is a hundred times better than just waiting for someone to drive you to the laundromat. I needed friends to pick me up all the time when I lived in New Jersey. It's like I was handicapped. Therefore, not until the sixth month did I flee that silent, small town and come to exciting, big New York.

That morning the train took me to a place called Long Island City in ₅ Queens. I was in a terrific suit that made me feel more confident. Appropriate dressing always impresses an interviewer and surprises oneself. When I graduated from high school in Hong Kong, I worked in different companies as a receptionist and a secretary. Through yesterday's telephone interview, I knew that this computer accessories wholesale company urgently needed a receptionist who could communicate in both Chinese and English. I was quite sure that the woman was satisfied with my working experience. Moreover, I needed a job desperately, so I figured that if she offered me the job and it was not far below my expectations, I probably would accept it.

Mary was in an old-fashioned scarlet dress that matched the color of ₆ her lipstick. Her hair was yellowish, short, and over-permed. The thing that impressed me the most was her eyes. They were small and sharp. She outlined her eyes with black and thick eyeliner that made them look very fearsome.

"This company was founded by me and my son, Tom. It has around ₇ ten employees, and all of them are Chinese. We have technicians and warehouse workers who work downstairs and salespeople who work on this floor." Mary spoke slowly and showed me a chair to sit in. The windows were all closed with window shades pulled down. Her desk was covered with thick dust. She pulled up the window shades and then wiped the office furniture and equipment. The environment of the office was not so pleasant because there was a construction site nearby.

Our interview lasted for about an hour, and it led to the result that ₈ Mary hired me as her personal assistant and receptionist. She told me that clerical work for new Chinese immigrants was rare and persuaded me to start working right after the interview. If I had not been desperately in need of a job, I wouldn't have accepted the offer because it didn't sound so reasonable. My hourly wage was $4.50. That was the minimum rate set by the city government. Mary told me that I was so lucky since I was a high school graduate, I was getting the same rate as a person with a Ph.D. Besides some public holidays, the company would provide not one fringe benefit, even to the full-time employees.

The next morning I met Mary at the entrance of the building. She 9 was standing up on the stairs, opening the door. It was not difficult to see that there were some big holes in her stockings. She had her badly fitting white rabbit fur on. Inside the building, she spotted my double-layer white skirt. Unexpectedly, she stepped forward and grasped my skirt. "Cute skirt!" she said. I was surprised and couldn't say anything for a second. It was so embarrassing that she walked away quickly.

The following months I spent most of the office hours doing clean- 10 ing, reorganizing invoices and files, preparing invoices, and answering calls. Mary supervised every single thing I did. She always stood next to me and looked over my shoulder to check what I was doing. There was an unspeakable pressure surrounding me that made me feel suffocated. It seemed that a pair of eyes was spying everywhere. It became not unusual that every day when it was just about time to leave, salespersons would hand me piles of new orders that needed to be delivered on the same day. So I always stayed late to prepare invoices. However, those warehouse workers stayed even later than I because they had to pack those new orders. We all worked so hard without any reward, not even a penny for overtime work. It was as if I should have known it even though it had never been mentioned in my interview.

I couldn't stand the way Tom and Mary yelled and argued in another 11 Chinese dialect that I don't understand. There was scarcely a day without a fight between them. I didn't like the way Mary treated any of us. I talked it over with John, who had worked there for a while.

"John, do you know that I thought you were a janitor when I first saw 12 you?" I laughed. "Now you are no better off than I am!" he said in his hoarse voice. We took the same train every day, and then we became very good friends. John was a salesman in our company, and I was surprised when he told me that he had graduated with a computer programming major. "So what are you here for? I don't think you like to work with this pushy Mary, do you?" I asked. "What for? I had sent out almost a hundred letters before I got this job. Life is hard, Ivy." "How about the other co-workers?" "They are all illegal workers here, don't you understand?" Then we were silent.

Now came the time when my probation was going to be over. I 13 realized that it would be a tragedy if I continued to work like a slave. So that morning I stood outside Mary's room. I breathed in deeply and knocked at the door. Then I left the "queen of Queens" who ruled over her people and kingdom, and I was going to celebrate a joyful Christmas.

Yim-Chi Lee, Hong Kong

After reading Lee's essay, think about the following questions, and discuss them with your class.

1. What specific details in this essay make this story personal and real?
2. How does Lee connect paragraphs 1 and 2? Which event happened first? How do you know?
3. How did Lee feel about Mary? What words and phrases tell you this?
4. Where in the essay does Lee use the present tense? Why?
5. Would you have quit the job? Explain your reason by referring to Lee's essay.

Write five questions that you will ask a classmate to help you revise your essay. You may want to adapt some of the questions listed here or look at the revision questions in another part of this book.

Show your classmate your essay, and discuss it using the questions you have written. Once you have decided on the changes you will make to improve your essay, revise it and share it with the same classmate.

Editing Strategies

Mechanics

Finding and Correcting Fragments

Sentence fragments (incomplete sentences) sometimes pose a big problem for writers. During editing, it may be hard to find and correct these errors. In the following paragraph, there are several fragments. Read the paragraph, and underline the fragments.

In each of our lives. There are certain important passages or steps. Such as graduating from high school, graduating from college, getting a job, and getting married. People mature. When it is the right time for them. They cannot just follow their friends. Because it is not right for them. Growing into adulthood. Is not an easy process.

The paragraph contains six fragments. If you missed any of them, study the information presented next.

A complete sentence must have a subject and a verb and express a complete thought. We will examine several sentences to determine how we can know when a sentence is complete and how we can repair a problem sentence. The following table can serve as a guide. If an entry has a checkmark in each column, it is a complete sentence. If it is missing a checkmark in any column, it is a fragment.

Sentences versus Fragments

	Subject	Verb	Complete Thought	
The baby. (This is a fragment. It has a subject but no verb, and it does not express a complete thought. The baby what?)	√			Fragment
The baby laughed. (This is a complete sentence.)	√	√	√	Sentence
Jumped. (This is a fragment. It has a verb but no subject, and it does not express a complete thought. Who or what jumped?)		√		Fragment
The horse jumped. (This is a complete sentence.)	√	√	√	Sentence
When the horse jumped. (This is a fragment. It has a subject and a verb, but it does not express a complete thought. What happened when the horse jumped?)	√	√		Fragment
When the horse jumped, the baby laughed. (This is a complete sentence.)	√	√	√	Sentence
Driving a car. (This is a fragment. It does not have a subject, it has only part of a verb, and it does not express a complete thought.)				Fragment
The teenager was driving a car. (This is a complete sentence.)	√	√	√	Sentence
To travel to Minneapolis. (This is a fragment. It does not have a subject, it does not have a complete conjugated verb, and it does not express a complete thought.)				Fragment
I want to travel to Minneapolis. (This is a complete sentence.)	√	√	√	Sentence
If I want to travel to Minneapolis.	√	√		Fragment

(continued)

	Subject	Verb	Complete Thought	
(This is not a complete sentence because it does not express a complete thought. What do I do if I want to travel to Minneapolis?)				
If I want to travel to Minneapolis, I will have to take a plane. (This is a complete sentence.)	√	√	√	Sentence
Such as chairs, tables, and sofas. (This is a fragment. It does not have a subject or a verb, and it does not express a complete thought.)				Fragment
A furniture store has many things, such as chairs, tables, and sofas. (This is a complete sentence.)	√	√	√	Sentence

□   □   □

EXERCISE   Using the criteria of subject, verb, and complete thought, decide whether each of the following is a complete sentence or a fragment. Then correct each fragment by making it into a complete sentence.

1. When I finish school.
2. I will look for a job.
3. Got married and moved to Wyoming.
4. Because he wanted to try engineering.
5. Cooking in the kitchen.
6. He cried.
7. Such as going to the movies, dancing at clubs, giving parties, and eating out with friends.

Editing Practice

Editing Other People's Writing

The following paragraph is a first draft that contains many errors. Find and correct the mistakes. Answers are on page 358.

According to Robbins, there are many factors involved in job satisfaction. People have to feel their jobs are meaningful and interesting it has to offer the workers a mental challenge. Even though there is individual differences in what people think is important, most people agree that their jobs should offer some challenge. Pay has greater importance for individuals which cannot gain other satisfactions from their jobs. Jobs who offer external recognition, good pay, and a mental challenge are sought by most people, each person want a feeling of fulfillment.

Editing Your Own Writing

Reread an essay that you wrote for this chapter, asking yourself the following questions:

1. Did I format my paper correctly?
2. Did I start new paragraphs when necessary?
3. Did I use final sentence punctuation and apostrophes correctly?
4. Did I use the past tenses correctly?
5. Did I use the present tenses correctly? Do my subjects and verbs agree?
6. Did I use quotation marks correctly?
7. Did I use pronouns correctly? Do the pronouns agree with their antecedents?
8. Did I form plurals correctly?
9. Did I use *the* correctly?
10. Did I use capital letters where they were needed?
11. Did I use commas correctly?
12. Did I use modals correctly?
13. Did I use comparatives correctly?
14. Are all the sentences complete, with no run-ons or fragments?
15. Did I use connecting words appropriately?

When you rewrite your essay, make any changes that will improve your writing.

Grammar Strategies

Relative Clauses

Relative clauses describe nouns; that is why they are also referred to as adjective clauses. They begin with relative pronouns such as *who, which, that, whose, whom, when, where,* and *why.*

People *who* work in repetitive jobs often become bored.
I hated my last job, *which* was very repetitive.
Jobs *that* bore people can cause accidents.
People *whose* jobs bore them often quit.
The people *whom* I interviewed were hired right away.

When is used to mean "at which time":

My boss still reminds me of the day *when* I arrived late for my interview.

Where is used to mean "at which place":

In the 1990s, computers and fax machines have enabled more people to work *where* they live.

Why means "for which":

Robbins suggested many reasons why people prefer to work at particular types of jobs.

Relative clauses can modify the subject of the main clause.

The house, which I bought last year, is beautiful.
The house that I bought is beautiful.

They can also modify the object of the main clause.

I took a course, which I liked very much.
I took a course that I liked very much.

The relative pronoun *whose* is the possessive form of *who* and can be used to introduce a relative clause.

The author *whose* books I admire gave me her autograph.

The relative pronoun *whom* is used in formal written English when the relative pronoun takes the place of a human object.

The person whom I met at the party was a student at this school.

Relative clauses may be *restrictive* or *nonrestrictive*. A restrictive clause is necessary for the meaning of the sentence. If you remove the clause, the sentence does not make sense or is false. For example, "Jobs that are repetitive bore people." If you remove "that are repetitive," the sentence reads "Jobs bore people," which is clearly untrue. Therefore, "that are repetitive" is a restrictive clause, a clause that is needed to make the sentence meaningful.

Restrictive clauses are never set off with commas and ordinarily use *that* to introduce the clause.

Nonrestrictive clauses provide additional information that is not necessary for the meaning of the sentence. If they were removed, the sentence would still make sense or be true.

> Unemployment, which is a worldwide problem, is decreasing in the United States.

"Which is a worldwide problem" adds information, but it is not necessary to understand the sentence "Unemployment is decreasing in the United States."

Nonrestrictive clauses *must* be set off by commas and *must* be introduced by *which*.

☐ ☐ ☐

EXERCISES

1. Simple sentences can be combined with the relative pronouns just described. Fill in the blanks in the following sentences. The first one is done for you. There may be more than one correct answer.

   a. Helene preferred a certain type of job.
      The job allowed her to be creative and intelligent.

      Helene preferred a job that allowed her to be creative and intelligent.

   b. Helene sent out many letters to big companies.
      The big companies had room for advancement.

      _____

      _____

   c. She received one reply to her letters.
      Her letters told about her background and requested an employment interview.

      _____

      _____

    d. The letter was sent to her home.
       The letter told her the time and place of the interview.

_____

_____

    e. Helene discussed her interview with a friend.
       The friend worked in the same company.

_____

_____

    f. The office building occupied a whole city block.
       The building was 100 stories high.

_____

_____

2. Finish the story about Helene. What was her experience at the interview? What was the job? Did she get the job?
3. Complete the following sentences with a relative clause.

    a. A good education is an education _____ .

    b. A good student is one _____ .

    c. A good career is one _____ .

    d. A computer is a machine _____ .

    e. A modem is a device _____ .

    f. A serious political problem is one _____ .

    g. A respectable politician is one _____ .

    h. A decent boss is one _____ .

    i. A fair income tax is one _____ .

    j. Violence is a problem _____ .

4. Reread one of the selections in the book that you have enjoyed. Notice the way relative clauses are used in the selection. Write down any relative clauses that confuse you. Discuss them with your teacher or a classmate.

□   □   □

CHECKING YOUR OWN WORK

1. Read through each essay you wrote for this chapter. Look at the way you used relative clauses. (It may be helpful to underline them lightly.) Did you use them appropriately and correctly? If you are not sure, check the explanation of uses of relative clauses in the previous section.
2. Repeat check 1 with other writing that you have done recently.
3. As an added check, work with a classmate to make sure that you have used relative clauses correctly in your writing.

Getting a Job

PREREADING ACTIVITIES

1. In a group, discuss the steps one should take to find a job.
2. Discuss your experiences on job interviews.
3. As a group, discuss and write the advice you would give to someone who has never gone on a job interview.

VOCABULARY DEVELOPMENT

Each of the following items contains a context clue that will help you understand the idiomatic expression indicated in italics. Underline the context clue that defines the idiom. The first one has been done for you.

1. The girl's family thinks she has *to have pull* before her letter of application will be considered. They think she has to have the help of someone who is important to get a job.

2. At the time Han Suyin writes of, no *ready-made clothes* existed. People could not just walk into a department store and buy clothes off the racks. All clothes were made by hand, usually at home.

3. The girl's father hopes that she will *make a good impression on* her future boss. He wants the comptroller to think good things about her when he meets her.

4. The secretary promises the girl that she will like Mr. Harned once she *gets used to* him. She has to grow accustomed to the kind of person he is.

Now answer the following questions.

1. Have you ever needed to have pull to do something?
2. Have you ever worn homemade clothes, or have your clothes always been ready-made?
3. What about a person is likely to make a good impression on you?
4. How long did it take you to get used to speaking English?

A Mortal Flower

Han Suyin

Han Suyin was born and raised in Beijing (at the time known as Peking). She is a pediatric physician and the author of many novels, including A Many Splendored Thing, *which was made into a movie.* A Mortal Flower *is the second of five volumes of history, biography, and autobiography, interweaving Chinese history of the past century with the experiences of the author and her family, both in and out of China. This excerpt describes the author's experience of looking for her first job.*

T he day after meeting Hilda I wrote a letter to the Rockefeller 1
Foundation, applying for a job.

Neither Father nor Mother thought I would get in. "You have to have 2
pull. It's an American thing, Rockefeller Foundation. You must have
pull."

Mother said: "That's where they do all those experiments on dogs and 3
people. All the Big Shots° of the Nanking government also came here to
have medical treatment, and sometimes took away a nurse to become 'a
new wife.' "

It made sense to me, typing in a hospital; I would learn about medi- 4
cine, since I wanted to study medicine. And as there was no money at
home for me to study, I would earn money, and prepare myself to enter
medical school. I had already discovered that a convent-school education was not at all adequate, and that it would take me at least three
more years of hard study before being able to enter any college at all.
Science, mathematics, Chinese literature and the classics . . . with the
poor schooling given to me, it would take me years to get ready for a university.

"I will do it." But clenched teeth, decision tearing my bowels,° were 5
not enough; there was no money, no money, my mother said it, said it
until I felt as if every morsel of food I ate was wrenched off my father's
body.

"No one is going to feed you doing nothing at home." Of course, one 6
who does not work must not eat unless one can get married, which is
called: "being settled at last." But with my looks I would never get married; I was too thin, too sharp, too ugly. Mother said it, Elder Brother
had said it. Everyone agreed that I should work, because marriage would
be difficult for me.

Within a week a reply came. The morning postman brought it, and I 7
choked over my milk and coffee. "I'm to go for an interview. At the
Peking Union Medical College. To the Comptroller's° office."

Father and Mother were pleased. Mother put the coffee pot down 8
and took the letter. "What good paper, so thick." But how could we dis-

°important people

°intestines

°chief accountant's

°counted, calculated

guise the fact that I was not [even] fifteen years old? I had claimed to be sixteen in the letter. In fact, said Papa, it was not a lie since Chinese are a year old when born, and if one added the New Year as an extra year, as do the Cantonese and the Hakkas, who became two years old when they reach their first New Year (so that a baby born on December 31st would be reckoned° two years old on the following January 2nd), I could claim to being sixteen.

"You look sixteen," said Mama; "all you have to do is to stop hopping   9
and picking your pimples. And lengthen your skirt."

°ruffles

°sheer fabric

What dress should I wear? I had two school uniforms, a green dress,   10
a brown dress, and one dress with three rows of frills° for Sunday, too dressy for an interview. I had no shoes except flat-heeled school shoes, and tennis shoes. There was no time to make a dress and in those years no ready-made clothes existed. Mother lengthened the green dress, and added her voile° scarf. I squeezed two pimples on my forehead, then went to the East market and bought some face powder, Butterfly brand, pink, made in Shanghai by a Japanese firm.

The next morning, straw-hatted, with powder on my nose, I went with   11
my father to the gates of the hospital.

"It's not this gate, this is for the sick. It's the other gate, round the cor-   12
ner," said the porter.

°complicated
°shinily painted
°woven floor covering

The Yu Wang Fu Palace occupied a whole city block. We walked along   13
its high grey outer wall, hearing the dogs scream in the kennels, and came to its other gate, which was the Administration building gate. It had two large stone lions, one male, one female. We crossed the marble courtyard, walked up the steps with their carved dragons coiling in the middle, into an entrance hall, with painted beams and intricate° painted ceiling, red lacquered° pillars, huge lamps. There was cork matting° on the stone floor.

"I'll leave you," said Papa. "Try to make a good impression." And he   14
was gone.

I found the Comptroller's office easily; there was a messenger in the   15
hall directing visitors. An open door, a room, two typewriters clattering and two women making them clatter.

I stood at the door and one of the women came to me. She had the   16
new style of hair, all upstanding curls, which I admired, a dress with a print round the hem; she was very pregnant, so that her belly seemed to be coming at me first. She smiled. "Hello, what can I do for you?"

"I have an interview."   17

She took the letter from my hand. "Glad you could come. Now,   18
just sit you down. No, sit down there. I'll tell Mr. Harned you've come."

The office had two other doors besides the one to the corridor, on   19

one was "Comptroller." That was the one she went through and returned from.

"Mr. Harned will see you now."   20

Mr. Harned was very tall, thin, [with] a small bald head, a long chin,   21
enormous glasses. I immediately began to quiver with fright. His head
was like a temple on top of a mountain, like the white pagoda° on the
hill in the North Sea Park. I could not hear a word of what he said. A paper and a pencil were in my hand, however, and Mr. Harned was dictat-
ing to me, giving me a speed test in shorthand.

°sacred temple

I went out of his office and the pregnant secretary sat me in front of   22
her own typewriter. I turned a stricken face to her, "I couldn't hear. I
couldn't hear what he said. . . ."

"Wait, I'll tell him." She bustled off. At the other desk was a blonde,   23
thin girl, who had thrown one look at me and then gone back to clattering. The pregnant one reappeared, a pink sheet in hand: "Now just
copy this on the typewriter, best you can."

I hit the keys, swiftly; the typewriter was the same make as mine, a   24
Royal.

"My, you are fast. I'll tell Mr. Harned."   25

°kindly, gentle
°large glasses that make
the eyes bulge

And Mr. Harned came out, benign° behind those enormous goggle   26
glasses.° "Well, Miss Chou, we've decided to take you on as a typist, at
thirty-five dollars a month. To start Monday. Is that all right?"

I nodded, unable to speak. Had he said ten dollars I would have ac-   27
cepted.

The kind secretary said: "Now take your time, and wipe your face.   28
How old are you, by the way?"

"Sixteen, nearly."   29

"Is that all? Why my eldest is bigger than you, and she isn't through   30
school yet. I told Mr. Harnard you were shy and upset, and that's why
you couldn't take dictation. He's all right, just takes getting used to,
that's all."

"I couldn't understand his English."   31

"Oh, you'll get used to it. Now, I won't be around on Monday, I'm go-   32
ing to have a baby. It's your letter that got them interested in you, you
wrote such good English, better than all the other letters we've had. Mr.
Harned will give you a try." She whispered, "I put in a good word for
you."

"Thanks, thanks a lot. . . . I need the money, I . . ."   33

"Yes, dear, we know." Obviously she wanted her typewriter back, and   34
her chair. I was still sitting on it. "Well, toodle-oo° for now; hope you enjoy yourself in this job. I've been here six months and I've enjoyed every
minute. Don't let Mr. Harned worry you; he's really great, once you get
used to him."

°good-bye

I had a job, had a job, had a job.   35

Reading and Thinking Strategies

Discussion Activities

Analysis and Conclusions

1. What happens during the interview with Mr. Harned?
2. Why isn't the girl's family more helpful and supportive? Is there anything in the story that makes you believe they care for her despite their behavior?
3. Do you think the young girl has confidence in herself when she goes for the interview? Support your point of view with evidence from the story.
4. Why does Miss Chou get the job?

Writing and Point of View

1. Why do you think Han Suyin titled her story "A Mortal Flower"? How does the title relate to the story?
2. Using evidence from "A Mortal Flower," show how Han Suyin made you aware of how she felt during the job interview. What descriptive words did she use?
3. "A Mortal Flower" is excerpted from an autobiography, as is "Age and Youth" by Pablo Casals in Chapter Nine. What is similar about these two pieces of writing? What is different about the two styles? Which did you prefer? Why?

Personal Response and Evaluation

1. If you were going on a job interview, what would you do that was similar to what the girl in this story did? What would you do that was different? Why?
2. What advantages are there for a young person to get a job while in school? What problems could develop? What is your advice to a young person thinking about getting a job while still in school?
3. What should you do on an interview so that you make a good impression? What shouldn't you do?
4. What steps should a person take to find a job?

Role Playing

In a small group, write the dialogue of an interview. It can be a job interview, a school interview, an interview with a landlord, or an interview with a loan official. Two people should be talking. Read the dialogue aloud in your group to make sure that it sounds natural. Each group should act out its dialogue in front of the class.

Journal Writing

Han Suyin's story is about success. A young girl whom many people had regarded as a failure goes off on her own to a strange place, meets a kind and supportive person, and has a successful experience: she gets a job. In your journal, write about your experience with success. Have you ever had an experience like this nervous young girl's in which you were afraid of failure but ultimately succeeded? If you have had this kind of experience, write about it.

The following quotation is taken from an article in *Self* magazine titled "Five Ways to Cash In on Your Mistakes":

Failure intimidates most people, but to the successful it is a challenge to try again. Look behind most successes and you'll find a solid foundation of failures they have learned from. Success is not something we are born to—we achieve it.

Think about this quote. What is failure? Can we learn from it? Has a failure ever led to a success in your life? For this journal entry, think about failure and success. What is the relationship between the two?

Writing Strategies

Essay Strategies

Résumé Writing

Write your résumé as though you were preparing to go for a job interview. What should employers know about you that will make them want to hire you? What special talents do you have? What education do you have? What job experience have you had? Your résumé may take the following form, or your teacher may suggest another style to you.

Name

Address

City, ST 00000

Telephone Number

Date of Birth

(This is optional.)

Educational Background

(List the schools you have attended, in reverse chronological order, the most recent one first. If you majored in something special or have any unique educational experience, mention it here.)

Work Experience

(List the jobs you have had, in reverse chronological order, the most recent one first. You may want to explain the duties of your jobs if you think it will help you get the job you are applying for.)

Special Abilities

(List the languages you speak and any other unique abilities you have that may help you get the job.)

References

(List the names and addresses of two or three people who know you well enough to recommend you for a job. You should contact these people before using their names. A former employer and a teacher would be good choices.)

Type or print your résumé on a typewriter or computer . If you use a typewriter, use 8½-by-11-inch white or off-white paper. Make sure that there are no typing or spelling errors. Your original should be neat and clean; make photocopies, keeping your original for future reference.

If you use a computer, be sure to save your résumé on the diskette. Use the spell-check function of your word processing program to make sure that all words are spelled correctly. You can be creative with your choice of fonts (typeface and size of letters) and formats (margins, spacing, use of bold and underlining), but remember to be consistent. See the sample résumé on page 263.

Transitional Words

The following paragraphs, which describe how to prepare yourself for a job interview, contain many transitional words. There are transitions that indicate importance or emphasis as well as transitions that indicate time. Underline all the transitional words in the paragraphs.

The first thing you have to do to prepare for a job interview is to write your résumé. Most of all, the résumé should emphasize all the related experience you have had. The résumé should be clear and should be written with an awareness that the person reading it will probably be

Résumé

Carmen Perozo
116 Broadway, Apt. 4B
Madison, NJ 07940
(201) 377-7802
Date of birth: 10/15/75

EDUCATIONAL BACKGROUND

September 1993–present
New Jersey State College
Major undecided; probably accounting or business
Grade point average: 3.2

April–July 1992
Riverside Learning Center, New York, New York—
studied English as a Second Language

1988–1992
San Sebastian High School, Bogotá, Colombia
Average: B+

WORK EXPERIENCE

August 1993–October 1995
Part-time bookkeeper and salesclerk,
Winston Gift Shop, Madison, New Jersey

June 1992–August 1993
Waitress, Three Brothers Restaurant,
Madison, New Jersey

SPECIAL ABILITIES

I speak fluent Spanish and French. I have studied English for seven years (four in Colombia and three in the United States). I have worked on both PCs and Macs and am familiar with WordPerfect 6.0 and Microsoft Word for Windows. I have also had some experience working with databases.

REFERENCES

Kay Winston, owner
Winston Gift Shop
331 Main Street
Madison, NJ 07940

Professor James Manley
Accounting Department
New Jersey State College
Madison, NJ 07940

reading many other résumés. The best thing you can do is to make it obvious why you can do the job better than anybody else. Your résumé should be neatly printed or typed.

Once you have organized your résumé, check your closet. Pay special attention to what you will wear for the interview. You don't want to be dressed up as if you were going to a party, but you also don't want to be underdressed. Consider getting your hair trimmed before the interview. Remember that neatness counts. You should be neat in your appearance as well as in your résumé.

Finally, you must keep in mind that employers do not like people to smoke or chew gum during an interview. The basic reason for this may be that you appear too casual. Remember, you are not visiting a friend; you are trying to get a job. If you follow all of the advice given here, you have a better chance of getting the job you desire.

If you had any difficulty, refer to the following lists. Transitional words add flow to your writing.

Time transitions: *first, next, then, before, after, during, now, while, finally*
Emphasis transitions: *keep in mind, remember, most of all, the most important, the best thing, the basic reason, the chief reason, the chief factor, special attention should be paid to*

□   □   □

EXERCISE   Rewrite the transitional words paragraphs, changing from the second person (*you*) to the third person (*he* or *she*). The first sentence should read "The first thing a person has to do to prepare for a job interview is to write a résumé" (or "his résumé" or "her résumé").

Essay Form

Writing a Business or Formal Letter

People write business letters to request information, to complain about a product they have bought, to explain why they haven't paid a bill on time. They write to request job interviews, to introduce their résumés. Business letters generally consist of an introduction, a body, and a conclusion. Formal essays consist of these same parts. The introduction to a business letter is usually found in the first paragraph. It is what makes the reader want to read more. It introduces the main idea that the letter will be about. The body of the letter offers specific details or examples to support the main idea that has been presented in the introduction. The letter ends with the conclusion, in which the ideas from the rest of the letter are summarized or restated.

The form of a business letter is important. At the upper right-hand side of the page goes the writer's full address. Under the address is the date when the letter is being written. One line below this, at the left-hand side of the page, is the address to which the letter is being sent. The writer skips a line and types "Dear _____:" and skips another line, indents five spaces, and begins the introductory paragraph. The entire letter is typed, indenting for each new paragraph. After the conclusion, the writer skips a line and types "Sincerely," or "Yours truly," aligned with the address and date at the right-hand side of the page, skips five lines, and types his or her name. The writer then signs the letter, folds it into thirds, and places it in a long, rectangular envelope on which the address has been typed. The writer finally places a stamp on the envelope and mails it.

A sample letter appears on page 266.

□   □   □

EXERCISES

1. Look at the sample business letter, and reread the directions for writing a business letter. Then write the answers to the following questions on the blank lines.

   a. What are the parts of a business letter?

   _____

   b. What is the purpose of the introduction?

   _____

   c. What is contained in the body of the letter?

   _____

   d. What goes in the upper right-hand corner of the page?

   _____

   e. Where is the date found in a business letter?

   _____

   f. What is at the upper left-hand side of the page?

   _____

   g. What punctuation mark is used after the salutation?

   _____

   h. How do you conclude a business letter?

   _____

2. With a partner or in a small group, write a formal letter applying for a job, requesting information, or complaining about a product you have bought.

116 Broadway, Apt. 4B
Madison, NJ 07940
October 15, 1995

Mr. Henry Walsh, Personnel Manager
Caldicott Publishing Company
177 West Vernon Boulevard
Madison, NJ 07940

Dear Mr. Walsh:

I am interested in applying for a weekend job as a word processor in your company. I saw your advertisement in the *Madison Sunday Record* this past Sunday, and I feel that I am qualified for this job. I have studied computers for two years at New Jersey State College in Madison. I know how to use PCs and Macs and have worked with WordPerfect 6.0, which you mention in your ad. I also am familiar with Microsoft Word for Windows and have some experience with databases. I am very accurate and fast. I enclose my résumé, and I will be glad to send you reference letters if you so desire.

I hope that you will consider me for the job. I can be reached at the above address, at (201) 377-7802 in the evenings, or by e-mail at cperozol2@aol.com. I look forward to hearing from you. Thank you for considering me for this job.

Sincerely,

Carmen Perozo

Carmen Perozo

3. Write a business letter applying for a job and introducing your résumé to a prospective employer.

Suggestions for Writing

Before you begin to write, try making a brainstorming list, as described in the next section, "Getting Started," or try one of the prewriting techniques described throughout the book. You may also want to refer to your journal for ideas.

1. Describe a job interview that you have been on. Create a mood so that your reader can feel what your experience was like. Use descriptive words.

2. First impressions do not always reveal the total person. Have you ever had an experience in which a first impression of a person turned out to be wrong? Describe what happened and what you learned from the experience.

3. Write a letter of recommendation to Mr. Harned, telling him why he should hire Miss Chou.

4. Write a dialogue that takes place between the girl and her parents when she returns home to tell them that she has gotten the job. (You may want to act out your dialogue in front of the class with two other classmates.)

5. Looking for a job can be very difficult. Use this as your thesis; then give examples and experiences to support your point of view.

6. "Success is not something we are born to—we achieve it." Explain the steps that you think a person has to go through to achieve success. What does success mean to you?

7. Many people learn more from their failures than they do from their successes. Give examples from your own life or from your observations of others to support this point of view.

8. Imagine that you are an employer who is interviewing someone for a job. In a well-developed essay, describe what you would expect in an employee. What are the characteristics you value, and why are they important?

Getting Started

Making a Brainstorming List

Before you start to write, take out a blank sheet of paper, and at the top of your page, write in five words or less your main idea or thesis—

what you want to write about. As soon as you finish writing this, look at it again, and start to make a list of any words or ideas that come to your mind. Your list should not contain sentences or fully developed ideas. It should be fragmentary and loose, recording ideas that will lead to your future essay development. Write the list for at least five minutes. Then spend five more minutes examining the list. Star the words or ideas that seem to relate to your main idea. Cross out words or ideas that do not seem to be related. As you are doing this, other words or ideas may occur to you; put them on your list. Use this list when you get ready to start writing your essay or story.

Revising

> One great aim of revision is to cut out. In the exuberance of composition it is natural to throw in—as one does in speaking—a number of small words that add nothing to meaning but keep up the flow and rhythm of thought. In writing, not only does this surplusage not add to meaning, it subtracts from it. Read and revise, reread and revise, keeping reading and revising until your text seems adequate to your thought.
>
> JACQUES BARZUN

Jacques Barzun's advice may seem surprising after our emphasis on adding detail to your writing to make your descriptions come alive. However, there is a difference between rich, exciting language and repetitive or wordy writing. Look critically at what you have written. Every time you see the words *in my opinion,* cross them out. It is obvious that your writing expresses your opinion because you have written it. Every time you see the words *you know,* cross them out. If your reader knows, why bother to say it again? Every time you find yourself repeating something you have already said a few sentences before, cross it out. In place of those excess bits of writing, add some new and exciting ideas. Keep reading and revising until "your text seems adequate to your thought."

A Student Essay

This student is responding to writing suggestion 6. Read her essay; then discuss it using one of the revising exercises from the book that has been helpful for you.

SUCCESS

Success is achieved by people who work hard. Success is good grades, the attainment of educational degrees, and good jobs in the future.   1

The first definition of success is for people to get good grades in   2
school. For instance, my boyfriend is a very smart person who gets good

grades in all his classes. Even though his courses are hard for other students who might get 50's and 60's on their tests, my boyfriend gets 90's. Therefore, most of his friends think he is a very successful person.

A second definition of success is for people to accomplish their educational degrees. As an illustration, my older sister graduated from City College with a nursing degree. All of my family and friends think she is very successful for this. They don't care whether she got the highest grades in her courses; they just care about her degree. 3

Another definition is that most of us think that people who have good jobs are also successful. For example, there is a girl in my church who doesn't know much English but has a very good job anyway. She works at New York Hospital as a medical lab technician. Once she told me that she was very satisfied with her job because she heard that all her friends admire what she does. It is true that most of our friends in church think she is an achiever. Her mother's friends all admire her. They want their children to be like her. 4

My observations of people tell me what success means. It means the kinds of achievements that any people who work hard can attain. 5

Jenny Wang, People's Republic of China

Editing Strategies

Mechanics

Using Semicolons

Semicolons are used for the following purposes:

1. To connect two complete (usually short) sentences with closely related ideas:

   Miss Chou mailed her letter; she got a quick response.

2. Before sentence connectors (see pages 224–25 for a list) used between sentences to create relationships:

   She was excited about getting the job; therefore, she responded immediately.

3. To separate a series of expressions that already contain commas:

   She tried on a long, green dress; a short, brown dress; and a loose, green plaid dress.

Using Colons

Colons are used in the following instances:

1. After a complete sentence that is followed by a list:

   Students have many problems when they first start college: registration, tuition costs, housing, and book prices.

2. After a complete sentence followed by a word, phrase, or sentence that explains the preceding sentence:

   One reason why so many marriages fall apart is clear: money.

3. After the salutation in a business letter

   Dear Sirs:
   Dear Mrs. Peabody:

4. To introduce a quotation:

   Han Suyin writes: "Neither Father nor Mother thought I would get in."

5. To separate minutes from hours in expressions of clock time:

   12:30 P.M.   9:45 A.M.

6. To separate a title from a subtitle:

   A Writer's Workbook: An Interactive Writing Text

Using Numbers in Your Writing

1. Numbers from one to nine or ten are usually written out as words. Higher numbers are usually written in numerals. However, if you use numbers very infrequently in your writing, you may choose to write out the numbers when you can do so in two or three words.

   five   seven   17   178   5,891   four thousand

2. When you use abbreviations in measurements, use numerals.

   5′6″   2 tsp.   88°F   99%   3 in.

3. When numbers begin a sentence, write them out.

One hundred students waited in line to get the new book.

4. Numbers that are being compared or contrasted should be kept in the same style. Look at the following excerpt from the text to see when Han Suyin wrote out the numbers and when she used numerals.

> But how could we disguise the fact that I was not [even] *fifteen* years old? I had claimed to be *sixteen* in the letter. In fact, said Papa, it was not a lie since Chinese are a year old when born, and if one added the New Year as an extra year, as do the Cantonese and the Hakkas, who became *two* years old when they reach their first New Year (so that a baby born on December *31st* would be reckoned *two* years old on the following January *2nd*), I could claim to being *sixteen*.

What patterns do you find in Han Suyin's use of numbers in this paragraph?

5. Reread the Naisbitt and Aburdene selection in Chapter Ten. Notice when they wrote out the numbers and when they used figures.

Editing Practice

Editing Other People's Writing

The following paragraph is an unedited draft that contains many errors. Find as many as you can, and correct them. Answers are on page 359.

Many students find it difficult to looks for a job the first time. They are not sure where to find listings of jobs for students, they do not know whether to say that they are students right away. They do not how much hours they should work a week. All this problems makes the interview difficult too, for one thing, the interviewee is never sure what to bring at the interview. Some people brings too much so when the interviewer asks for a paper it is hard finding. I suggest that you bring only the following documents; your résumé, your birth certificate, your passport, and your high school diploma. If you have a green card bring that too. In addition: I try to impress an interviewer by dressing very neatly and never chewing gum or candy. I always look directly into an interviewer's eyes. I want interviewer to believe that I can be trusted. If I remember to follow mine own advice. I believe I will get a job soon.

Extra Practice

articles

All the articles (*the*, *a*, and *an*) have been omitted from the following paragraph. Rewrite the paragraph, adding articles where necessary.

Trying to get job at Rockefeller Foundation is difficult for girl who does not have pull. Finally, morning postman brings letter. She is to go for interview at Peking Medical College, to Comptroller's office. She prepares her clothes and goes to East market to buy face powder to cover her pimples. Next morning, she goes with her father to Yu Wang Fu Palace to Administration Building. They cross marble courtyard and go into entrance hall. Her father leaves. She finds office and meets her future employer, Mr. Harned. His bald head reminds her of white pagoda on hill in North Sea Park. She takes required typing test and gets job.

Check your answers on page 359.

Editing Your Own Writing

Reread an essay that you wrote for this chapter, asking yourself the following questions:

1. Did I format my paper correctly?
2. Did I start new paragraphs when necessary?
3. Did I use final sentence punctuation and apostrophes correctly?
4. Did I use the past tenses correctly?
5. Did I use the present tenses correctly? Do my subjects and verbs agree?
6. Did I use quotation marks correctly?
7. Did I use pronouns correctly? Do the pronouns agree with their antecedents?
8. Did I form plurals correctly?
9. Did I use *the* correctly?
10. Did I use capital letters where they are needed?
11. Did I use commas correctly?
12. Did I use other punctuation marks correctly?

13. Did I use modals correctly?
14. Did I use comparatives correctly?
15. Are all the sentences complete, with no run-ons or fragments?
16. Did I use connecting words appropriately?

When you rewrite your essay, make any changes that will improve your writing.

Grammar Strategies

Use of Participle Forms

A *participle* is a verb form that can function as an adjective or as a verb. The present participle ends in *-ing;* the past participle ends in *-ed* or *-en.* (Past participles are listed in Appendix A.)

Participles as Adjectives

Participles can be used as adjectives. When the participle ends in *-ing,* the adjective describes or characterizes the thing or noun phrase it describes.

The movie was boring. (*Boring* tells about the movie.)
The play was frightening. (*Frightening* tells about the play.)

When the participle ends in *-ed,* the adjective describes a response or feeling.

I was bored by the class. (I did not feel interested in the class.)
My friend was frightened by the noise. (My friend felt scared when he heard the noise.)

A selection of verbs and their participles follows.

Base form of verb	*Present participle*	*Past participle*
amaze	amazing	amazed
amuse	amusing	amused
annoy	annoying	annoyed
bore	boring	bored
confuse	confusing	confused

depress	depressing	depressed
determine	determining	determined
disappoint	disappointing	disappointed
disgust	disgusting	disgusted
excite	exciting	excited
exhaust	exhausting	exhausted
fascinate	fascinating	fascinated
frighten	frightening	frightened
interest	interesting	interested
overwhelm	overwhelming	overwhelmed
please	pleasing	pleased
relieve	relieving	relieved
satisfy	satisfying	satisfied
surprise	surprising	surprised
thrill	thrilling	thrilled
worry	worrying	worried

□   □   □

EXERCISE   Decide which participle you need to complete each of the following sentences.

a. Miss Chou was _____ when she received a reply to her letter.
   (exciting/excited)

b. My father was _____ with me for coming home late.
   (annoying/annoyed)

c. The story had a _____ ending.
   (disappointing/disappointed)

d. After traveling all night, I was _____.
   (exhausting/exhausted)

e. That physics class was _____.
   (overwhelming/overwhelmed)

f. Violence on television is _____.
   (disgusting/disgusted)

g. The car accident was _____.
   (frightening/frightened)

h. They were _____ at the thought of graduating.
   (exciting/excited)

i. My brother was _____ because I used his cellular phone.
   (annoying/annoyed)

j. I was _____ with my grade.
   (satisfying/satisfied)

Participles as Verbals

Participles can also be used as verbals at the beginning of sentences.

Surprising people is a magician's job.

Determined, I marched into the registrar's office.

Hoping to make more money, she looked for another job. (The participle, *hoping,* and the subject, *she,* must refer to the same person or idea.)

Excited about graduating, he tried on his cap and gown in front of the mirror. (The participle, *excited,* and the subject, *he,* must refer to the same person or idea.)

Note that errors occur when the participle and the subject of the sentence are not the same.

INCORRECT: Hoping to avoid the red light, the car came to a quick stop. (This sentence says, illogically, that the *car* was hoping.)

CORRECT: Hoping to avoid the red light, the driver stepped on the brake and brought the car to a quick stop.

INCORRECT: Excited by graduation, a big party was planned. (This sentence says that the *party* was excited.)

CORRECT: Excited by graduation, the students planned a big party.

□   □   □

EXERCISES

1. Complete the following sentences.

   a. Disgusted by the violence on television, I _____

   _____.

   b. Realizing I had too much work to do, I _____

   _____.

   c. Bored by the book, I _____.

   d. Hearing the phone ring as I opened the door, I _____

   _____.

e. Annoyed by my friend's attitude, I ⸻⸻⸻ .

f. Amazed by the fast response, I ⸻⸻⸻ .

g. Feeling quite sick, I ⸻⸻⸻ .

h. Relieved to be home, I ⸻⸻⸻ .

i. Exhausted by the trip, I ⸻⸻⸻ .

j. Hoping to win the contest, I ⸻⸻⸻ .

2. In the following sentences, underline the participle. Then decide whether the participle is functioning as an adjective or a verbal, and explain how you made your choice.

a. Miss Chou was thrilled to get a job.

b. The thrilling story kept me up all night.

c. Thrilled to be alive, the survivor thanked everyone for helping him.

d. Enjoying her moment of success, she called all her friends and told them about it.

e. The confused witness could not remember anything about the thief.

f. The confusing story did not help the police very much.

g. Confused by the case, the lawyer consulted with a colleague.

h. The bored student fell asleep in class.

i. The boring teacher woke him up.

j. Bored by my job, I stared out the window.

3. Reread the Han Suyin story, looking for participles. Notice how they are used in the story.

4. Reread one of the selections in the book that you have enjoyed. Notice the way participles are used as adjectives and as verbals in the selection. Write down any participles that confuse you. Discuss them with your teacher or a classmate.

□   □   □

CHECKING YOUR OWN WORK

1. Read through each essay you wrote for this chapter. Look at the way you used participles as adjectives and as verbals. (It may be helpful to underline them lightly.) Did you use them appropriately and cor-

rectly? If you are not sure, check the explanation of uses of participles in the previous section.

2. Repeat check 1 with other writing that you have done recently.
3. As an added check, work with a classmate to make sure that you have used participles correctly in your writing.

Thinking about Roots

Chapter Thirteen: Returning Home

Chapter Fourteen: Focusing on Behavior

Chapter Fifteen: Responding to Change

Returning Home

PREREADING ACTIVITIES

1. This essay is about a person who came to the United States from Cuba at a young age. In a small group, discuss Cuba. Where is it? What is its history? Why did some people leave Cuba and move to other countries?
2. As a class, find out what Cuba is like today. Can all people from the United States visit Cuba? If so, how? If not, why not?
3. What do you think the title of the essay "Back, but Not Home" means? In a group, discuss what you consider to be home—the United States or the country in which you were born. Why? When does a country become "home"?

VOCABULARY DEVELOPMENT

A useful way to increase vocabulary is to learn new forms of words that you already know. In this way you more than triple the number of words that you can understand and use.

The underlined forms of the following words appear in "Back, but Not Home." They are all words that are commonly used in college-level material.

Adjective	*Adverb*	*Noun*	*Verb*
sympathetic	sympathetically	sympathy	sympathize
communicative	communicatively	communication	communicate
persistent	persistently	persistence	persist
hesitant	hesitantly	hesitation	hesitate
hesitating	(un)hesitatingly		

Fill in the blanks with the appropriate forms of the listed words. Think about each word's meaning and function as you decide which form of the word to use.

People learn new languages in order to _____ with others. _____ listeners are patient with new users of a language, who often _____ as they speak. _____ requires _____ and hard work.

Back, but Not Home

Maria L. Muñiz

Maria L. Muñiz was born in 1958. She and her family came to the United States in 1963. In 1978, she graduated from New York University. She has written and edited many articles and books. In this 1979 essay, Muñiz describes her feelings about returning to Cuba.

With all the talk about resuming diplomatic relations with Cuba, and with the increasing number of Cuban exiles returning to visit friends and relatives, I am constantly being asked, "Would you ever go back?" In turn, I have asked myself, "Is there any reason for me to go?" I have had to think long and hard before finding my answer. Yes.

I came to the United States with my parents when I was almost five years old. We left behind grandparents, aunts, uncles and several cousins. I grew up in a very middle-class neighborhood in Brooklyn. With one exception, all my friends were Americans. Outside of my family, I do not know many Cubans. I often feel awkward visiting relatives in Miami because it is such a different world. The way of life in Cuban Miami seems very strange to me and I am accused of being too "Americanized." Yet, although I am now an American citizen, whenever anyone has asked me my nationality, I have always and unhesitatingly replied "Cuban."

Outside American, inside Cuban.

I recently had a conversation with a man who generally sympathizes with the Castro regime. We talked of Cuban politics and although the discussion was very casual, I felt an old anger welling° inside. After 16 years of living an "American" life, I am still unable to view the revolution with detachment or objectivity.° I cannot interpret its results in social, political or economic terms. Too many memories stand in my way.

And as I listened to this man talk of the Cuban situation, I began to remember how as a little girl I would wake up crying because I had dreamed of my aunts and grandmothers and I missed them. I remembered my mother's trembling voice and the sad look on her face whenever she spoke to her mother over the phone. I thought of the many letters and photographs that somehow were always lost in transit. And as the conversation continued, I began to remember how difficult it often was to grow up Latina in an American world.

It meant going to kindergarten knowing little English. I'd been in this country only a few months and although I understood a good deal of

°filling up

°absence of personal feelings

what was said to me, I could not express myself very well. On the first day of school I remember one little girl's saying to the teacher: "But how can we play with her? She's so stupid she can't even talk!" I felt so helpless because inside I was crying, "Don't you know I can understand everything you're saying?" But I did not have words for my thoughts and my inability to communicate terrified me.

^oassigned

As I grew a little older, Latina meant being automatically relegated^o to 7 the slowest reading classes in school. By now my English was fluent, but the teachers would always assume I was somewhat illiterate or slow. I recall one teacher's amazement at discovering I could read and write just as well as her American pupils. Her incredulity^o astounded^o me. As a child, I began to realize that Latina would always mean proving I was as good as the others. As I grew older, it became a matter of pride to prove I was better than the others.

^odisbelief
^oamazed

As an adult I have come to terms with these memories and they 8 don't hurt as much. I don't look or sound very Cuban. I don't speak with an accent and my English is far better than my Spanish. I am beginning my career and look forward to the many possibilities ahead of me.

But a persistent little voice is constantly saying, "There's something 9 missing. It's not enough." And this is why when I am now asked, "Do you want to go back?" I say "yes" with conviction.

I do not say to Cubans, "It is time to lay aside the hurt and forgive and 10 forget." It is impossible to forget an event that has altered and scarred all our lives so profoundly. But I find I am beginning to care less and less about politics. And I am beginning to remember and care more about the child (and how many others like her) who left her grandma behind. I have to return to Cuba one day because I want to know that little girl better.

When I try to review my life during the past 16 years, I almost feel as 11 if I've walked into a theater right in the middle of a movie. And I'm afraid I won't fully understand or enjoy the rest of the movie unless I can see and understand the beginning. And for me, the beginning is Cuba. I don't want to go "home" again; the life and home we all left behind are long gone. My home is here and I am happy. But I need to talk to my family still in Cuba.

Like all immigrants, my family and I have had to build a new life from 12 almost nothing. It was often difficult, but I believe the struggle made us strong. Most of my memories are good ones.

But I want to preserve and renew my cultural heritage. I want to 13 keep "la Cubana" within me alive. I want to return because the journey back will also mean a journey within. Only then will I see the missing piece.

Reading and Thinking Strategies

Discussion Activities

Analysis and Conclusions

1. Why does the author feel awkward visiting her relatives in Miami? What difference does the author suggest between her life in Brooklyn and the lives of her family in Florida?

2. Why did the author find it difficult to grow up Latina in an American world?

3. How did she prove that her work was as good as or better than the work of the other students in her class? What is she doing now that shows that her English is excellent?

4. What is the missing piece to which Muñiz refers in the last sentence of the essay?

Writing and Point of View

1. What is this essay about? What is Muñiz trying to make you aware of? Does she make you feel what she has been through? If so, how does she do this? Are her examples good ones? Are there enough examples to convince you?

2. Reread paragraph 3. What is the effect of a one-sentence paragraph? What does the sentence mean?

3. Which piece of writing seems more personal, the article about Berenice Belizaire in Chapter One or Maria Muñiz's essay? Why? How do you decide when your writing should be more personal or more impersonal?

Personal Response and Evaluation

1. Compare Muñiz's experience with her teachers to your own experiences and those of your classmates. Then compare Muñiz's experiences to Berenice Belizaire's. What similarities do you find? What differences?

2. Many people experience disappointment when they return to a place they left when they were children. Places change, and so do people. What kind of experience do you think the author will have in Cuba? Have you ever returned to a place that you left years before? What was your experience?

3. Is it important to hold on to the customs and cultural patterns of your native country? Is it important to maintain your first language when you are living in a new country?

4. What does it mean to be too "Americanized"? Reread the Klein selection in Chapter One and the Namioka story in Chapter Six. Compare the various attitudes toward being Americanized.

Collaborative Story Writing

In a group of no more than five students, work together to write a story beginning with one of the following lines.

1. When Maria arrived in Cuba one sunny morning, the first thing she did was . . .
2. Maria talked to a friend who visited relatives that she hadn't seen in many years. Her friend said . . .
3. Maria receives a letter from a childhood friend who has just moved to the United States from Cuba. The letter begins . . .

After your group has agreed on which story to write, one student writes the first line of the story and then passes the paper to another student, who writes the next line. Pass the story around, each person adding a line, until you reach a satisfying ending. Then each group should share its story with the class.

If you are working on computers, students can take turns at the keyboard typing in their contributions to the story. This is especially enjoyable if your classroom's computers are networked together and all the students can follow the story as it develops on the screen.

Journal Writing

The theme of this chapter is going home, returning to a way of life that still lives in memories. The upheaval of confronting a new country, a new language, and a new way of life is probably one of the most emotionally charged experiences a person can have in life. By this time, you have made many adjustments to your new life; there is probably a part of you, however, that thinks of the past with sadness, joy, or a bit of both.

In this journal entry, you may want to think about home. A famous American writer, Thomas Wolfe, wrote a book titled *You Can't Go Home Again*. Do you agree with the title? Do you ever think about returning to your home country? Do you still have friends and family in your country? Where do you feel your real home is?

If you have difficulty writing about this, you might want to try the clustering technique (see pages 58–59), using *home* as the nucleus word.

Writing Strategies

Essay Strategies

Time Transitions

In the essay in this chapter, Maria Muñiz tells a story about 16 years of her life. The essay begins when Muñiz is almost 5 years old and arriving in the United States and continues until she is 21 years old and writing the essay. She makes transitions between various paragraphs using phrases that signify time. Time transitions are a good way to connect ideas and to help your readers follow the events you are describing. Here are some of the time indicators Muñiz uses:

I came to the United States when I was almost five years old. (paragraph 2; past tense)

I began to remember how as a little girl . . . (paragraph 5; past tense)

As a child, I began to realize . . . (paragraph 7; past tense)

As I grew older, it became a matter of pride . . . (paragraph 7; past tense)

As an adult I have come to terms . . . (paragraph 8; present perfect tense)

When I try to review my life during the past 16 years, I almost feel as if . . . (paragraph 11; present tense)

You can use time phrases like these to create your own paragraph, for example:

I came to the United States when I was almost 9 years old. I began to remember how as a little boy I had to try extra hard to do well in school. I was left back in the fourth grade because I was shy and my English was not good. As I grew older, I began to do better in school than a lot of the students who were born in this country. As an adult, I feel proud of my accomplishments. When I try to review my life, I realize that there were many difficult moments, but there were also many great times.

Use time phrases to create a paragraph about yourself or someone you know.

Details make stories rich. And as we have observed in Muñiz's writing, a sense of time, a chronology that we can follow, makes a story easier to understand.

In the Hemingway story we read in Chapter Three, we followed one day in the life of a family. The story began in the morning, continued into the afternoon, and ended later that day. That time framework made the story easy to follow. In the writing exercises for this chapter, keep in mind the elements that make a story work for you. You may want to go back to the stories you have written and revise them, keeping in mind detail and chronology.

□ □ □

EXERCISE   Read the following poem. Then read it again, thinking about the Muñiz essay.

THESE DAYS

whatever you have to say, leave
the roots on, let them
dangle

And the dirt
       just to make clear
       where they have come from.

CHARLES OLSON

1. Why do you think this poem has been included in this chapter? What is this poem about?
2. Poems are condensations of emotional feelings into a short, tight form. In a few words, they can say many things. Therefore, each word must be selected very carefully. The words resonate—like the sun, their meaning beams out in many directions. Poems are often symbolic. What might *roots* refer to other than roots of plants in the soil? What might *dirt* symbolize?
3. Do Charles Olson and Maria Muñiz have similar ideas? If so, what are these ideas?

Essay Form

Writing a Cause-and-Effect Essay

In writing, we sometimes try to make connections between experiences and their consequences. For instance, we might try to show that being forced to leave our homes as children, as Maria Muñiz was, has affected the way we see the world as adults. Usually, when writers try to establish these connections, they use particular words and phrases to focus the reader's attention on the ways that events are tied together in the writer's mind. Some of the words and phrases traditionally used for this purpose are *as a result, consequently, for this reason, due to, therefore, because, since,* and *the reason why*.

In addition, to establish a cause-and-effect relationship, writers may tell a story or describe an event. They develop this in chronological or time order to show how one event led to another. Review the time transition words in "Essay Strategies."

Keep in mind, however, that it is difficult to state with certainty that one event "caused" a specific response. Life is complicated, and there are almost always multiple reasons—immediate, obvious reasons and distant, underlying reasons—to explain why an event occurred.

Therefore, it is the ability of the writer to join together ideas, using stories, description, words, and phrases, that makes this type of essay effective or not.

Keep the following steps in mind when you write a cause-and-effect essay.

1. *Define* the cause. Put the event or occurrence in a historical context—tell what happened immediately before, and briefly outline the steps that led to the major event. Tell your readers why it is important for them to know about and understand this event. Which event does Muñiz describe in her essay? How does she set it in a historical context?

2. *Describe* in detail what followed the event or occurrence you define in step 1. Readers follow your reasoning through your words, so make them clear and direct. What specific descriptive details did the selection authors use? How do they add to the overall effectiveness of the essay?

3. *Analyze* the details you are explaining. Tell in what ways these details are direct responses to the cause you have defined in step 1. Explain the history and the future of your subject to your readers.

4. *Evaluate* why the cause led to the effect you describe. You may generalize about what this may mean to others or to the future. Does Muñiz convince you that she should visit Cuba and that her decision is important to you and the decisions you make in your life?

□   □   □

EXERCISE   As a class, write a cause-and-effect essay using the information from the Muñiz essay establishing the connection between Muñiz's childhood experiences and her feelings about returning to Cuba today.

Suggestions for Writing

Take some time to think about your ideas before you start to write. You may want to look at your journal for ideas, or you may want to try reminiscing, as described in the "Getting Started" section that follows.

Choose one of the following topics to write about.

1. "Outside American, inside Cuban." What does Muñiz mean by these words? Have you ever felt this way in relation to your country? Write a cause-and-effect essay in which you connect the experience of living in a new country or learning a new language with your feelings about yourself and your culture and language.

2. Write a cause-and-effect essay in which you explain how a political event has caused a change in your life. Establish the connection between the occurrence and the effect it has had on your life and your perceptions.

3. "Like most immigrants, my family and I have had to build a new life from almost nothing. It was often difficult, but I believe the struggle made us strong." Write a cause-and-effect essay on the relationship between struggle and personal strength. Use your experiences or those of someone you know or have heard about to support your ideas. You may want to interview someone in your class or your neighborhood.

4. In his acceptance speech for the 1992 German Publishers' Peace Prize, the Israeli writer Amos Oz stated:

> Here is my dilemma: what should a man of words do if he happens to live next door to injustice, to prejudice, and to violence? . . . What do you do when basic decency demands that you try to combat political evil, rather than just observe, describe, and decipher it?

Do individuals have a responsibility to be political? What effect can being political have on people's lives? Write an essay in which you connect between being political with the effect it can have on someone's life.

Getting Started

Reminiscing

In Maria Muñiz's essay, she wrote about her own past and the past of her family. In doing this, she reminisced about her family history. This helped make her writing more powerful and real to her readers.

As you prepare to write one of the essays proposed in "Suggestions for Writing," think about your past and your family history. Focus on the personal experiences or observations that relate to the question you will answer. Jot down a few words that will help you recall these events. Write down as many events or memories as you can recall in five to ten minutes. Then, before you write your essay, look through these reminiscences or memories and choose the ones that, developed more fully, will enrich your writing.

A Student Essay

ROOT AND BRANCH

"Ding . . . ding . . . ding." The phone made noises during our din- 1
nertime. I stood up quickly and ran to pick up the phone. "Hello. Who
is speaking?" I asked. I had swallowed down my food. "May I speak to
your mother?" said a soft lady's voice that I had heard a million times
before.

I called my mother. She picked up the phone and said some pleas- 2
antries to her first, and then I heard, "What! . . . Oh, OK . . . OK . . .
I would . . . thank you for telling me." She finished talking and said to
me, "After dinner, come to my room." I nodded, "Ah." "Pun! pun!" I
heard my heart beat very fast, and my hands were shaking a little.

It was seven years ago. When I was in junior high school, it was hard 3
for me to learn to read English. I memorized the words that the teacher
spoke in a second, but I forgot them the next day. Later, I learned from
my neighbor when he wrote down Chinese characters with similar
sounds to English. I still can remember some words now, such as "bee"
and "knife." Their sounds were very similar to English. So I could look
at the characters and pronounce them easily. However, those sounds
were very strange when someone else heard them.

One day, the teacher found out I was using Chinese characters when 4
she checked my homework in the book. She was angry and told me,
"Sau, we need to have a talk after school! Please come to my office!" I
nodded. Unfortunately, I forgot to meet her after school. She called my
mother in the evening. She told my mother what I had done in school.
My mother seemed also very angry. She wanted me to come to her
room. I was very frightened, and I had never thought that using these
characters was such a serious problem. When I came in my mother's
room, the room was so quiet that I could hear a pin drop. My mother
was sitting on her bed. I thought that she would scold me that night. But
in fact, my thinking was totally wrong. She wanted me to sit beside her,
and she said, "Sau, do you know why I called you to come?" I nodded
and I slowly put down my head. She continued, "If you can't read, you
can ask your brothers for help. Do you think using Chinese characters
helps you to learn English? I don't want you to lie; I want to be proud of
you." I felt very sorry for her when I heard the last sentence because she
was hurt by me. I promised her that I wouldn't do that anymore. After
that, I paid more attention to English. I learned how to pronounce
words during the second semester without using Chinese characters.

My family immigrated to the United States after I graduated from ju- 5
nior high school, except for my oldest brother because he was over the
age limit. My mother and older brother still encouraged me to go to
high school. My older brother worked in a French restaurant. My
mother worked in a factory. Sometimes I went there to help her sewing

after school. But anyway, we still had the same feelings toward each other. We still talked and laughed as before.

My brother mentioned that I should speak English to him. He said, 6 "Sau, we must speak English starting now. It will help you to improve your speaking." I agreed with him. Since then, we spoke English most times, except some words we didn't know in English. So when I spoke English to my brother, my mother just smiled or sometimes she walked away. Sometimes she wanted me to translate TV shows for her, such as *American Funny People, Wild Animals,* and some interesting movies. I would be glad to do that because I thought that she was the greatest mother in the world.

The time passed very fast. I went to college last semester. All of my 7 family members were very happy because I was the first generation to go to college. My father graduated only from elementary school; my mother was educated for only three years; both brothers graduated from junior high school; my youngest sister is in high school now. Sometimes we speak English, but usually we speak the family language, Fuzhounese.

My older brother has been attending evening school after work since 8 last semester. He said that he wanted to improve his English. He also said that his English would be far away from mine if he didn't improve it now. Sometimes, he wants me to go over his homework and correct the errors. I am always glad to help him because he really is a nice brother, and I have no reason to refuse him.

If I think of my future, I will choose to learn more about medical 9 knowledge because my forefathers were doctors. After them, no one could take up the duty. I hope that I can do something to renew this family tradition.

Therefore, I would say that my family and learning English are like a 10 tree. My family is the most important root of the tree. English is like the branches of the tree. The jobs are like leaves. So if a tree is without one of these, it wouldn't survive or it will lose its appearance. So the family and English are important to me. I can't lose either one. On the contrary, I will learn more English, and I will be closer to my family.

Sau Nga, China

After you have read Sau Nga's essay, answer the following questions.

1. What does Nga seem to feel about English in the beginning of the essay? What does she feel about it at the end of the essay? What causes the change in her feelings?

2. What is the connection between Sau Nga's family and her learning of English? What events does she describe that help her readers to make this connection?

3. What time transition words and phrases does Sau Nga use to help her readers follow her story?

4. What is the purpose of beginning the essay with a story?

5. How does the conclusion of the essay connect to the beginning?

Now review some of the other student essays in this book. What have you learned from reading these essays and doing revision exercises on them? How has their writing influenced your writing? What are you more careful about when you write now that you were not aware of earlier in the term?

Revising

After discussing Sau Nga's essay with your classmates, review the draft of the essay you wrote as you prepare to revise it. Rewrite the questions so that they will be helpful in revising your own essay. Read your essay aloud, and ask yourself questions about it; you may want to write these questions on a separate piece of paper. Use these questions to help you during the rewriting process. Try to be a helpful critic. Focus on the organization of the essay. Does one idea lead to the next? Are there enough details so that you can form pictures in your mind? How can this piece of writing be made to come alive to its readers?

Editing Strategies

Mechanics

Parallelism

Words in pairs or in series in sentences should be parallel or similar in structure so that the writing is clearer and more readable. This means that all the verbals should be in the same form—all infinitives or all gerunds—or that all the words be nouns, adjectives, or adverbs.

> I enjoy *singing, dancing,* and *having* a good time.
> I like *to sing, to dance,* and *to have* a good time.
> I enjoy going to *restaurants, parties,* and *dance clubs.*

A sentence like "I enjoy singing, dancing, and to have a good time" would be incorrect because *singing* and *dancing* are gerunds but *to have* is an infinitive; the structure of the sentence is not parallel.

Maria Muñiz writes:

> I am still unable to view the revolution with *detachment* or *objectivity*. (Both these words are nouns.)
> I cannot interpret its results in *social, political,* or *economic* terms. (All three words are adjectives.)

Han Suyin writes:

> But with my looks I would never get married; I was *too thin, too sharp, too ugly.* (All three expressions are adjectives modified by *too.*)
> "You look sixteen," said Mama; "all you have to do is to stop *hopping* and *picking* your pimples." (Both words are in the same verb form.)

□   □   □

EXERCISE   Fill in the blanks with appropriate words in parallel structure. There can be many correct answers, so share what you have written with a partner.

Muñiz explains that some of the steps that she went through to make a difficult decision included talking with others, _____, and _____. She decided to return to Cuba so that she could visit her old house, _____, and _____. She wants to know, to _____, and to _____. After living in the United States for many years, she still thinks about her grandmother, _____, and _____. She has letters, _____, and _____ to remind her of her family, but that is not enough. She wants to return to the place where she was born, _____, and _____ until she moved to the United States. She thinks it is time to _____ and to _____.

Editing Practice

Editing Other People's Writing

The following paragraph is an unedited first draft. Read it and edit the paragraph, looking for errors of any kind. If you have difficulty, discuss it with a classmate. To check your answers, turn to page 359.

The essay "Back, but Not Home" by maria l. muñiz made me think about returning to my country. I grown up thinking that their was no reason to go back, but now I am not sure. Its interesting for me to think about the world that I left behind, I feel mixed emotions. Such as happiness, sadness, and regret. My aunts and uncle still lives in my country. They still live in the same town; in the same house. I have never seen most of my cousins, the youngest one is five month old and I would like to know him to. My brother visited my family last year, and he told me all the news. Its strange hearing about my best girlfriends which are getting married and one even has a baby. The Muñiz essay, my brother's visit, and my dreams makes me: want to return to my country for a visit.

Editing Your Own Writing

Reread an essay that you wrote for this chapter, asking yourself the following questions:

1. Did I format my paper correctly?
2. Did I start new paragraphs when necessary?
3. Did I use final sentence punctuation and apostrophes correctly?
4. Did I use the past tenses correctly?
5. Did I use the present tenses correctly? Do my subjects and verbs agree?
6. Did I use quotation marks correctly?
7. Did I use pronouns correctly? Do the pronouns agree?
8. Did I form plurals correctly?
9. Did I use *the* correctly?
10. Did I use capital letters where they are needed?
11. Did I use commas correctly?
12. Did I use other punctuation marks correctly?
13. Did I use modals correctly?
14. Did I use comparatives correctly?
15. Are all the sentences complete, with no run-ons or fragments?
16. Did I use connecting words appropriately?
17. Are all series—places where I have used *and, or,* or *but*—parallel?

When you rewrite your essay, make any changes that will improve your writing.

Grammar Strategies

Direct and Indirect Speech

When we report what another person has said in our writing, we can use direct quotations, the exact words that a person has spoken or written. To do this, we use quotation marks and appropriate capital letters and punctuation marks.

> I am constantly being asked, "Would you ever go back?"
> One little girl said, "She's so stupid, she can't even talk."

We can divide a long sentence in a quotation.

> "She's so stupid," said one little girl, "she can't even talk."

We can also restate what the person has said without quoting the exact words. This is referred to as indirect or reported speech.

> I am constantly being asked whether I would ever go back.
> One little girl said that I was so stupid, I couldn't even talk.

Particular rules help readers understand that what they are reading has already been said or written in the past. The indirect sentence normally begins by identifying the person who spoke. For example, the sentence *"It is raining out," she said* becomes *She said that it was raining out.*
In indirect speech, the tense changes:

1. From present to past:

   > Mei Mei said, "The clock *is* broken."
   > She said that the clock *was* broken.

2. From past to past perfect:

   > Jose said, "I *bought* a new television."
   > He said that he *had bought* a new television.

In indirect speech, the modal auxiliary changes:

1. From *may* to *might:*

   > Lynn said, "It *may* rain."
   > She said that it *might* rain.

2. From *can* to *could:*

Pak said, "I *can* speak Mandarin."
He said that he *could* speak Mandarin.

3. From *will* to *would:*

Reinaldo said, "I *will* go to the movies."
He said that he *would* go to the movies.

4. From *must* to *had to:*

Estelle said, "I *must* finish my paper."
She said that she *had to* finish her paper.

In indirect speech, the demonstrative changes:

1. From *this* to *that:*

Will said, "I can't carry *this* table alone."
He said that he couldn't carry *that* table alone.

2. From *these* to *those:*

Sonia said, "*These* books are overdue at the library."
She said that *those* books were overdue at the library.

In indirect speech, the adverbials of time and place change:

1. From *today* to *that day:*

Leslie said, "I want to leave *today.*"
She said that she wanted to leave *that day.*

2. From *tomorrow* to *the following day* or *a day later.*
3. From *yesterday* to *the previous day* or *the day before.*
4. From *next month* or *next year* to *the following month/year* or *a month/year later.*
5. From *this* to *that:*

Her father said, "We waited for you *this* Thursday."
Her father said that they had waited for her *that* Thursday.

6. From *now* to *then:*

"I am waiting for you *now*," the woman said to her husband.
The woman told her husband that she was waiting for him *then*.

In indirect speech, the word order of questions changes to a statement word order:

Maria asked, "What time *is it?*"
She asked what time *it was*.

If or *whether* is added if there is no question word:

Michael asked, "Is it raining?"
He asked *if* it was raining.

In indirect speech, pronouns sometimes change:

1. From *I* to *she* or *he* in a third person narrative:

"*I* need some advice," she said.
She said that *she* needed some advice.

but in a first person narrative, the pronoun does not change:

"*I* am tired," I told my friend.
I told my friend that *I* was tired.

2. From *you* to *she, he,* or *they* in the third person:

"Where do *you* want to go?" one of the men asked.
One of the men asked where *they* wanted to go.

or to *I* in the first person:

One of the men asked where *I* wanted to go.

3. From *my* to *her* or *his:*

She asked them, "Didn't you get *my* message?"
She asked them if they had gotten *her* message.

□   □   □

EXERCISES

1. Using the information just given, change the following direct quotations to indirect or reported speech. The first one has been done for you.

a. "I am so happy to have a job," says Miss Chou.

Miss Chou said that she was happy to have a job.

b. "I left Cuba when I was five years old," Maria said.

_____

c. "Some students worry about high tuitions," the college president said.

_____

d. "I can speak Russian and Uzbek," Alevtina said.

_____

e. "Ming will present her paper tomorrow," the teacher said.

_____

f. "We just became American citizens," the couple announced.

_____

g. Wendy said, "My brother is meeting me after class."

_____

h. Juan asked, "When is the final?"

_____

i. "Is this the right classroom?" Mikhail asked.

_____

j. "I am happy to see you," she said to her father.

_____

k. "Things have really changed here," he told her.

_____

1. "Do you have a phone?" Feri asked her brother.

    _____

2. For additional practice, with a partner change the dialogue in "A Day's Wait" (Chapter Three), "The All-American Slurp" (Chapter Six), or "A Mortal Flower" (Chapter Twelve) into indirect speech. You can also do this with other selections from the book for extra practice.
3. Reread selections in this book, looking for instances of indirect speech. Write down any uses of indirect speech that confuse you. Discuss them with your teacher or a classmate.

                              □   □   □

CHECKING YOUR OWN WORK

1. Read through each essay you wrote for this chapter. Look at the places in which you used indirect speech. (It may be helpful to underline them lightly.) Did you handle this material appropriately and correctly? If you are not sure, check the explanation of uses of indirect speech in the previous section.
2. Repeat check 1 with other writing that you have done recently.
3. As an added check, work with a classmate to make sure that you have used indirect speech correctly in your writing.

CHAPTER FOURTEEN

Focusing on Behavior

PREREADING ACTIVITIES

1. What is culture?
2. What are some of the positive images you have of culture?
3. What are some of the negative images you have of culture?
4. What do you want to know about culture that has not been taught in your classes up to now?

VOCABULARY DEVELOPMENT

We learn many words in contrast or by looking at the opposites that are presented in a piece of writing. In the selection in this chapter, Patricia Miller contrasts some ideas to help her readers understand these concepts.

1. Miller contrasts *independence* and *interdependence*. Which one means to be on one's own?

   _____ Which one means to be connected with others? _____ How did you make your choice?

2. *Invisible* is contrasted with *presence*. Which one is something that can be seen?

   _____ Which one is something that cannot be seen? _____ How did you make your choice?

3. *Separate* is contrasted with *dependent*. Which one means to be connected with others?

   _____ Which one means to be apart from others? _____

4. *Passive* is contrasted with *active*. Which one refers to involvement and movement?

   _____ Which refers to quiet and little action? _____

5. *Nonverbal interactions* are contrasted with *verbal discourse*. Which one refers to talk?

   _____ Which refers to physical but not speaking activities? _____

What do these words suggest the selection will be about?

Cross-Cultural Research

Patricia H. Miller

*Patricia H. Miller teaches psychology at the University of Florida. The follow-
ing reading is excerpted from her textbook* Theories of Developmental
Psychology. *In this book, Miller includes the following quotation by Albert
Einstein: "Perhaps the most incomprehensible thing about the world is that it
is comprehensible." In her description of cross-cultural research, Miller attempts to make the world a bit more comprehensible.*

Cross-cultural research contributes to our understanding of devel- 1
opment in two main ways. First, it identifies universal characteristics of development and mechanisms by which culture affects development. Second, it shows us that certain child behaviors, stages, and
child-rearing activities are not universal. Rather, they are the product of
particular cultural-social-historical circumstances. In this way, our attention is drawn to what is "invisible" in our own culture because we are so
accustomed to its presence. For example, nearly all middle-class babies
in the United States sleep in their own bed and often in a different room
from the parents. And U.S. parents encourage their babies to sleep
through the night. In contrast, parents do not push babies toward sleeping through the night in cultures where parents and infants share a bed
so that nursing on demand is possible, where parents need not live by
the clock, and where babies are strapped to their mothers' backs while
they work during the day—all true of rural Kenyan children (Super &
Harkness, 1983). Families in each culture consider their sleeping
arrangement as the only reasonable one. Mayan mothers, for example,
expressed pity for babies in the United States when told that they slept
in their own rooms (Morelli, Rogoff, Oppenheim, & Goldsmith, 1992).
They considered this harmful for the babies. Japanese parents believe
that babies are born separate beings who must be taught feelings of interdependence with other people, and sleeping with parents is thought
to encourage this process (Caudill & Weinstein, 1969). In contrast, parents in the United States (and most Western social developmental theorists) believe that babies are born dependent and must develop inde-
°make easier   pendence; a separate bed is thought to facilitate° this. . . .

Cross-cultural studies describe many striking cultural differences in 2
verbal interaction patterns between parents and their children (Rogoff,
1990). In some cultures, children are expected to play a passive role in
this activity—responding when spoken to but not initiating verbal interactions or participating equally in conversations. Mayan adults, for example, think that a child is challenging adults with her greater knowledge if she tells them something. In many cultures most of the care of
young children comes from older sisters, who consequently may be the

young children's main conversational partners. In these cultures, children still may learn a great deal from adults through nonverbal interactions—observing them in adult work settings in particular. Although this interaction pattern may work quite well in everyday settings, it may not prepare them for the verbal discourse° expected by teachers in formal schooling, such as asking questions and making eye contact with the teacher. Navajo children, for example, sit quietly and observe their teachers more than twice as much as do Caucasian children in the same classroom (Guilmet, 1979).

°exchange of ideas

Another cultural difference in adult-child interaction patterns is that North American middle-class mothers usually hold their infants facing toward them, whereas in many cultures, such as in the Marquesas Islands in the South Pacific, mothers hold their infants facing away from them (Martini & Kirkpatrick, 1981). Facing babies outward may reflect both the deemphasis on parent-child verbal interaction described above and an attempt to encourage children to observe and interact with older siblings° and other members of the community. This orientation° of children away from the parent to the larger community may indicate the sense of community typically found in such villages. Community members may share in the socialization of the young, reprimanding° misbehavior in other people's children.

°brothers and sisters
°positioning

°criticizing

Bornstein and his colleagues (Bornstein, Toda, Azuma, Tamis-LeMonda, & Ogino, 1990; Bornstein, Tal, & Tamis-LeMonda, 1991) have observed American and Japanese (Tokyo) mothers interacting with their 5-month-old infants. At this point infants in both cultures show equal amounts and types of orientation to their mothers and to physical objects in the environment. However, their mothers respond differently in the two cultures. American mothers are more responsive when babies orient to physical objects; Japanese mothers are more responsive when their babies orient to them. Mothers even tried to change their babies' attention to fit their preferences—toward themselves for the Japanese and toward objects for Americans. Japanese mothers in general continue to encourage their young children's dependence on them. These specific behaviors are a concrete expression of a very general cultural belief system. The Japanese culture values social ties and dependency; American culture values autonomy and independence. Culture clearly is directing development.

When Japanese children enter preschool, the value placed on group harmony° continues to be instilled° in them (Cole, 1992). For example, American educators viewing a videotape of Japanese preschool were shocked that there were 30 preschoolers and only one teacher. In contrast, Japanese educators viewing the American classroom with only a few students per teacher expressed concern for the children: "A class that size seems kind of sad and underpopulated" and "I wonder how you teach a child to become a member of a group in a class that small" (Tobin, Wu, & Davidson, 1989). In the Japanese mind, "A child's humanity is realized most fully not so much in his ability to be independent

°agreement, pleasant
 relations
°taught, trained

3

4

5

from the group as [in] his ability to cooperate and feel part of the group" (Tobin et al., 1989, p. 39). As Markus and Kitayama (1991) observe, in America "the squeaky wheel gets the grease" and in Japan "the nail that stands out gets pounded down."

Even something as universal-sounding as mathematics is touched by culture. First, numerical symbol systems differ. Certain cultures in New Guinea, for example, use the names of parts of the body for their counting system. Counting begins with the thumb of one hand and progresses through 29 separate locations (each finger, wrist, elbow, shoulder, right ear, right eye, nose, left eye, and so on) through the far side of the other hand (Saxe, 1981). Second, the form of mental calculation varies as a function of the culture's symbol system. In the Orient, people often use abacuses to solve math problems. At least among older children who achieve expertise, these devices encourage people to solve calculation problems in their head by forming a mental image of the abacus (Stigler, 1984). As evidence, when they make an error, it is of the type that would be expected if they were reading from such a mental image rather than the type made by people in cultures where the abacus is not used. Third, certain social-cultural contexts encourage the development of mathematical skills. One example comes from Saxe's (1988) research on child candy vendors° on the streets of Brazil. They must very quickly perform various numerical activities—purchase candy, decide on a sale price, negotiate the price, make change, and so on. Despite their generally disadvantageous childhood environment, they develop impressive mental calculation abilities. Interestingly, when child street vendors are asked to solve similar math problems outside the vending context, they perform much more poorly (Carraher, Carraher, & Schliemann, 1985). Another example is that Asian children surpass° American children in their mathematical prowess.° One cause may be that Asian mothers generally attribute mathematical performance to trying hard and not giving up, and instill these behaviors in their children. In contrast, American mothers tend to emphasize inherent° ability, an attribution that does not encourage studying hard (Stevenson, Lee, & Stigler, 1986). Moreover, the Japanese language system encourages attention to the quantitative° aspect of reality. There are separate words for counting people, birds, four-legged animals, broad thin objects such as sheets of paper, and long thin objects such as sticks. And Japanese mothers encourage even very young children to play counting games, such as "Let's count birds" (Hatano, 1989; cited in Siegler, 1991, pp. 163–164).

°sellers

°outperform
°ability

°inborn

°numerical

References

Bornstein, M. H., J. Tal, & C. S. Tamis-LeMonda (1991). Parenting in cross-cultural perspective: The United States, France, and Japan. In M. H. Bornstein, ed., *Cultural approaches to parenting*. Hillsdale, N.J.: Erlbaum.

Bornstein, M. H., S. Toda, H. Azuma, C. S. Tamis-LeMonda, & M. Ogino (1990). Mother and infant activity and interaction in Japan and in the United States: II. A comparative microanalysis of naturalistic exchanges focused on the organization of infant attention. *International Journal of Behavioral Development, 13,* 289–308.

Carraher, T. N., D. W. Carraher, & A. D. Schliemann (1985). Mathematics in the streets and in schools. *British Journal of Developmental Psychology, 3,* 21–29.

Caudill, W., & H. Weinstein (1969). Maternal care and infant behavior in Japan and America. *Psychiatry, 32,* 12–43.

Cole, M. (1992). Culture in development. In M. Bornstein and M. Lamb, eds., *Developmental Psychology: An advanced textbook,* 3rd ed. Hillsdale, N.J.: Erlbaum.

Guilmet, G. M. (1979). Navajo and Caucasian children's verbal and nonverbal-visual behavior in the urban classroom. *Anthropology and Education Quarterly, 9,* 196–215.

Hatano (1989) cited in Siegler, R. S. (1991). *Children's thinking,* 2nd ed. Englewood Cliffs, N.J.: Prentice Hall.

Markus, H. R., & S. Kitayama (1991). Culture and the self: Implications for cognition, emotion, and motivation. *Psychological Review, 98,* 224–253.

Martini, M., & J. Kirkpatrick (1981). Early interactions in the Marquesas Islands. In T. M. Field, A. M. Sostek, P. Vietze, and P. H. Leiderman, eds. *Culture and early interventions.* Hillsdale, N.J.: Erlbaum.

Morelli, G. A., B. Rogoff, D. Oppenheim, and D. Goldsmith (1992). Cultural variations in infants' sleeping arrangements: Questions of independence. *Developmental Psychology, 28,* 604–613.

Rogoff, B. (1990). *Apprenticeship in thinking: Cognitive development in social context.* New York: Oxford University Press.

Saxe, G. B. (1981). Body parts as numerals: A developmental analysis of numeration among the Oksapmin in Papua New Guinea. *Developmental Psychology, 52,* 306–316.

Saxe, G. B. (1988). The mathematics of street vendors. *Child Development, 59,* 1415–1425.

Stevenson, H. W., S. Lee, & J. W. Stigler (1986). Achievement in mathematics. In H. Stevenson, H. Azuma, and K. Hakuta, eds., *Child development and education in Japan.* New York: Freeman.

Stigler, J. W. (1984). "Mental abacus": The effects of abacus training on Chinese children's mental calculation. *Cognitive Psychology, 16,* 145–176.

Super, C. M., & S. Harkness (1983). *Looking across at growing up: The cultural expression of cognitive development in middle childhood.* Unpublished manuscript, Harvard University.

Tobin, J. J., D. Y. H. Wu, & D. H. Davidson (1989). *Preschool in three cultures.* New Haven, Conn.: Yale University Press.

Reading and Thinking Strategies

Discussion Activities

Analysis and Conclusions

1. According to Miller, in human development, what is universal? What is not universal?

2. What does Miller mean by the expression *cultural-social-historical circumstances?* What example of this does she provide?

3. What specific differences does Miller point out about the sleeping arrangements of babies in different cultures?

4. What evidence does Miller provide that interacting with the community is more important in some cultures than it is in others?

5. In what ways is mathematics influenced by culture? What specific examples are included in the reading?

Writing and Point of View

1. Circle the connecting or transitional words in paragraph 1 (*First, Second, Rather,* and so on). Discuss how each of these words ties together the ideas in that paragraph.

2. What words and phrases in this reading indicate contrast or differences? Make a list of these words and phrases. Notice the sentence that precedes and follows each of them.

3. What words and phrases in this reading indicate comparison or similarities? Make a list of these words.

4. Look at the first sentence in each paragraph. What words and phrases connect the ideas between paragraphs?

5. What is the writer's point of view about the research she presents? Why?

Personal Response and Evaluation

1. What do you think the best sleeping arrangement is for babies? Why?

2. Do you usually hold a baby facing toward you or away from you? Why? Look around your neighborhood, and notice how babies are held. What did you discover? How does this correspond with Miller's findings?

3. Discuss with members of your class the way that plurals are indicated in your first language. How are numbers indicated in that language?

4. What does the expression "the squeaky wheel gets the grease" mean in the context of this selection? What does "the nail that stands out gets pounded down" mean? What expressions in your first language have similar meanings?

Small Group Discussion

As a class, choose an aspect of culture that you would like to know more about, such as ways in which children are fed, helped with homework, or cared for. In a small group of three to five students, discuss the differences and similarities in the various cultures represented in your class. Present your findings to the class as a whole.

Journal Writing

We do not live to think, but, on the contrary, we think in order that we may succeed in surviving.

JOSÉ ORTEGA Y GASSETT

When you think about your own culture, how does it help you understand your own behavior? How does culture help you to identify the values in your life that are most important to you? Thinking about specific behaviors and values in your life, write in your journal.

Writing Strategies

Essay Strategies

Getting Information from Your Textbook

One important skill for college students is being able to get information from various sources. One source is your textbook. When you read a textbook, you cannot expect to remember every detail. However, the text itself is constructed in a way that can help you find and remember the most important ideas. Some students highlight these important ideas with specially colored pens; other students copy them into their notebooks or onto index cards. Copying the main ideas and supporting details is a good idea because most people find it easier to remember material that they have written down than material that they have simply read and underlined.

In your classes, when you read textbook material, you should make notes that you will refer to later. One way to break down the notes into a usable form is to label them with the authors' names, the title, and the page number. If you write down the authors' exact words, put them in quotation marks and record the page number. This will help you if you need to find this information again. It will also help if you are writing a research paper and want to quote or paraphrase the material.

Summary Writing

Students often write short summaries of textbook material. These summaries include the names of the writers, the title of the piece, and the pages on which it appears. The summary should contain the most important ideas from the original piece of writing, expressed in your own words. Your summary should be no longer than one-third or one-fourth of the original piece of writing. You may include a quotation from the original selection, but if you do this, put it in quotation marks so that you will remember that this is not your own writing.

When you write your summary, look for key words or phrases. Be sure to include important names, places, dates, and facts. Answer the *who, what, where, when, why,* and *how* questions as clearly and concisely as possible. See pages 242–43 for more information about summary writing.

□ □ □

EXERCISES

1. Write a summary of "Cross-Cultural Research."
2. Make an outline of "Cross-Cultural Research" (see page 244–45 for more information about summary writing on outlining).
3. Compare your summary and your outline. Which is more helpful for you to remember the ideas presented in the Miller selection?

Essay Form

Using Examples in Your Writing

In much of the college writing we do, we make generalizations and state opinions. Writers must support their generalizations with examples or evidence. Writing that generalizes without examples is uninteresting, vague, and meaningless.

The examples you choose must support your generalization. If you are writing about the importance of cross-cultural research, as Miller does, you must give specific examples that show the differences or similarities between cultural attitudes and behaviors. Showing that babies all over the world are treated differently by their parents supports the main idea that the subject is worth investigating. Showing that babies all over the world are treated exactly the same would also be interesting, but it would lead a reader to think the researcher had not done very careful work.

Readers usually require that writers make the connection between their generalizations and their examples. Some words and phrases that are used to make these connections are *for example, for instance, to illustrate, specifically, a case in point, thus, hence, an illustration of this, as an example, consider,* and *to show what I mean.* It is not always necessary to include these words and phrases if the example is placed right next to the generalization or if it is the second of two examples. It is only important that the writer help the reader make the connection through the placement or choice of words.

Be aware, however, that writers can overuse examples. The writer who states that tuition increases are bad and then describes only his or her own financial problems will not have provided enough support for the generalization. On the other hand, the writer who states that tuition increases are bad and then proceeds to list five or ten students who have been affected by them is overdoing it and risks losing the readers' ability to connect with the main idea. After all, examples are helpful to prove or support the generalizations but should not overpower them.

Let's take a look at the examples Miller used to support the generalizations in paragraph 1 that "certain child behaviors, stages, and child-rearing activities are not universal" and that they "are the product of particular cultural-social-historical circumstances." Miller tells her readers about middle-class babies in the United States and introduces this illustration with the words *for example*. She contrasts the U.S. child-rearing practices with those practiced in Kenya and uses the words *in contrast* to tell us what she is doing. Next, she describes Mayan child rearing and again writes *for example*. Next, she writes about Japanese babies and connects back to the United States. She has compared and contrasted sleeping patterns of babies in four parts of the world—North America, Africa, South America, and Asia. These examples support her generalizations.

☐ ☐ ☐

EXERCISES

1. Look at paragraph 2, and decide what generalizations Miller is making. Then make a list of the examples she uses to support the generalizations and the words she uses to make connections.
2. Do the same thing for paragraphs 3 through 6.
3. What did you discover about the numbers of generalizations, the numbers and types of examples, and the words used to make connections between ideas? How can you use this information to help you when you write?

Suggestions for Writing

1. Use the library, conduct interviews, or do both to find out about one aspect of culture that you would like to understand better. Reread the Miller selection to get some ideas. Write an essay in which you describe your findings. Explain what you learned from doing this research.
2. Find out about the infant sleeping arrangements in cultures other than the ones described in the Miller selection. Write an essay in which you describe your findings and compare them to the ones presented in the Miller article.
3. Find out about child care arrangements in your culture and about those in the United States. Write an essay in which you describe your findings. What do you think are the ideal child care arrangements? Explain your reasons for this choice.

4. Find a study describing some aspect of culture in your native country. Read the study, and write an essay in which you describe it. What would you have liked the researchers to do that they did not do? Why do you think this is important? Do you agree with the findings of the researchers? Explain your answer.

Extra Class Project

After completing the writing assignments, students can meet in groups with classmates who have worked on similar writing projects to share their findings and make short oral presentations to the class about what they have discovered.

Getting Started

Freewriting with a Purpose: Creating Your Own Context

According to Miller, "cross-cultural research contributes to our understanding of development." This means that we are all affected by the culture in which we live. For the next ten minutes, write about the culture in which you live. Think about where you live, the people you see on the street, the newspaper you read, the television programs you watch, the music you listen to, and the school you attend. Describe as many of these and any other influences that occur to you. Look at the world that surrounds you, and write about how it has affected your values, ambitions, and daily life.

Revising

A Student Essay

Diego Ferro writes about the different attitudes toward time in the United States and in his native Colombia.

WHAT TIME IS IT?

As an immigrant who came from Colombia, a country where the pace 1
of life is slower, I have experienced differences in how rules of time act
in a culture. In the United States, we are dominated by the concept of
time.

An Italian proverb says, "Man measures time and time measures 2
man." Although it is an old proverb it sounds real for today. For exam-

ple, here wherever you go you can see a time clock. In the houses there is a clock in almost every room. Banks, offices, streets, and even highways have time clocks. But what is the reason for so many clocks? The answer is, "It seems clear that time talks," and it looks like it is telling us that we are on time or late for our duties. Because of this I had to bear some discomfort when I went to my country. Every time that I wanted to know the time I could not find a clock as I do here. I felt as if I was always out of time.

Another aspect that I found a lot different here is the walking pace. I remember one of my teachers used to say, "Whenever somebody is walking slow in New York we know that he or she is a foreigner." I did not understand that statement before, but now it is clear to me. I have read that the United States is in third place in the world for walking speed. In my country we walk slowly. And when I went to New York, as I was walking, I remembered that I had to get to the side in order to let people that were walking faster pass. In my country we cannot say to somebody, "Will you walk a little faster?" You hear, "Pass to the side." 3

Fast food is also something that I cannot get used to here. When I left my country, there were not places like McDonald's, Burger King, Wendy's, not even the popular lunch trucks. There is a reason for that. There the office workers have two hours for lunch, and no office worker has less than one hour. Hence the people there have the time to go to a restaurant and enjoy a peaceful lunch. Here I cannot get used to it. My work obligates me to be on the road the major part of the time. It is impossible for me to have a "peaceful lunch." There is only a half hour of lunch here. This situation has brought me some trouble. Sometimes when I am having lunch, I get a call from my boss who wants me to go to another place at that moment. Nothing can get me more upset than that, because in my country we do not like to be bothered when we are having lunch. Despite this, I have to say that I admire the service offered here from public agencies. For example, in my country, fulfilling the income tax requirement takes as long as one day. Also, this requirement has to be done personally. However, here, all that can be done in even less than one hour. Of course, technology plays an important part in this matter. 4

Another service that I admire is the one related to colleges and universities. For instance, here a student who wants to go to college for the first time doesn't need to go there to get an application. This is a waste of time. Applications can be obtained by simply making a phone call. On the other hand, getting an application in my country sometimes takes more than one day. 5

But customs don't stay where they belong; they travel along with people. Although we have been living here for several years, these influences from our country still persist. For instance, many times when a group of Colombians plans to get together, the agreement about the 6 meeting time is made by the question "Colombian time or American time?" which means that if it is American time, we will attempt to meet at that exact time. However, if it is Colombian time, we know that there will be at least 30 minutes' delay.

To conclude, I have to say that my culture is very different from   7
American culture. And how time is used is also very different between both countries.

Diego Ferro, Colombia

After reading Ferro's essay, think about the following questions in relation to his writing.

1. What is the main idea of Ferro's essay?
2. What comparison does Ferro make about the use of clocks in the United States and in Colombia? How does this comparison relate to the main idea of the essay?
3. How does "fast food" relate to the time concept?
4. What is the purpose of the proverb in paragraph 2? Try moving the proverb to another part of the essay. Which location do you prefer? Why?
5. How does the conclusion connect to the introduction? What could you do to make this connection stronger?

Rewrite these questions so they can be used to help you as you prepare to revise your essay. Using your questions, discuss your essay with a classmate. When you have decided which changes to make in the next draft of your essay, rewrite it and share it with your classmate.

Editing Strategies

Mechanics

Types of Verbs

The three types of verbs are linking, intransitive, and transitive.

linking verbs

Linking verbs are followed by complements, which are words that describe or rename the subject. These words can be nouns:

Jin Won *is* a teacher.
Hiroko *is* a doctor.

Or adjectives:

> Irina *is* intelligent.
> The book *was* lost.

The verb *be* (*be, am, is, are, was, were, being, been*) usually functions as a linking verb unless it is used as a helping verb (*is buying, was collecting*). Sometimes verbs such as *appear, become, feel, look, make, seem, sound,* and *taste* are also used as linking verbs:

> Boris *seems* happy.
> Juana *feels* better.

intransitive verbs

Intransitive verbs do not require an object or a noun phrase to make a complete sentence. Their pattern is always subject-verb. All linking verbs are intransitive. Intransitive verbs cannot be used in the passive voice (see pages 315–17 for information on the passive voice):

> They *go.*
> Children *sleep.*
> She is *walking.*

Intransitive verbs are often followed by prepositional phrases (see pages 201–205 for more information on prepositions):

> They go to school.
> Children sleep in their beds.
> She is walking in the park.

transitive verbs

Transitive verbs must be followed by a direct object or a noun phrase:

> The player threw the ball.

Transitive verbs can take more than one object:

> The player threw the ball and the bat.

Transitive verbs can take both a direct and an indirect object:

> The player threw the batter a ball.

One or more prepositional phrases can follow the object:

> The player thew the ball to the catcher at home plate.

Transitive and intransitive verbs are identified in the dictionary. Some verbs may be used transitively or intransitively:

> She was writing.
> She was writing a letter.

Certain intransitive verbs have different forms for transitive use:

Intransitive	Transitive	Examples
lie	lay	She will lie down now.
		He laid the paper down.
rise	raise	The sun rises in the east.
		She raised her hand in class.
sit	set	They sat down.
		He set the chair near the table.

□   □   □

EXERCISES

1. Look up the following verbs in the dictionary and find out if they are transitive (shown as *v.t.* in many dictionaries) or intransitive (shown as *v.i.* in dictionaries).

   a. travel
   b. send
   c. follow
   d. study
   e. like

2. In the following sentences, underline each verb and identify it as transitive, intransitive, or linking.

   a. Nearly all middle-class babies in the United States sleep in their own bed.

   b. Parents encourage their babies to sleep through the night.

   c. Rural Kenyan mothers strap their children to their backs.

   d. Children learn a great deal from adults.

   e. Navajo children sit quietly and observe their teachers.

   f. American mothers are more responsive when babies orient to physical objects.

   g. Asian children surpass American children in their mathematical prowess.

Editing Practice

Editing Other People's Writing

The paragraph that follows is an unedited draft that contains many errors. Find and correct as many as you can. If you have difficulty, discuss the paragraph with a classmate. Answers are on page 359.

Cross-cultural research interests to me. Miller wrote that American parents want their children to sleep on their own beds as soon as possible. It is important for babies learn to sleeping through night by herself. She said that Mayan mothers express the pity on American babies because she has to sleep alone. Japanese parents believe babies should sleeps with their parent too. Cultures who want children to developing independence wants children to sleep alone. Cultures who value interdependence likes babies to sleep with the parent. When mother nurse her baby, it is good for baby to sleep her mother. If baby wake up the night, mother can hold and nurse baby back sleep. Mother can fall asleep with baby too. Then mother is not so tired a next day. Learning about how cultures around world live fascinate to me.

Editing Your Own Writing

Reread an essay that you wrote for this chapter, asking yourself the following questions:

1. Did I format my paper correctly?
2. Did I start new paragraphs when necessary?
3. Did I use final sentence punctuation and apostrophes correctly?
4. Did I use the past tenses correctly?
5. Did I use the present tenses correctly? Do my subjects and verbs agree?
6. Did I use quotation marks correctly?
7. Did I use pronouns correctly? Do the pronouns agree?
8. Did I form plurals correctly?
9. Did I use *the* correctly?
10. Did I use capital letters where they are needed?

11. Did I use commas correctly?

12. Did I use other punctuation marks correctly?

13. Did I use modals correctly?

14. Did I use comparatives correctly?

15. Are all the sentences complete, with no run-ons or fragments?

16. Did I use connecting words appropriately?

17. Are all series—places where I have used *and, or,* or *but*—parallel?

When you rewrite your essay, make any changes that will improve your writing.

Grammar Strategies

Passive Verbs

We sometimes want to emphasize the object of a verb more than the subject of the verb. Compare these two sentences:

Someone *stole* my car last week. (active verb)
My car *was stolen* last week. (passive verb)

If you want to emphasize *car* rather than *someone,* you can use passive verb forms. It is usually better to use active verbs in English. However, there are some situations when you need to or prefer to use passive verbs. Remember, however, that you *cannot* use intransitive verbs (see page 312) in the passive construction.

The passive construction is appropriate in the following situations:

1. When the performer of the action is less important or is not essential to the meaning of the sentence:

   The Declaration of Independence was signed in 1776. (The unidentified performer of the action is not important.)
   Pine trees were planted all around my campus.
   Your citizenship papers were approved.

2. When the writer wants to emphasize the receiver of the action:

   The couple was married in June.
   The house was painted last summer.

3. When the writer wants to make an impersonal or objective statement:

It is expected that students using this book will do well.
It is thought that the idea will succeed.

By is often used to indicate the person doing the action in a passive construction:

The stock was sold by a broker.
The sink was repaired by a plumber.

Passive verbs can occur in any tense:

Simple present

ACTIVE: The stylist *cuts* my hair every six weeks.
PASSIVE: My hair *is cut* every six weeks.

Present continuous

ACTIVE: She *is* cutting my hair now.
PASSIVE: My hair *is being cut* now.

Present perfect

ACTIVE: She *has cut* my hair every six weeks for most of my life.
PASSIVE: My hair *has been cut* every six weeks for most of my life.

Present perfect continuous

ACTIVE: She *has been cutting* my hair every six weeks for most of my life.
PASSIVE: My hair *has been being cut* every six weeks for most of my life.

Simple past

ACTIVE: The stylist *cut* my hair last week.
PASSIVE: My hair *was cut* last week.

Past continuous

ACTIVE: The stylist *was cutting* my hair when the phone rang.
PASSIVE: My hair *was being cut* when the phone rang.

Future

ACTIVE: The stylist *will cut* my hair tomorrow.
PASSIVE: My hair *will be cut* tomorrow.

The passive construction can also occur with modals (see list of modals on pages 158–59):

ACTIVE:　You *can study* Spanish by listening to tapes.
PASSIVE:　Spanish *can be studied* by listening to tapes.

ACTIVE:　You *may improve* your voice and intonation through practice.
PASSIVE:　Voice and intonation *may be improved* through practice.

ACTIVE:　Parents *must learn* proper child care.
PASSIVE:　Proper child care *must be learned.*

Passive verbs are sometimes used by politicians and other powerful people as a way of avoiding responsibility for their acts or deflecting attention from the performer of the action.

The tuition increase *was agreed* to by the state legislators.
The law *was passed* by the House.
The criminal *was sentenced* to five years in jail.
Your appeal *was denied.*
Your loan application *was turned down.*

Passive verbs are also frequently used in textbooks, especially books about scientific or technological subjects. (Passive verbs are reviewed in Appendix B.)

□　□　□

EXERCISES

1. The following sentences come from the Miller selection at the start of this chapter. Underline the passive verbs in each sentence.

   a. In this way, our attention is drawn to what is "invisible" in our own culture because we are so accustomed to its presence.

   b. Japanese parents believe that babies are born separate beings who must be taught feelings of interdependence with other people, and sleeping with parents is thought to encourage this process.

   c. In contrast, parents in the United States (and most Western social developmental theorists) believe that babies are born dependent and must develop independence; a separate bed is thought to facilitate this.

    d. In some cultures, children are expected to play a passive role in this activity—responding when spoken to but not initiating verbal interactions or participating equally in conversations.

2. Reread the rest of the Miller selection, and note any other uses of passive verbs. Then, with a classmate, reread the selection by Craig in Chapter Eight or by Robbins in Chapter Eleven, looking for any uses of passive verbs. Next, reread the Muñiz selection in Chapter Thirteen, looking for any uses of passive verbs. Compare the numbers of passive verbs you find in various selections. Which writers use the most? Which the least? Why might this be so?

3. Change the following sentences from active to passive construction.

    a. People speak English in many parts of the world.

        _____

    b. He filmed the movie in Seattle, Washington.

        _____

    c. She hung the O'Keeffe paintings in the National Gallery.

        _____

    d. They performed *Porgy and Bess* at the Kennedy Center.

        _____

    e. He replaced all my windows in three hours.

        _____

    f. The dentist filled my teeth with an amalgam.

        _____

4. The following paragraph is written entirely in the passive voice. Add variety to the paragraph by changing some of the sentences to the active voice.

In the past in many countries around the world, marriages were arranged by a matchmaker hired by the family. This matchmaker was expected to make a lasting match. An unhappy marriage was feared by many young people. However, the parents' wishes were respected by the children. Young people were reminded of their obligations by their family and their community. It was expected by everyone that the marriages would lead to love and mutual respect. Divorce was looked down on by most of the community and religious leaders. Marriage was regarded as a lifetime commitment by most people in those days.

5. Reread any selections in this book that interested you. Write down any uses of passive verbs that you want to remember. If the uses of the passive voice confuse you, discuss them with your teacher or a classmate.

□   □   □

CHECKING YOUR OWN WORK

1. Read through each essay you wrote for this chapter. Look at the places in which you used passive verbs. (It may be helpful to underline them lightly.) Did you use them appropriately and correctly? If you are not sure, check the explanation of uses of passive verbs in the previous section.
2. Repeat check 1 with other writing you have done recently.
3. As an added check, work with a classmate to make sure that you have used passive verbs correctly in your writing.

CHAPTER FIFTEEN

Responding to Change

PREREADING ACTIVITIES

1. This story is about a person who left Iran to come to the United States. In a small group, discuss Iran. Where is it? What is its history? What do you know about the relationship between the United States and Iran?
2. The main character in the story is returning to Iran after being away for 14 years. What do you expect her to feel when she returns to her country, home, and family?
3. What do you think the title of the story "Foreigner" means? In a group, discuss the feeling of being a foreigner in a country. Do you think you might feel like a foreigner if you returned to your home country? Have you ever felt like a foreigner in the United States?
4. If there is a Moslem student in the class, that student might inform the other class members about the Islamic religion and traditions.
5. You might want to consult your library to find out more about Islam or about other religions. Write a short paper to hand in to your teacher or present to the class.

VOCABULARY DEVELOPMENT

"Foreigner" introduces us to the special vocabulary of the country of Iran and the religion of Islam. As you read about different countries and peoples, you will be exposed to such new vocabulary.

chador: a garment that Iranian women wear, which is draped around the body, across the shoulders, over the head, and across the lower part of the face.

tomans: Iranian money

mosque: a Moslem place for the worship of God

muezzin: a crier who calls faithful Moslems to prayer

Islam: the religion taught by the Prophet Mohammed in the 600s (Mohammed, who was born in Mecca in 570, taught the worship of one God, Allah, and proclaimed that he, Mohammed, was Allah's messenger. *Islam* is an Arabic word that means "submission." Islam is the faith of approximately one-fifth of the world's population.)

Moslems (Muslims): Believers in Allah who accept Mohammed as

God's messenger. (In Arabic, *Moslem* means "one who submits to God.")

Foreigner

Nahid Rachlin

This excerpt is from the novel Foreigner *by Nahid Rachlin, an Iranian woman who now lives and writes in the United States. It is about a woman returning home to Iran after 14 years. She has to learn to deal with changes in herself, her family, and her country.*

As I boarded the plane at Logan Airport in Boston I paused on the top step and waved to Tony. He waved back. I pulled the window curtain beside me and closed my eyes, seeing Tony's face falling away, bitten by light. 1

In the Teheran airport I was groggy° and disoriented.° I found my valise° and set it on a table, where two customs officers searched it. Behind a large window people waited. The women, mostly hidden under dark chadors, formed a single fluid shape. I kept looking towards the window trying to spot my father, stepmother, or stepbrother, but I did not see any of them. Perhaps they were there and we could not immediately recognize each other. It had been fourteen years since I had seen them. 2

A young man sat on a bench beside the table, his task there not clear. He wore his shirt open and I could see bristles of dark hair on his chest. He was making shadow pictures on the floor—a rabbit, a bird—and then dissolving the shapes between his feet. Energy emanated° from his hands, a crude, confused energy. Suddenly he looked at me, staring into my eyes. I turned away. 3

I entered the waiting room and looked around. Most people had left. There was still no one for me. What could possibly have happened? Normally someone would be there—a definite effort would be made. I fought to shake off my groggy state. 4

A row of phones stood in the corner next to a handicraft° shop. I tried to call my father. There were no phone books and the information line rang busy, on and on. 5

I went outside and approached a collection of taxis. The drivers stood around, talking. "Can I take one of these?" I asked. 6

The men turned to me but no one spoke. 7

"I need a taxi," I said. 8

"Where do you want to go?" one of the men asked. He was old with stooped shoulders and a thin, unfriendly face. I gave him my father's address. 9

°dazed, half awake
°confused
°suitcase

°flowed

°handmade wares

"That's all the way on the other side of the city." He did not move 10
from his spot.

"Please . . . I have to get there somehow." 11

The driver looked at the other men as if this were a group project. 12

"Take her," one of them said. "I would take her myself but I have to 13
get home." He smiled at me.

"All right, get in," the older man said, pointing to a taxi. 14

In the taxi, he turned off the meter almost immediately. "You have to 15
pay me 100 tomans for this."

"That much?" 16

"It would cost you more if I left the meter on." 17

There was no point arguing with him. I sat stiffly and looked out. We 18
seemed to be floating in the sallow° light cast by the street lamps. Thin
old sycamores° lined the sidewalks. Water flowed in the gutters. The
smoky mountains surrounding the city, now barely visible, were like a
dark ring. The streets were more crowded and there were many more
tall western buildings than I had remembered. Cars sped by, bouncing
over holes, passing each other recklessly, honking. My taxi driver also
drove badly and I had visions of an accident, of being maimed.°

We passed through quieter, older sections. The driver slowed down 19
on a narrow street with a mosque at its center, then stopped in front of
a large, squalid° house. This was the street I had lived on for so many
years; here I had played hide-and-seek in alleys and hallways. I had a
fleeting sensation that I had never left this street, that my other life with
Tony had never existed.

I paid the driver, picked up my valise, and got out. On the cracked 20
blue tile above the door, "Akbar Mehri," my father's name, was written.

I banged the iron knocker several times and waited. In the light of the 21
street lamps I could see a beggar with his jaw twisted sitting against the
wall of the mosque. Even though it was rather late, a hum of prayers, like
a moan, rose from the mosque. A Moslem priest came out, looked past
the beggar and spat on the ground. The doors of the house across the
street were open. I had played with two little girls, sisters, who had lived
there. I could almost hear their voices, laughter. The April air was mild
and velvety against my skin but I shivered at the proximity° to my childhood.

A pebble suddenly hit me on the back. I turned but could not see any- 22
one. A moment later another pebble hit my leg and another behind my
knee. More hit the ground. I turned again and saw a small boy running
and hiding in the arched hallway of a house nearby.

I knocked again. 23

There was a thud from the inside, shuffling, and then soft footsteps. 24
The door opened and a man—my father—stood before me. His cheeks
were hollower than I had recalled, the circles under his eyes deeper, and
his hair more evenly gray. We stared at each other.

°pale and yellowish
°trees

°physically harmed

°dirty and neglected

°nearness

°making a twisted facial
expression

"It's you!" He was grimacing,° as though in pain.   25

"Didn't you get my telegram?"   26

He nodded. "We waited for you for two hours this morning at the air-   27
port. What happened to you?"

I was not sure if he was angry or in a daze. "You must have gotten the   28
time mixed up. I meant nine in the evening."

My father stretched his hands forward, about to embrace me but, as   29
though struck by shyness, he let them drop at his sides. "Come in now."

I followed him inside. I too was in the grip of shyness, or something   30
like it.

"I thought you'd never come back," he said.   31

"I know, I know."   32

"You aren't even happy to see me."   33

"That's not true. I'm just . . ."   34

"You're shocked. Of course you are."   35

He went towards the rooms arranged in a semicircle, on the other   36

°porch

side of the courtyard. A veranda° with columns extended along several
of the rooms. Crocuses, unpruned rosebushes, and pomegranate trees
filled the flower beds. The place seemed cramped, untended. But still it
was the same house. Roses would blossom, sparrows would chirp at the
edge of the pool. At dawn and dusk the voice of the muezzin would mix
with the noise of people coming from and going to the nearby bazaars.

We went up the steps onto the veranda and my father opened the   37
door to one of the rooms. He stepped inside and turned on the light. I
paused for a moment, afraid to cross the threshold. I could smell it:
must, jasmin, rosewater, garlic, vinegar, recalling my childhood. Shut
doors with confused noises behind them, slippery footsteps, black,

°lazy

golden-eyed cats staring from every corner, indolent° afternoons when
people reclined on mattresses, forbidden subjects occasionally reaching
me—talk about a heavy flow of menstrual blood, sex inflicted by force,
the last dark words of a woman on her death bed.

My father disappeared into another room. I heard voices whispering   38
and then someone said loudy, "She's here?" Footsteps approached. In
the semidarkness of a doorway at the far end of the room two faces appeared and then another face, like three moons, staring at me.

"Feri, what happened?" a woman's voice asked, and a figure stepped   39
forward. I recognized my stepmother, Ziba. She wore a long, plain cotton nightgown.

"The time got mixed up, I guess." My voice sounded feeble and hesi-   40
tant.

A man laughed and walked into the light too. It was my stepbrother,   41
Darius. He grinned at me, a smile disconnected from his eyes.

"Let's go to the kitchen," my father said. "So that Feri can eat some-   42
thing."

They went back through the same doorway and I followed them. We   43

°one in front of another

walked through the dim, intersecting rooms in tandem.° In one room all the walls were covered with black cloth, and a throne, also covered with a black cloth, was set in a corner—for monthly prayers when neighborhood women would come in and a Moslem priest was invited to give sermons. The women would wail and beat their chests in these sessions as the priest talked about man's guilt or the sacrifices the leaders of Islam had made. They would cry as if at their own irrevocable° guilt and sorrow.

°unchangeable

We were together in the kitchen. Darius, Ziba, my father—they 44 seemed at once familiar and remote like figures in dreams.

Reading and Thinking Strategies

Discussion Activities

Analysis and Conclusions

1. Do you think Feri is wearing a chador, or is she dressed in Western style? Do you think this affects the way she is treated by the men at the airport and the little boy throwing the pebbles?

2. What are some of the details from the story that suggest that Feri feels like a foreigner in her own country?

3. Her father stretches his hands forward as though to embrace her but then drops them. Why does he drop his hands? How does this make her feel?

Writing and Point of View

1. Writers try to create a mood through their choices of words and images. This story is dreamlike. What words and images does Rachlin use to make this story dreamlike?

2. Like Hemingway, Rachlin uses dialogue throughout the story. Do you enjoy stories in which there is dialogue? Why or why not?

3. "A Mortal Flower" in Chapter Twelve is excerpted from an autobiography; "Foreigner" is excerpted from a novel. Are there differences in writing style? Are there any indications that "Foreigner" is fictional? If so, what are they?

Personal Response and Evaluation

1. Rachlin says that the veranda seems "cramped and untended." Sometimes when we return to a place that we knew as children, it seems cramped and smaller than we remember it. Have you ever had that experience? Why do you think this occurs?

2. Do you think Feri will remain in Iran or return to her life in the United States? What in the story helps you decide?

3. Have you ever had an experience similar to Feri's? How did it make you feel?

Response Paragraph

After you have read "Foreigner," write a paragraph about how this story made you feel and what you thought about as you read it. Share your paragraphs with your classmates.

One student wrote the following paragraph:

After I read "Foreigner," it made me think about me visiting my country, Korea, after I had been gone for some time. I'd been gone only four and a half years, but I understand Feri's feelings. Everyone was strange, even my friends, but the places and streets were the same. I talked about our past with my friends. After a few hours, I could feel that they were my friends and they still are. Then I felt I really had come to my hometown. It was hard to catch up to the distance made by four and a half years that we'd been apart, but I believe it was more difficult for Feri. It will take time for her to fit in her family as she was before.

Sohyung Kim, South Korea

Did you feel any of the same feelings as this student felt when she read "Foreigner"?

Extra Reading

A Wagner Matinée
Willa Cather

Willa Cather (1873–1947) was born in Virginia but grew up in the Nebraska countryside. Cather's novels O Pioneers! *and* My Ántonia *focus on life in this part of the United States and the hard lives of the immigrants who settled there. "A Wagner Matinée" is about an experience shared by a young man and his elderly aunt.*

The title of the story refers to a matinée or afternoon performance of music by the German composer Richard Wagner (1813–1883). The two characters in "A Wagner Matinée" have many shared experiences involving music. Knowing about the music may help you understand the context and meaning of the story.

Euryanthe is a nineteenth-century romantic opera written by Carl Maria von Weber (1786–1826), a composer whose work influenced Wagner. Weber was one of the greatest of the German romantic opera composers. Euryanthe tells the love story of Addlor and Euryanthe, who, after many conflicts, are united in the end.

Les Huguenots is a romantic opera that involves religious differences between Catholics and Protestants. It is by Giacomo Meyerbeer (1791–1864), whose compositions also influenced Wagner. This opera ends in the union in death of the two lovers, Raoul and Valentine.

The Flying Dutchman (1840), Tannhäuser *(1844),* Tristan and Isolde *(1859), and* The Ring of the Nibelungs *(1874) are all romantic operas written by Richard Wagner. Many of these operas are based on legends and myths and involve passionate but often tragic love stories.*

Il Trovatore is a romantic opera telling the tragic love story of Leonora and Manrico written by the Italian composer Giuseppe Verdi (1813–1901). Cather also mentions the great Austrian composer Wolfgang Amadeus Mozart (1756–1791) in the story.

I received one morning a letter, written in pale ink on glassy, blue-lined note-paper, and bearing the postmark of a little Nebraska village. This communication, worn and rubbed, looking as if it had been carried for some days in a coat pocket that was none too clean, was from my uncle Howard, and informed me that his wife had been left a small legacy° by a bachelor relative, and that it would be necessary for her to go to Boston to attend to the settling of the estate. He requested me to meet her at the station and render° her whatever services might be necessary. On examining the date indicated as that of her arrival, I found it to be no later than tomorrow. He had characteristically delayed writing until, had I been away from home for a day, I must have missed my aunt altogether.

°inheritance, money left after death

°provide

The name of my Aunt Georgiana opened before me a gulf of recollection so wide and deep that, as the letter dropped from my hand, I felt suddenly a stranger to all the present conditions of my existence, wholly ill at ease and out of place amid the familiar surroundings of my study. I became, in short, the gangling° farmer-boy my aunt had known, scourged° with chilblains° and bashfulness, my hands cracked and sore from the corn husking.° I sat again before her parlor organ, fumbling the scales° with my stiff, red fingers, while she, beside me, made canvas mittens for the huskers.

°awkward, long-legged
°troubled
°a rash from the cold
°removing the outer covering
°musical exercises

The next morning, after preparing my landlady for a visitor, I set out for the station. When the train arrived I had some difficulty finding my aunt. She was the last of the passengers to alight,° and it was not until I got her into the carriage that she seemed really to recognize me. She had come all the way in a day coach; her linen duster° had become black with soot and her black bonnet grey with dust during her journey. When we arrived at my boarding-house the landlady put her to bed at once and I did not see her again until the next morning.

°get off

°light coat

1

2

3

°admiration

°youthful

°ran away to be married
°disapprovals

°open fields

°food and supplies
°roaming, wandering

°respectful

°verb forms
°tired

°mending clothing

°shakily

°not fully conscious

Whatever shock Mrs. Springer experienced at my aunt's appearance,   4
she considerately concealed. As for myself, I saw my aunt's battered figure with that feeling of awe° and respect with which we behold explor-
ers who have left their ears and fingers north of Franz-Joseph-Land, or
their health somewhere along the Upper Congo. My Aunt Georgiana
had been a music teacher at the Boston Conservatory, somewhere back
in the latter sixties. One summer, while visiting in the little village among
the Green Mountains where her ancestors had dwelt for generations,
she had kindled the callow° fancy of my uncle, Howard Carpenter, then
an idle, shiftless boy of twenty-one. When she returned to her duties in
Boston, Howard followed her, and the upshot of this infatuation was that
she eloped° with him, eluding the reproaches° of her family and the crit-
icism of her friends by going with him to the Nebraska frontier.
Carpenter, who, of course, had no money, took up a homestead in Red
Willow County, fifty miles from the railroad. There they had measured
off their land themselves, driving across the prairie° in a wagon, to the
wheel of which they had tied a red cotton handkerchief, and counting
its revolutions. They built a dug-out in the red hillside, one of those cave
dwellings whose inmates so often reverted to primitive conditions. Their
water they got from the lagoons where the buffalo drank, and their slender stock of provisions° was always at the mercy of bands of roving°
Indians. For thirty years my aunt had not been farther than fifty miles
from the homestead.

I owed to this woman most of the good that ever came my way in my   5
boyhood, and had a reverential° affection for her. During the years
when I was riding herd for my uncle, my aunt, after cooking the three
meals—the first of which was ready at six o'clock in the morning—and
putting the six children to bed, would often stand until midnight at her
ironing-board, with me at the kitchen table beside her, hearing me re-
cite Latin declensions° and conjugations, gently shaking me when my
drowsy° head sank down over a page of irregular verbs. It was to her, at
her ironing or mending, that I read my first Shakespeare, and her old
textbook on mythology was the first that ever came into my empty
hands. She taught me my scales and exercises on the little parlor organ
which her husband had bought her after fifteen years during which she
had not so much as seen a musical instrument. She would sit beside me
by the hour, darning° and counting, while I struggled with the "Joyous
Farmer." She seldom talked to me about music, and I understood why.
Once when I had been doggedly beating out some easy passages from an
old score of *Euryanthe* I had found among her music books, she came up
to me and, putting her hands over my eyes, gently drew my head back
upon her shoulder, saying tremulously,° "Don't love it so well, Clark, or
it may be taken from you."

When my aunt appeared on the morning after her arrival in Boston,   6
she was still in a semi-somnambulant° state. She seemed not to realize

that she was in the city where she had spent her youth, the place longed for hungrily half a lifetime. She had been so wretchedly trainsick throughout the journey that she had no recollection of anything but her discomfort, and, to all intents and purposes, there were but a few hours of nightmare between the farm in Red Willow County and my study on Newbury Street. I had planned a little pleasure for her that afternoon, to repay her for some of the glorious moments she had given me when we used to milk together in the straw-thatched cowshed and she, because I was more than usually tired, or because her husband had spoken sharply to me, would tell me of the splendid performance of the *Huguenots* she had seen in Paris, in her youth.

At two o'clock the Symphony Orchestra was to give a Wagner program, and I intended to take my aunt; though, as I conversed with her, I grew doubtful about her enjoyment of it. I suggested our visiting the Conservatory and the Common before lunch, but she seemed altogether too timid[°] to wish to venture out. She questioned me absently about various changes in the city, but she was chiefly concerned that she had forgotten to leave instructions about feeding half-skimmed milk to a certain weakling calf, "old Maggie's calf, you know, Clark," she explained, evidently having forgotten how long I had been away. She was further troubled because she had neglected to tell her daughter about the freshly-opened kit[°] of mackerel[°] in the cellar, which would spoil if it were not used directly.

I asked her whether she had ever heard any of the Wagnerian operas, and found that she had not, though she was perfectly familiar with their respective situations, and had once possessed the piano score of *The Flying Dutchman*. I began to think it would be best to get her back to Red Willow County without waking her, and regretted having suggested the concert.

From the time we entered the concert hall, however, she was a trifle[°] less passive and inert,[°] and for the first time seemed to perceive her surroundings. I had felt some trepidation[°] lest she might become aware of her queer, country clothes, or might experience some painful embarrassment at stepping suddenly into the world to which she had been dead for a quarter of a century. But, again, I found how superficially I had judged her. She sat looking about her with eyes as impersonal, almost as stony, as those with which the granite[°] Rameses[°] in a museum watches the froth and fret that ebbs and flows about his pedestal. I have seen this same aloofness in old miners who drift into the Brown hotel at Denver, their pockets full of bullion,[°] their linen soiled, their haggard faces unshaven; standing in the thronged corridors as solitary as though they were still in a frozen camp on the Yukon.[°]

The matinée audience was made up chiefly of women. One lost the contour of faces and figures, indeed any effect of line whatever, and there was only the color of bodices[°] past counting, the shimmer of fabrics soft and firm, silky and sheer; red, mauve, pink, blue, lilac, purple,

7

8

9

10

Margin glosses:

[°]shy

[°]container
[°]type of fish

[°]slightly
[°]unmoving
[°]anxiety

[°]stone
[°]Egyptian king

[°]gold

[°]Canadian river

[°]upper parts of dresses

écru, rose, yellow, cream, and white, all the colors that an impressionist finds in a sunlit landscape, with here and there the dead shadow of a frock coat. My Aunt Georgiana regarded them as though they had been so many daubs of tube-paint on a palette.

When the musicians came out and took their places, she gave a little 11 stir of anticipation, and looked with quickening interest down over the rail at that invariable grouping, perhaps the first wholly familiar thing that had greeted her eye since she had left old Maggie and her weakling calf. I could feel how all those details sank into her soul, for I had not forgotten how they had sunk into mine when I came fresh from plow-ing° forever and forever between green aisles of corn, where, as in a treadmill, one might walk from daybreak to dusk without perceiving a shadow of change. The clean profiles of the musicians, the gloss of their linen, the dull black of their coats, the beloved shapes of the instru-ments, the patches of yellow light on the smooth, varnished bellies of the 'cellos and the bass viols in the rear, the restless, wind-tossed forest of fiddle necks and bows—I recalled how, in the first orchestra I ever heard, those long bow-strokes seemed to draw the heart out of me, as a conjurer's° stick reels out yards of paper ribbon from a hat.

The first number was the *Tannhäuser* overture. When the horns drew 12 out the first strain of the Pilgrim's chorus, Aunt Georgiana clutched my coat sleeve. Then it was I first realized that for her this broke a silence of thirty years. With the battle between the two motives,° with the frenzy of the Venusberg theme and its ripping of strings, there came to me an overwhelming sense of the waste and wear we are so powerless to com-bat; and I saw again the tall, naked house on the prairie, black and grim as a wooden fortress; the black pond where I had learned to swim, its margin pitted with sun-dried cattle tracks; the rain-gullied clay banks about the naked house, the four dwarf-ash seedlings° where the dish-cloths were always hung to dry before the kitchen door. The world there was the flat world of the ancients; to the east, a cornfield that stretched to daybreak; to the west, a corral that reached to sunset; between, the conquests of peace, dearer-bought than those of war.

The overture° closed, my aunt released my coat sleeve, but she said 13 nothing. She sat staring dully at the orchestra. What, I wondered, did she get from it? She had been a good pianist in her day, I knew, and her musical education had been broader than that of most music teachers of a quarter of a century ago. She had often told me of Mozart's operas and Meyerbeer's, and I could remember hearing her sing, years ago, cer-tain melodies of Verdi. When I had fallen ill with a fever in her house she used to sit by my cot° in the evening—when the cool, night wind blew in through the faded mosquito netting tacked over the window and I lay watching a certain bright star that burned red above the corn-field—and sing "Home to our mountains, O, let us return!" in a way fit to break the heart of a Vermont boy near dead of homesickness al-ready.

°doing field work

°magician's

°musical themes

°young trees

°musical introduction

°bed

°figure out
°silently

°arms of an octopus

°male singer

°wanderer
°cowboy
°cowboys'

°card game

°humor

I watched her closely through the prelude to *Tristan and Isolde,* trying 14
vainly to conjecture° what that seething turmoil of strings and winds
might mean to her, but she sat mutely° staring at the violin bows that
drove obliquely downward, like the pelting streaks of rain in a summer
shower. Had this music any message for her? Had she enough left to at
all comprehend this power which had kindled the world since she had
left it? I was in a fever of curiosity, but Aunt Georgiana sat silent upon
her peak in Darien. She preserved this utter immobility throughout the
number from *The Flying Dutchman,* though her fingers worked mechan-
ically upon her black dress, as if, of themselves, they were recalling the
piano score they had once played. Poor hands! They had been stretched
and twisted into mere tentacles° to hold and lift and knead with;—on
one of them a thin, worn band that had once been a wedding ring. As I
pressed and gently quieted one of those groping hands, I remembered
with quivering eyelids their services for me in other days.

Soon after the tenor° began the "Prize Song," I heard a quick drawn 15
breath and turned to my aunt. Her eyes were closed, but the tears were
glistening on her cheeks, and I think, in a moment more, they were in
my eyes as well. It never really died, then—the soul which can suffer so
excruciatingly and so interminably; it withers to the outward eye only;
like that strange moss which can lie on a dusty shelf half a century and
yet, if placed in water, grows green again. She wept so throughout the
development and elaboration of the melody.

During the intermission before the second half, I questioned my aunt 16
and found that the "Prize Song" was not new to her. Some years before
there had drifted to the farm in Red Willow County a young German, a
tramp° cow-puncher,° who had sung in the chorus at Bayreuth when he
was a boy, along with the other peasant boys and girls. Of a Sunday
morning he used to sit on his gingham-sheeted bed in the hands'° bedroom which opened off the kitchen, cleaning the leather of his boots
and saddle, singing the "Prize Song," while my aunt went about her work
in the kitchen. She had hovered over him until she had prevailed upon
him to join the country church, though his sole fitness for this step, in
so far as I could gather, lay in his boyish face and his possession of this
divine melody. Shortly afterward, he had gone to town on the Fourth of
July, been drunk for several days, lost his money at a faro° table, ridden
a saddled Texas steer on a bet, and disappeared with a fractured collar-
bone. All this my aunt told me huskily, wanderingly, as though she were
talking in the weak lapses of illness.

"Well, we have come to better things than the old *Trovatore* at any rate, 17
Aunt Georgie?" I queried, with a well-meant effort at jocularity.°

Her lip quivered and she hastily put her handkerchief up to her 18
mouth. From behind it she murmured, "And you have been hearing this
ever since you left me, Clark?" Her question was the gentlest and saddest
of reproaches.

The second half of the program consisted of four numbers of the 19 *Ring,* and closed with Siegfried's funeral march. My aunt wept quietly, but almost continuously, as a shallow vessel overflows in a rain-storm. From time to time her dim eyes looked up at the lights, burning softly under their dull glass globes.

The deluge of sound poured on and on; I never knew what she found 20 in the shining current of it; I never knew how far it bore her, or past what happy islands. From the trembling of her face I could well believe that before the last number she had been carried out where the myriad° ⁰countless graves are, into the grey, nameless burying grounds of the sea; or into some world of death vaster yet, where, from the beginning of the world, hope has lain down with hope and dream with dream and, renouncing, slept.

The concert was over; the people filed out of the hall chattering and 21 laughing, glad to relax and find the living level again, but my kinswom-an° made no effort to rise. The harpist slipped the green felt cover over ⁰relative his instrument; the flute-players shook the water from their mouth-pieces; the men of the orchestra went out one by one, leaving the stage to the chairs and music stands, empty as a winter cornfield.

I spoke to my aunt. She burst into tears and sobbed pleadingly. "I 22 don't want to go, Clark, I don't want to go!"

I understood. For her, just outside the concert hall, lay the black 23 pond with the cattle-tracked bluffs; the tall, unpainted house, with ⁰bent weather-curled boards, naked as a tower; the crook-backed° ash ⁰thin seedlings where the dish-cloths hung to dry; the gaunt,° moulting ⁰garbage turkeys picking up refuse° about the kitchen door.

Discussion Activities

1. What is the theme of "A Wagner Matinée"?
2. What is the symbol of music in this story?
3. How does the setting help the reader understand the characters in this story?
4. Describe the characters. What moral lessons, psychological princi-ples, or philosophical insights do you gain from reading about them?
5. What similarities and what differences are there between the excerpt from Casals's autobiography in Chapter Nine and the Cather story?

Journal Writing

What is writing, if it is not the countenance of our daily experience: sensuous, contemplative, imaginary, what we see and hear, dream of, how it strikes us, how it comes into us, travels through us, and emerges in some language hopefully useful to others.

M. C. RICHARDS, *Centering: Poetry, Pottery and the Person*

Journals let us record our impressions of the world and make sense of them with our words. Sometimes we record dreams and sometimes real events; regardless, we try to use our journal entries to deepen our understanding of ourselves and, at the same time, to improve our writing.

When you write this time, think of dreams, of returning to places that you have thought about and had mixed feelings about. Before you write, you might want to cluster around the word *foreigner* or *dream*. You may want to write a story, a poem, or prose (writing that is not a poem). This short poem by a Russian poet may help you reflect on these ideas and stimulate your mind and pen.

TO MY SISTER

I dreamt of the old house   1
where I spent my childhood years,
and the heart, as before, finds
comfort, and love, and warmth.

I dreamt of Christmas, the tree,   2
and my sister laughing out loud,
from morning, the rosy windows
sparkle tenderly.

And in the evening gifts are given   3
and the pine needles smell of stories,
And golden stars risen
are scattered like cinder above the rooftop.

I know that our old house   4
is falling into disrepair
Bare, despondent branches
knock against darkening panes.

And in the room with its old furniture,   5
a resentful captive, cooped up,
lives our father, lonely and weary—
he feels abandoned by us.

Why, oh why do I dream of the country   6
where the love's all consumed, all?
Maria, my friend, my sister,
speak my name, call to me, call . . .

OLGA BERGGOLTS

Writing Strategies

Essay Strategies

Setting the Mood in Your Writing

images

To understand how images can create a feeling or understanding on the part of the reader, let's examine some of the images Rachlin uses.

In the Teheran airport, Rachlin tells us about the relationships between men and women.

The women, mostly hidden under dark chadors, formed a single fluid shape.

What does this sentence tell us about the women in the airport?

_____

Do you think Feri is wearing a chador? Why would Rachlin want the reader to know if Feri were wearing a chador?

_____

A young man sat on a bench beside the table, his task there not clear. He wore his shirt open and I could see bristles of dark hair on his chest.

Contrast these two descriptions. What is Rachlin telling us about the differences between men and women in Teheran?

_____

The April air was mild and velvety against my skin but I shivered at the proximity to my childhood.

There is an interesting contrast of images in this sentence. What does it tell the reader about Feri's childhood?

_____

mood

Rachlin creates a dreamlike mood with her choice of descriptive words.

We seemed to be floating in the sallow light cast by the street lamps.

"Floating" creates a very dreamy feeling. "Sallow light" is a shadowy light, as contrasted with bright, sunny light.

The smoky mountains surrounding the city, now barely visible, were like a dark ring.

"Smoky mountains" conveys an image that is vague, cloudy, and dreamy. "Barely visible" gives the reader the same feeling.

Read through the story, looking for other images that suggest dreams.

Rachlin has used many delicate poetic images to convey strong feelings. What do you think Rachlin wants the reader to think about Feri?

_____

What do you think Rachlin wants the reader to think about Feri's family?

_____

What do you think Rachlin wants the reader to think about Teheran?

_____

Similes and Metaphors

Writers use comparisons to enrich their writing. One type of comparison is the *simile*—a comparison of unlike things, usually using the word *like* or *as:*

In the semidarkness of a doorway at the far end of the room two faces appeared and then another face, *like* three moons staring at me. (Moons are known to us, yet they are remote and mysterious.)

Writers also use *metaphors* to describe feelings and events. A metaphor uses a word or term that usually stands for one thing to represent another:

I pulled the window curtains beside me and closed my eyes, seeing Tony's face falling away, bitten by light. (This implies that Tony is disappearing, being eaten up by the light.)

The women, mostly hidden under dark chadors, formed a single fluid shape. (This suggests that the women look the same and seem to melt into each other, to form a liquid mass.)

The April air was mild and velvety against my skin. . . . (This implies a softness in the air.)

Poets use words very carefully. They are always looking for exactly the right word to convey meaning. Poets work with fewer words than prose writers do; however, prose writers must also be concerned with finding the right word. The examples illustrate some of the ways in which Rachlin was able to influence the reader's view of her characters and the city she describes. When you write, keep in mind the power of words. Search for the right word to help your reader understand what you have written.

Essay Form

Writing about Literature

Writing about literature is complicated and is the subject of many specialized courses. We will look at only the basic aspects of writing about literature that will help you as you read and write about what you have read.

When you write about a poem, story, play, or novel, you explore the work's meaning. Usually, you are expected to do a straightforward discussion of one or two of its techniques. For example, if you were writing about a short story, you might describe the theme of the story and examine the attitudes of one of its characters. You might analyze an action of one of the characters, interpret a symbol, or comment on the form of the writing. Or you might explain the social context or world within which the story is situated.

To do any of these, you are expected to have done a close reading of the piece of literature. Your interpretations should refer to the text itself, and you must support your ideas by referring to specific passages in the text itself.

describing a theme

The theme of a piece of literature is its central or dominant idea, its comment on life. This is not a summary of the work; it involves looking for a larger meaning. Is "Foreigner" simply the story of a young woman returning home after 14 years? Is it rather about the theme of loss and gain? Is the theme the constancy of family love? These are just two possibilities. As a writer, you must explain your interpretation of the theme by citing incidents or lines or phrases from the work that support your interpretation. It is important that your teacher understand how you constructed your interpretation.

□   □   □

EXERCISES

1. What is the theme of "To My Sister," by Olga Berggolts, on page 332? What in the poem supports your answer?
2. What is the theme of "These Days" by Charles Olson, on page 287? What in the poem supports your answer?

analyzing action

Looking at the action that takes place in literature allows us to examine how characters handle dilemmas, difficult situations, and ordinary circumstances. From the way these characters behave, we learn moral lessons, psychological principles, and philosophical insights. When we describe what particular characters did at particular times, we analyze their behavior by looking for such lessons, principles, and insights. Again, it is necessary to support the analysis with examples from the writing itself.

interpreting symbols

A symbol is a thing that stands for something else. Apple pie is a symbol of home and family to people in the United States. A dove is a symbol of peace. A hawk is a symbol of war. Symbols differ from culture to culture. In literature, a symbol is created when a person, an action, an object, or an idea seems to have significance beyond itself. For example, in "These Days," what is the symbolism of roots? What in the poem supports your reading of this?

The reader discovers symbolism through careful reading and analysis. The writer must include examples from the text to support the interpretation of something as symbolic. Because symbols may be specific to a particular culture, the writer may have to explain the importance of the symbol in that culture. Does this mean that a piece of literature could have a different meaning depending on the cultural background of the reader?

commenting on form

Looking at form, the writer describes the author's vocabulary and sentence structure to examine how the writer expresses ideas. You may want to look at how the writer uses similes, metaphors, and images. You may also describe the use of flashbacks, flashforwards, and other literary techniques.

This type of analysis will be taught in greater detail in literature classes in your college.

explaining social context

Examining the social context, the place and historical time in which a piece of literature takes place, provides other insights into the meaning of the writing. If "Foreigner" had been written about a different country or in a different time period, would its meaning be altered? Explain this by referring to the text and to other texts written about the same place in a different time period, the same theme in a different place or time, and the same time period in a different place.

Basic ideas to keep in mind

1. Before you write about any piece of literature, read it carefully.
2. Your ideas must be supported with examples, actual passages, statements, or phrases from the text you have read.

3. Explain how the examples support or prove your interpretation of what you have read.

4. Most well-known pieces of literature have been written about and studied many times. As you continue studying literature, you will want to read some of the other interpretations of the texts about which you are writing.

□   □   □

EXERCISES

1. As a class, discuss "Foreigner." What is its theme? What is the significance of the action that takes place? What symbols can you find in the story? What do you notice about its form? Where and when does the story take place?

2. Do the same set of activities for "A Day's Wait" by Ernest Hemingway in Chapter Three.

3. Do the same set of activities for "The All-American Slurp" by Lensey Namioka in Chapter Six.

4. Do the same set of activities for "A Mortal Flower" by Han Suyin in Chapter Twelve.

5. Do the same set of activities for "A Wagner Matinée" by Willa Cather earlier in this chapter.

6. What did you learn about each piece of literature from examining it in these ways?

Suggestions for Writing

1. Write an analysis of "Foreigner" using one or two of the techniques discussed in the "Essay Form" section and some of the results of your class discussion about the story. Focus on theme, one of the characters, action, symbols, form, or social context. Make sure you include passages from the text to support your point of view.

2. Do an analysis of the poem "To My Sister" or one of the stories in this book.

3. Choose a favorite poem or story from your own culture, and write an analysis as described in "Essay Form." Bring the poem or story to class. Be prepared to share it with your classmates.

4. Choose a student essay from one of the chapters in the book that you particularly liked or thought was well written. Write an essay describing the piece, explaining why you chose it and what you have learned as a writer from reading it.

5. Choose a favorite poem or story written by a North American writer, and write an analysis. Bring the poem or story to class, and be prepared to share it with your classmates.

Class Project

Read the novel *Foreigner* in its entirety. As a class, discuss the theme, characters, action, form, symbolism, and setting. What does the book mean in light of these considerations? How does this discussion provide a deeper and richer experience in reading? Write about what you have learned by doing this.

Getting Started

Focused Clustering with a Partner

On your own or with a partner, write the name of your literary selection at the top of your page, and draw a circle around it. Then write the words *theme, actions, characters, symbols,* and *setting* underneath it from left to right, and draw lines from the name of the selection to each of these words. Look at the words, and start fillng in any ideas that occur to you beneath them. Put your ideas in the appropriate column on the page.

Work in this way for about 15 minutes. Read down the columns that have developed. One may seem more interesting than the others. Or you may notice that you have more words in one column than in another. This may be the area on which you want to focus your literary analysis.

Revising

After you have finished writing the first draft of your essay, separate yourself from your writing by reading the following essay written by a student about a book she had read in class. Think about how well this student has followed some of the ideas presented in this chapter for writing about a piece of literature.

A Student Essay

WRITING ABOUT A BOOK

The book *Hunger of Memory* by Richard Rodriguez is an autobiography, 1 and it has important themes in it. The author has written six chapters, "Aria," "The Achievement of Desire," "Credo," "Complexion," "Profession," and "Mr. Secrets." The titles tell something about the themes of the book.

The first chapter of the book covers Rodriguez's childhood and 2 school education. He describes his experiences when he went to a Catholic school where they spoke only English. He says, "I was astonished" when he entered the classroom and heard his name in English for the first time. This is a simple statement, but it is honest. Every child at home is a child in a special atmosphere, but when he goes to school, he becomes a "student." The formality of the new experience shocks the child. Rodriguez writes, "Quickly I turned to see my mother's face dissolve in a watery blur behind the pebbled glass door" (p. 11). This is a significant expression of the child's feelings as he was left among strangers by his own mother. This is also a symbolic moment when a child begins his own life separate from his mother, his family, and in this case, his language. Rodriguez is a very emotional and sensitive child. Sometimes words can become a mirror image of a person's mind. Rodriguez's words are rich enough to offer a good sense of the writer's feelings the very first time he entered school.

This connects back to Rodriguez's feelings about language, a theme 3 that occurs throughout the book. Rodriguez thinks his native language, Spanish, is the language that is his own alone and cannot be shared among the people outside his family. He writes: "It is not possible for a child—any child—ever to use his family's language in school" (p. 12).

Rodriguez has given a good description of being an immigrant in a 4 new place. He feels so much surrounded by strangers speaking a strange language that he feels uncomfortable quite constantly. At times he seems overconscious of this feeling. A constant feeling of alienation keeps him occupied analyzing each and every small action or comment around him. He helps his readers feel his alienation as he does this.

He felt sorry for himself in the beginning. He felt sorry for his par- 5 ents. He felt sorry and ashamed because they did not know English and could not converse with their neighbors or with his teachers. He was engrossed with his own feeling of inferiority because of his poor command of English at the start. "I was unable to hear my own sounds, but I knew very well that I spoke English poorly. My words could not stretch far enough to form complex thoughts" (p. 14).

Rodriguez does not believe in bilingual education. He says, "As a so- 6 cially disadvantaged child, I considered Spanish to be a private language" (p. 19). He suggests that outside the home, children should be taught the public language as early as possible. Rodriguez writes about the themes of alienation, family, and the power of language in this important and beautifully written book.

Sampada Arya, India

After you have finished reading this essay, think about the following questions.

1. Did the writer let you know how she had interpreted the piece of literature she had read?

2. Did the student use passages from the text to support her ideas?

How did she let you know where in the text these passages appeared?

3. What did you like best about this essay?

4. What additional information would you have liked to see?

Reread your own draft, asking yourself the same questions. Think about the best way to improve your essay. Rewrite it, making any revisions you think will make the essay stronger, clearer, and more informative. Share the revised essay with a classmate.

Editing Strategies

Mechanics

Adjective Word Order

When we describe, we use adjectives—sometimes series of adjectives. In English, there is a required order for these adjectives. Following is a chart illustrating adjective word order. After studying the chart, read the sentences that follow it, using the words provided to fill in the blanks in the proper order. The first two have been done for you. Check your answers by referring to the chart. This chart is meant to help you when you write, but you do not have to memorize it. The more you write, the more familiar you will become with word order, and it will eventually become natural to you.

The Order of Adjectives in English

Articles and Possessives	Numbers: Ordinal and Cardinal	General Descriptive Adjectives and Some Adjectives Ending in -ed, -ing, -y, ful, -ous*	Size*	Shape	Age	Color	Adjectives of Nationality and Religion and Some Adjectives Ending in ic, -al, -ed, -y	Noun Adjuncts	Nouns
the	two		big	angular	old	green	air-conditioned	convertible	cars
her	three	lovely	little	slender	newborn	gray	Burmese		cats
Louise's		famous		long		blue	lacy	evening	gown
a		chipped	huge	square		blue and white	English	soup	bowl
a		weeping	tiny	round	old	gray-haired	French		lady
a	first	quick					comic		scream

*These positions are sometimes interchangeable.

1. <u>*Thin, old sycamores*</u> lined the sidewalks.
   (sycamores, old, thin)

2. Facing the open windows stood <u>*a comfortable, roomy armchair*</u>.
   (roomy, comfortable, a, armchair)

3. _____ surrounding the city, now barely visible,
   (smoky, the, mountains)

   were like _____.
   (dark, ring, a)

4. The doctor examined the boy and then left prescriptions for

   _____.
   (medicines, three, different)

5. It was _____, the ground covered with sleet.
   (cold, a, day, bright)

6. Papa took _____ for a walk on the road.
   (two, the, setters, young, Irish)

7. _____ emanated from his hands.
   (energy, a, confused, crude)

8. I had _____, a green dress, a brown dress, and one
   (two, uniforms, school)

   dress with three rows of frills for Sunday, too dressy for an inter-

   view.

9. I had no shoes except _____ and tennis shoes.
   (shoes, flat-heeled, school)

10. We walked along _____ , hearing the dogs
    (outer, high, wall, gray, its)

    scream in the kennels, and came to its other gate, which was

    _____.
    (gate, administration, the, building)

11. It had _____, one male, one female.
    (two, stone, large, lions)

12. Mr. Harned was tall and thin, with _____, a long chin,
    (bald, small, head, a)

    and enormous glasses.

13. Feri walked up _____ to her house.
    (winding, the, staircase, long, empty)

14. She sat at _____ and began to write.
    (desk, old, wooden, carved, her)

15. Staring at his son's picture, he held _____ in
    (old, his, pen, green, fountain)

    his hand.

16. He wanted to write, but suddenly he felt very tired; he sat on

_____ and fell asleep.
(plaid, the, soft, old, brown, chair)

☐ ☐ ☐

EXERCISE   Describe a person you saw on the street today, using long strings of descriptive words. After you have finished, refer to the chart to check the order of your adjectives.

Editing Practice

Editing Other People's Writing

The following paragraph is a first draft. It contains many errors. Edit and rewrite the paragraph, correcting the errors. Answers are on page 360.

Returning home can be very difficult. As we see in Nahid Rachlin's story *foreigner.* People return to their home countries they often find many changes. The familiar, old streets may not look the same. People they remember may not recognized them. If they go back to their own childhood house. The house may look very different. It may appear small and cramped. One women wrote that she returned to her neighborhood and her house was gone. In its place was a little grocery modern store. No one remembers her. She is extremely depressed. It is also possible to return to a place where everyone remember you. That makes a person happy inside; at least you were not forgotten.

Editing Your Own Writing

Reread an essay that you wrote for this chapter, asking yourself the following questions:

1. Did I format my paper correctly?
2. Did I start new paragraphs when necessary?
3. Did I use final sentence punctuation and apostrophes correctly?
4. Did I use the past tenses correctly?
5. Did I use the present tense correctly? Do my subjects and verbs agree?

6. Did I use quotation marks correctly?
7. Did I use pronouns correctly? Do the pronouns agree?
8. Did I form plurals correctly?
9. Did I use *the* correctly?
10. Did I use capital letters where they are needed?
11. Did I use commas correctly?
12. Did I use other punctuation marks correctly?
13. Did I use modals correctly?
14. Did I use comparatives correctly?
15. Are all the sentences complete, with no run-ons or fragments?
16. Did I use connecting words appropriately?
17. Are all series—places where I have used *and, or,* or *but*—parallel?
18. Did I use the passive construction correctly?
19. Are all adjectives presented in the correct order?

When you rewrite your essay, make any changes that will improve your writing.

Grammar Strategies

Conditionals Using *if*

Conditionals are used in English for a number of reasons and in a number of forms:

1. To express relationships that are true and unchanging:

If you lower the temperature of water to 0°C, it freezes.
If you boil water, it vaporizes.

Note that the present tense is used in both clauses. This kind of conditional is often used in scientific writing.

2. To express relationships that are habitual:

If I wash the car, it rains.
If I had washed the car, it would have rained.

Note: In 1 and 2, it is possible to substitute *when* or *whenever* for *if* without changing the meaning of the sentence:

When (whenever) you lower the temperature of water to 0°C, it freezes.

Try using *when* or *whenever* with the other examples.

3. To express inferences:

   If the police can't solve that crime, no one can.
   If you'll go to Pierre's party, I'll go too.
   If you act happy, the baby will stop crying.

4. To express a condition in the future:

   If it snows, I'll wear my boots.
   If you do your homework, you'll pass the course.
   If you call me tonight, I'll call you tomorrow.

   The first clause uses the present tense, and the second clause uses the future tense.

5. To express unlikely but possible events:

   If I had the energy, I would jog tonight.
   If he had left work early, he would be home by now.

   The first clause uses *had,* and the second clause uses *would.*

6. To express impossible events:

   If I had your face, I would become a model.
   If Gandhi were alive today, he would make peace in the world.

7. To express past contrary-to-fact situations:

   I would have done better in my English class if I had studied more.
   If workers had protested poor conditions sooner, employers might have been forced to make changes sooner.
   If employment had been available in their homelands, many immigrants would not have moved to this country.

   Note that we use the past perfect tense (*had* + past participle) to express the untrue condition and the past conditional tense (*would have, could have,* or *might have*) to express the main clause of the sentence. The *if* clause can come at the beginning or the end of the sentence.

Using *were* in Conditionals

English uses *were* to indicate unlikely or impossible circumstances. "If I were a genius" means that the writer is not a genius. *Were* is used with all subjects (*I, you, we, he, she, it, they*) to indicate an unlikely or untrue situation:

> If he were to win the lottery, he would buy his parents a new house. (He does not expect to win the lottery.)
> If they were to quit their jobs, they would go to Hawaii. (They do not expect to quit their jobs.)
> If I were you, I would study harder. (I am not and could never be you.)

Notice that the independent clause that follows the *were* part of the sentence uses *would* and no ending on the verb that follows. You can also use *should, could, ought to,* and *might* in this structure.

☐ ☐ ☐

EXERCISES

1. Complete the following sentences using the structure just described.

a. If he were to win the contest, he ought to _____

_____ .

b. If I were you, I might _____ .

c. If a student were to fail a course, she might _____ .

d. If schools were to give automatic passing grades to all students, stu-

dents could _____ .

e. If I were to win the lottery, I would _____ .

2. Write conditional sentences about the following situations.

a. I don't have time to clean my house, so it is very messy. If

_____ .

b. They want to learn to dance, but they don't have money for

lessons. If _____ .

c. Marcella had to work last night, so she couldn't go to the party. If

_____ .

d. Wendy forgot her friend's birthday, so she didn't call her.   If

_____ .

e. It is supposed to rain, but I don't own an umbrella.   If

_____ .

Using the Verb *wish*

1. To express a present wish, the verb after *wish* is in the past tense. If that verb is *be*, use *were* with all subjects, just as in *if* clauses.

Po Ching *wishes* she *were* able to see her family more often. (This means that she cannot see her family as much as she wants to.)
Lee *wishes* he *had moved* into the dorm when he had the chance. (He did not.)
Rana *wishes* she *would* win the lottery.

2. To express a past wish, we use the past perfect.

I wish I hadn't missed your birthday party. (I did miss the party.)
Marguerite wishes she had found her lost book. (She did not find her book.)

□   □   □

EXERCISES

1. Complete this paragraph.

In this unit, we read about cultural change and customs. What would

I do if I were Maria Muñiz? If I were Maria Muñiz, I _____

_____ . What kind of research would I do if I were a researcher

like Patricia Miller? If I _____ Miller, I _____

_____ . What would I do if I went home and my family

treated me the way that Feri's family treats her in the Rachlin story?

If I _____ Feri, I _____ .

It is hard to predict what would you do if you _____

_____ in someone else's footsteps. Of course, we all think we know

what we _____ do, but in real life, the decisions

and the situations are always different from what we expect.

2. Reread any selections in this book that interested you. Write down any uses of the conditional that you want to remember. If the uses of conditional voice confuse you, discuss them with your teacher or a classmate.

□   □   □

CHECKING YOUR OWN WORK

1. Read through each essay you wrote for this chapter. Look at the places in which you used the conditional. (It may be helpful to underline them lightly.) Did you use them appropriately and correctly? If you are not sure, check the explanation of uses of the conditional in the previous section.
2. Repeat check 1 with other writing you have done recently.
3. As an added check, work with a classmate to make sure that you have used the conditional correctly in your writing.

Principal Parts of Irregular Verbs

Base	Past	Past participle
awake	awoke, awaked	awoken, awaked
be	was, were	been
bear	bore	borne
beat	beat	beat, beaten
become	became	become
begin	began	begun
bend	bent	bent
bet	bet	bet
bind	bound	bound
bite	bit	bit, bitten
bleed	bled	bled
blow	blew	blown
break	broke	broken
breed	bred	bred
bring	brought	brought
build	built	built
burst	burst	burst
buy	bought	bought
catch	caught	caught
choose	chose	chosen
come	came	come
cost	cost	cost
creep	crept	crept
cut	cut	cut
deal	dealt	dealt
dig	dug	dug

Base	*Past*	*Past participle*
dive	dived, dove	dived
do	did	done
draw	drew	drawn
dream	dreamed, dreamt	dreamed, dreamt
drink	drank	drunk
drive	drove	driven
eat	ate	eaten
fall	fell	fallen
feed	fed	fed
feel	felt	felt
fight	fought	fought
find	found	found
fit	fit, fitted	fit, fitted
flee	fled	fled
fly	flew	flown
forbid	forbade	forbidden
forget	forgot	forgotten, forgot
freeze	froze	frozen
get	got	gotten, got
give	gave	given
go	went	gone
grind	ground	ground
grow	grew	grown
hang (an object)	hung	hung
hang (a person)	hanged	hanged
have	had	had
hear	heard	heard
hide	hid	hidden, hid
hit	hit	hit
hold	held	held
hurt	hurt	hurt
keep	kept	kept
kneel	knelt, kneeled	knelt, kneeled
knit	knitted, knit	knitted, knit
know	knew	known

Base	Past	Past participle
lay (put)	laid	laid
lead	led	led
lean	leaned, leant	leaned, leant
leave	left	left
lend	lent	lent
let (allow)	let	let
lie (recline)	lay	lain
light	lighted, lit	lighted, lit
lose	lost	lost
make	made	made
mean	meant	meant
pay	paid	paid
prove	proved	proved, proven
quit	quit, quitted	quit, quitted
read	read	read
rid	rid, ridded	rid, ridded
ride	rode	ridden
ring	rang	rung
rise	rose	risen
run	ran	run
say	said	said
see	saw	seen
seek	sought	sought
sell	sold	sold
send	sent	sent
set	set	set
shake	shook	shaken
shine	shone, shined	shone, shined
shoot	shot	shot
show	showed	shown, showed
shrink	shrank	shrunk
shut	shut	shut
sing	sang	sung
sink	sank	sunk
sit	sat	sat

Base	*Past*	*Past participle*
sleep	slept	slept
slide	slid	slid, slidden
speak	spoke	spoken
speed	sped, speeded	sped, speeded
spend	spent	spent
spin	spun	spun
split	split	split
spread	spread	spread
spring	sprang	sprung
stand	stood	stood
steal	stole	stolen
stick	stuck	stuck
sting	stung	stung
strike	struck	struck, stricken
swear	swore	sworn
swim	swam	swum
swing	swung	swung
take	took	taken
teach	taught	taught
tear	tore	torn
tell	told	told
think	thought	thought
throw	threw	thrown
wake	woke, waked	woken, waked
wear	wore	worn
weave	wove	woven
weep	wept	wept
win	won	won
wring	wrung	wrung
write	wrote	written

Models for Tenses

Active Voice

SINGULAR	PLURAL	SINGULAR	PLURAL

Simple Present Tense

I go	we go		
you go	you go		
he goes			
she goes	they go		
it goes			

Simple Past Tense

I lived	we lived	
you lived	you lived	
he lived		
she lived	they lived	
it lived		

Simple Future Tense

I will learn	we will learn
you will learn	you will learn
he will learn	
she will learn	they will learn
it will learn	

Present Perfect Tense

I have seen	we have seen
you have seen	you have seen
he has seen	
she has seen	they have seen
it has seen	

Past Perfect Tense

I had jumped	we had jumped
you had jumped	you had jumped
he had jumped	
she had jumped	they had jumped
it had jumped	

Present Continuous Tense

I am helping	we are helping
you are helping	you are helping
he is helping	
she is helping	they are helping
it is helping	

Past Continuous Tense

I was sleeping	we were sleeping
you were sleeping	you were sleeping
he was sleeping	
she was sleeping	they were sleeping
it was sleeping	

Future Continuous Tense

I will be playing	we will be playhing
you will be playing	you will be playing
he will be playing	
she will be playing	they will be playing
it will be playing	

Present Perfect Continuous Tense

I have been trying	we have been trying
you have been trying	you have been trying
he has been trying	
she has been trying	they have been trying
it has been trying	

Past Perfect Continuous Tense

I had been running	we had been running
you had been running	you had been running
he had been running	
she had been running	they had been running
it had been running	

Active Voice

SINGULAR	PLURAL	SINGULAR	PLURAL
Future Perfect Tense		*Future Perfect Continuous Tense*	
I will have left	we will have left	I will have been getting	we will have been getting
you will have left	you will have left	you will have been getting	you will have been getting
he will have left		he will have been getting	
she will have left	they will have left	she will have been getting	they will have been getting
it will have left		it will have been getting	

Passive Voice

SINGULAR	PLURAL	SINGULAR	PLURAL
Simple Present		*Present Continuous*	
I am given	we are given	I am being taken	we are being taken
you are given	you are given	you are being taken	you are being taken
he is given		he is being taken	
she is given	they are given	she is being taken	they are being taken
it is given		it is being taken	
Simple Past		*Past Continuous*	
I was brought	we were brought	I was being carried	we were being carried
you were brought	you were brought	you were being carried	you were being carried
he was brought		he was being carried	
she was brought	they were brought	she was being carried	they were being carried
it was brought		it was being carried	
Simple Future			
I will be found	we will be found		
you will be found	you will be found		
he will be found			
she will be found	they will be found		
it will be found			
Present Perfect			
I have been offered	we have been offered		
you have been offered	you have been offered		
he has been offered			
she has been offered	they have been offered		
it has been offered			
Past Perfect			
I had been loved	we had been loved		
you had been loved	you had been loved		
he had been loved			
she had been loved	they had been loved		
it had been loved			

Passive Voice

SINGULAR	PLURAL

Future Perfect

SINGULAR	PLURAL
I will have been seen	we will have been seen
you will have been seen	you will have been seen
he will have been seen	
she will have been seen	they will have been seen
it will have been seen	

Answers to Exercises

page 17

My Earliest Memory about Learning English

I was about fifteen years old in Azerbaijan, my country, when I started to study English. I spent a lot of time on it. I really wanted to know this language just for myself. I studied it in my elementary school, but it was too hard for me then. I tried to study and do my homework by myself. Memorizing words and English grammar was awful for me. Then I got a tutor. That helped a lot. Now I know much more and I try to use English all the time.

page 40

Becoming a Successful Language Learner

Twenty-five students from Columbia University talked about their experiences learning English. They thought that students needed to use English in a natural way. They should practice and try to think in the new language as much as possible. A lot of students thought that they should be in an English-speaking country to learn English. Some students said that it was important to learn the grammar and vocabulary. They think people learn from making mistakes. Personal factors such as personality and aptitude for learning are also important. I learned a lot from reading this article.

page 64

A Bad Communication

I want to tell you the story about my visit to the hospital in the United States. One year ago I came to this country with my parents, my husband, and my nine-month-old son. Last month my mother had a bad stomach problem, and she decided to go to the hospital. When we got there, the nurse asked her for information about herself. My mother got so confused! She told the nurse the wrong street number. "No, she gave you our address in San Salvador," I shouted. My mother finally saw the doctor. After several tests, the doctor said she had eaten too fast and her stomach was upset. We were all relieved. She felt much better the next day. Now we all are trying to eat our food slowly and chew it carefully.

page 68

Once upon a time there was a smart young man who decided to trick a wise old man. He caught a little bird and held it in one hand behind his back. The boy approached the wise man and said, "Sir, I have a question for you. I want to

355

see how very wise you are. I am holding a bird in my hand. Is it alive, or is it dead?"

The boy thought that if the man said the bird was dead, he would open his hand to reveal the live bird, but if the man said the bird was alive, he would crush the bird, killing it. The old man stared into the boy's eyes for a long time. Then he said, "The answer, my friend, is in your hands."

page 83

Fashion is one of the biggest industries in the United States today. Thousands of men and women make their livings in the fashion industry. Unfortunately, there are few high-paying jobs and many low-paying jobs in fashion. The designers make lots of money creating clothing for millions of people. Highly paid models pose for pictures in magazines and newspapers. They perform in fashion shows. But the garments are made by poor people, often immigrants. They sew in factories all over the world and get paid very little money for their hard work. Despite the many problems of such employment, these jobs provide work and money for many men, women, and children in the world.

page 88

Each morning, Henry gets up at 6 o'clock and prepares to go to work. After taking a shower, he combs his hair and puts on his shirt, pants, and tie. He shaves every other day because his skin is delicate and his beard is thin. This morning he shaved in the steamy shower. Then he blew his hair with one of the hair dryers in his closet. He put on hair mousse because it smelled nice and fresh. He brushed his teeth with an electric toothbrush because he thought it saved time. He boiled water and made coffee for his family. They ate cereal or toast together, and then they all ran off to their different buses.

page 113

Flying over the Pacific Ocean from California to the United States' most distant, Hawaii, is exciting. I visited the Hawaiian Islands last year to celebrate my twenty-first birthday. More than twenty islands make up the Hawaiian group. Hawaii has a nickname, "Aloha State"—*aloha* means "greetings" in the Hawaiian language. People live on seven of the eight main islands. Hawaii covers 4,021 square miles and is the biggest island. It was built by volcanoes. Mauna Kea and Mauna Loa are the highest volcanoes in the Hawaiian group. Honolulu is the capital and the largest city and is located on the island of Oahu. Hawaii is the most beautiful place I have ever seen. I recommend that you visit there soon.

page 117

In my class last week, we had to interview a student in our class. The student I interviewed came to the United States from Poland. Her name is Irina, and she wants to become a nurse. She is majoring in nursing in college, but she wants to take courses in psychology too. First, she has to take courses in English. Irina studies very hard, and she also likes to play the violin and read books. Her favorite books are mysteries, especially ones about hospitals and medicine. We had a good conversation, and I am happy to be in the class with Irina.

page 135

Tatyana moved to Illinois from Russia. She attends the University of Illinois in Champaign-Urbana and lives in a dorm with a roommate from Missouri. In March, Tatyana began to work on Wednesday, Thursday, and Friday afternoons in the college library. It is one of the biggest college libraries in the United States. She practices English with everyone who borrows books. One day a student borrowed *Anna Karenina* by Leo Tolstoy. She asked Tatyana about the book and soon invited her to a Saturday night buffet dinner at St. Joseph's Church. She met some interesting people from the college at the dinner. They took her to a school game, where she learned "Hail to the Orange," the school song. Tatyana is starting to feel more at home in the midwest. She is teaching some of her new friends Russian, and they are helping her with English. She bought an old Chevrolet Blazer from a student and plans to visit Chicago and Lake Michigan in July.

page 136

When Mikhail and Fatima volunteered to work one afternoon in the Western College Post Office, they were in for a surprise. In one corner, there were many boxes piled high. They found three cartons of French language tapes addressed to Professor Maude Cousteau, now of the Ford Foundation. She had left the school back in February and had moved to New Mexico. Fatima accidentally opened a box filled with the Microsoft Windows programs needed for the college IBM computers. "Mr. Smith, this post office is a mess," Mikhail told the postmaster. "I know it, son. We just have to get a little more organized. The U. S. mail has to go through, and we will do it soon." Mikhail and Fatima left there wondering if the college mail would ever get through.

page 137

Marie learns languages very easily. She was born in Haiti and has spoken French and Creole all her life. Now Marie also knows English, Spanish, and Italian. She has a special technique that always works for her. At night she goes to sleep by hypnotizing herself as she stares at a poster of the stained-glass windows of Nôtre-Dame Cathedral in Paris. Her Sony Walkman tape deck is on her head, and she listens to a different language tape each night.

page 154

5516 Buena Vista Avenue
Miami, FL 33158
March 14, 1996

Dear Aunt Millie,

Because I am so excited, I had to write to you today. I have some special news, so I wanted you to be one of the first people to know about it. I just got engaged to Jorge, your best friend Luisa's oldest son. Just like that, you have a wedding to attend. After we made our plans, we talked for hours about everything. When he told me about his memories of you and Luisa, I knew I had to write to you right away. He remembers you, of course, from when he was a little boy. He said you always treated him like he was worth $1,000,000. You do remember him, don't you? If you do, write soon. Millie, send me any pictures or tell me any stories you recall. By the way, my parents are doing very well, and we just opened a new store. Even though you have not seen our first store yet, I am sure you will be impressed with this one. The new store is big, elegant, and beautifully decorated. Working so hard together, we all feel very proud. Everyone says, "Hi!" Please write soon.

Love always,

Blanca

page 156

Traveling to a different country, whether it is returning home or going to a new destination, is exciting. When the airplane arrives in the airport safely, even people who travel often are glad. Suddenly, they are in a new, exciting world. Feeling tired, they get off the plane, and they head for their destination. They convert their money, wait in line for taxis, and spend too much money on foolish things. On the way home, they feel mixed emotions, but overall, most of them are glad they took the chance and traveled.

page 183

Anyone who has a baby cares more that the baby is healthy than if it is a boy or a girl. But each mother and father has expectations. Some people think a boy baby should be stronger than a girl baby. He is supposed to be bigger, faster, and smarter. People need to know that girl and boy babies all over the world are more similar than different. Some girl babies are bigger, faster, and smarter, but it doesn't matter. When one of the babies is your baby, then all that matters is that the baby is alive and healthy.

page 200

Jacqueline Kennedy Onassis died in May 1994 at the age of 64. She was loved by many Americans because of her grace, beauty, and style. Jackie, as people called her, was the first lady for a shorter time than almost any other first lady, yet she made a huge impact on people all over the world. Her first husband, President John Kennedy, was assassinated in 1963, so Jackie became a widow at the age of 34. She raised her two children, Caroline and John, alone. Later, she married one of the richest men in the world, Aristotle Onassis. After he died, Jackie never remarried. She worked as an editor, and she enjoyed her friends, children, and grandchildren until the end. Everyone will miss Jackie. She was a great woman.

page 250

According to Robbins, there are many factors involved in job satisfaction. People have to feel their jobs are meaningful and interesting. They have to offer the workers a mental challenge. Even though there are individual differences in what people think is important, most people agree that their jobs should offer some challenge. Pay has greater importance for individuals who cannot gain other satisfactions from their jobs. Jobs that offer external recognition, good pay, and a mental challenge are sought by most people. Each person wants a feeling of fulfillment.

page 271

Many students find it difficult to look for a job the first time. They are not sure where to find listings of jobs for students. They do not know whether to say that they are students right away. They do not know how many hours they should work a week. All these problems make the interview difficult too. For one thing, the interviewee is never sure what to bring to the interview. Some people bring too much so when the interviewer asks for a paper, it is hard to find. I suggest that you bring only the following documents: your résumé, your birth certificate, your passport, and your high school diploma. If you have a green card, bring that too. In addition, I try to impress an interviewer by dressing very neatly and never chewing gum or candy. I look directly into the interviewer's eyes. I want the interviewer to believe that I can be trusted. If I remember to follow my own advice, I believe I will get a job soon.

page 272

Trying to get a job at the Rockefeller Foundation is difficult for a girl who does not have pull. Finally, the morning postman brings the letter. She is to go for an interview at Peking Medical College, to the Comptroller's office. She prepares her clothes and goes to the East market to buy face powder to cover her pimples. The next morning, she goes with her father to Yu Wang Palace to the Administration Building. They cross the marble courtyard and go into the entrance hall. Her father leaves. She finds the office and meets her future employer, Mr. Harned. His bald head reminds her of the white pagoda on the hill in North Sea Park. She takes the required typing test and gets the job.

page 294

The essay "Back, but Not Home," by Maria L. Muñiz, made me think about returning to my country. I grew up thinking that there was no reason to go back, but now I am not sure. It's interesting for me to think about the world that I left behind. I feel mixed emotions such as happiness, sadness, and regret. My aunts and uncles still live in my country. They still live in the same town, in the same house. I have never seen most of my cousins; the youngest one is five months old, and I would like to know him, too. My brother visited my family last year, and he told me all the news. It's strange hearing about my best girlfriends who are getting married, and one even has a baby. The Muñiz essay, my brother's visit, and my dreams make me want to return to my country for a visit.

page 314

Cross-cultural research interests me. Miller wrote that American parents want their children to sleep in their own beds as soon as possible. It is important for babies to learn to sleep through the night by themselves. Miller said that Mayan mothers express pity for American babies because they have to sleep alone. Japanese parents believe babies should sleep with their parents too. Cultures that want children to develop independence want children to sleep alone. Cultures that value interdependence like babies to sleep with their parents. When a mother nurses her baby, it is good for the baby to sleep with her mother. If the baby wakes up in the night, the mother can hold and nurse her baby back to sleep. The mother can fall asleep with the baby too. Then the mother is not so tired the next day. Learning about how cultures around the world live is fascinating to me.

page 342

Returning home can be very difficult, as we see in Nahid Rachlin's story, "Foreigner." When people return to their home countries, they often find many changes. The familiar old streets may not look the same. People they remember may not recognize them. If they go back to their own childhood house, the house may look very different. It may appear small and cramped. One woman wrote that she returned to her neighborhood and her house was gone. In its place was a little, modern grocery store. No one remembered her. She was extremely depressed. It is also possible to return to a place where everyone remembers you. That makes a person feel happy inside; at least you were not forgotten.

Acknowledgments (continued from page iv)

Gary Althen, "American Ways," from *American Ways: A Guide for Foreigners in the United States.* Copyright © 1988. Reprinted with permission of Intercultural Press, Inc., Yarmouth, ME.

Lensey Namioka, "The All-American Slurp," from *Visions,* edited by Donald R. Gallo. Copyright © 1987. All rights reserved by Lensey Namioka. Reprinted by permission of the author.

Laura Ullman, "Will You Go Out With Me?" *Newsweek,* April 1984. Copyright © 1984. Reprinted by permission of the author.

Grace Craig, "Gender-Role Identity," pages 82–83 from *Human Development,* 6th ed. Copyright © 1992. Reprinted by permission of Prentice Hall, Upper Saddle River, New Jersey.

Kate Chopin, "The Story of an Hour," from *The Awakening and Selected Stories of Kate Chopin,* edited by Barbara Solomon. New American Library (1976). Originally published in 1894.

Albert E. Kahn, "Age and Youth," excerpt from *Joys and Sorrows: Reflections by Pablo Casals as told to Albert E. Kahn.* Copyright © 1970 by Albert E. Kahn. Reprinted with the permission of Simon & Schuster and Aitkens, Stone & Wylie, Ltd., London.

John Naisbitt and Patricia Aburdene, "Looking at the Economy," originally titled "The Global Boom of the 1990s" from *Megatrends 2000* by John Naisbitt and Patricia Aburdene. Copyright © 1990 by Megatrends Ltd. Reprinted by permission of the authors and William Morrow & Company, Inc.

Stephen P. Robbins, "Job Satisfaction," pages 184–185 from *Organizational Behavior: Concepts, Controversies, and Applications,* 6th ed. Copyright © 1993. Reprinted by permission of Prentice Hall, Upper Saddle River, New Jersey.

Han Suyin, "Getting A Job," from volume 2 of a 5 volume history, biography and autobiography of the author and her family. Putnam 1965, pp. 136–139. Reprinted by permission of the author.

Maria L. Muñiz, "Back, but not Home," from *The New York Times,* July 13, 1979. Copyright © 1979 by The New York Times Company. Reprinted by permission.

Patricia Miller, "Cross-Cultural Research," from *Theories of Developmental Psychology,* 3rd ed. by Patricia Miller. Copyright © 1993 by W. H. Freeman and Company. Used with permission.

Nahid Rachlin, pages 9–14 from *Foreigner.* Copyright © 1978 by Nahid Rachlin. Reprinted with the permission of W. W. Norton & Company, Inc. and Curtis, Brown Ltd.

Willa Cather, "A Wagner Matinée," from *Youth and A Bright Medusa.* A. A. Knopf (1975). Reprinted with permission.

Index